M

Stanley Knowles

Stanley Knowles

The Man From Winnipeg
North Centre

Susan Mann Trofimenkoff

Western Producer Prairie Books
Saskatoon, Saskatchewan

Printed and bound in Canada by
Modern Press ⟨logo⟩1
Saskatoon, Saskatchewan

Cover design by John Luckhurst

Western Producer Prairie Book publications are produced and
manufactured in the middle of Western Canada by a unique
publishing venture owned by a group of prairie farmers who are
members of Saskatchewan Wheat Pool. From the first book published
in 1954, a reprint of a serial originally carried in the weekly
newspaper, *The Western Producer*, to the book before you now, the
tradition of providing enjoyable and informative reading for all
Canadians is continued.

The publisher has endeavoured to obtain permission to reproduce
illustrative material which appears in this book. Any errors or
omissions which are brought to the publisher's attention will be
rectified in future editions.

Canadian Cataloguing in Publication Data

Trofimenkoff, Susan Mann, 1941-
    Stanley Knowles, the man from Winnipeg
  North Centre

    Includes index
    ISBN 0-88833-100-2

    1. Knowles, Stanley, 1908-   2.
  Politicians — Canada — Biography.
  FC601.K59T76   971.064'092'4   C82-091305-7
  F1034.3.K59T76

To my parents who cared for him

CONTENTS

PREFACE

This is a biographical memoir. It is as close to an autobiography as Stanley Knowles was ever willing or now able to undertake, and is interpreted through the eyes, ears, and pen of one who has known him all her life. He told me the story in 1975 in a lengthy series of interviews conducted in the studios of the sound archives division of the Public Archives of Canada where the original taped versions now are. Each interview was designed around an important day in Knowles' life and the tale wove its way into the past and the future from that starting point. I have maintained that structure in this book with two alterations in the days originally chosen, Chapters 11 and 16, clearly indicated in the notes. My historian's training has taken me to the public record to confirm, clarify, or amplify the account but the book does not pretend to be a comprehensive survey of all of Knowles' political activities. For one could be buried alive in Hansard alone before going near Knowles' own voluminous files. I have therefore tackled each gingerly and selectively. As the Knowles papers are gradually deposited at the Public Archives they will constitute one of the more important collections of political papers for the mid-twentieth century. They will add to the colour and complexity of the story that follows, but not, I trust, to its accuracy.

Ottawa, June 1982.

ACKNOWLEDGEMENTS

Many of the illustrations which appear in this book come from the private collection of Stanley Knowles and his son David Knowles and I wish to thank them for granting me unrestricted access to them. Permission was granted for use of the following illustrations: p. 77 *The Globe and Mail,* Toronto, 12 March 1947; p. 139, *Toronto Star,* 25 April 1975; p. 152, *Free Press,* Winnipeg, 1961; p. 157, Photo Illustrations of Canada, Montreal; p. 166, Dominion-Wide Photographs, Ottawa; p. 176, *Toronto Star;* p. 186, *The Gazette,* Montreal; p. 196, United Press Limited, Toronto; p. 205, *The Citizen,* Ottawa.

1

MOTHER

2 June 1919

She was thirty-eight and she was dying. A slim woman of medium height, with brown hair and eyes, Margaret Blanche Murdock Knowles now lay wasted, struggling for breath and for the strength to say good-bye to her dear family and precious sons. Perhaps she knew of her husband's notion that life was at its lowest ebb in the early morning hours; certainly he knew that the time had come, between four and five A.M. on 2 June 1919. He summoned the two boys — Stanley, not yet eleven, a thin and solemn lad, understanding what was happening but rebelling silently against the cruelty of it all, and Warren, five and round, and usually mischievous but now too sleepy and too awed to acknowledge or even to register much in the early morning light. The elder boy took it all in and has kept it close to his heart ever since. Were her parting words of comfort or encouragement? Or was the scene itself sufficient to impress on this sensitive child that not only death but life too was a lonely struggle in the half-light. Physically, he let her go — how could a mere boy put a stop to the disease that she had been fighting for years but had only known as the killer tuberculosis for the last two months? But spiritually he would cling to her.

She had come a long way from her New Brunswick birth to a Los Angeles death. Like most women in history, however, she is difficult to summon from the past. If she had in her from birth the weakness that led to death from tuberculosis, she must also have had strength. For she spent most of her childhood alone and in bondage. Margaret Murdock did not even have the opportunity to choose the major paid occupation of women of the time; she was born into domestic service in 1880 as the daughter of a servant in a home on Germain Street in St. John, New Brunswick. She never knew her father who either died or disappeared during her infancy. Nor did she have relatives or even any acquaintances; there was only her mother and the family which fed and tolerated her in exchange for a child's services. After her mother's death, when Margaret was twelve, she was even more alone. The family on Germain Street kept her for a while, as a servant. And she probably worked in that capacity in the small village of Hampton, east of St. John, where she seems to have spent a few years. After that she set out at about age eighteen to see the world, following the well-trod Maritime path to Boston. There a job was easy enough to find for she could read and write and she had her domestic skills; she was also modest, reserved, and used to hard work. She was accustomed to the loneliness that was so much a part of the servant's life. Some solace, some entertainment, and even some friends could always be found in that other centre of nineteenth-century women's lives — the church. What she was never to know was that her son Stanley would retrace her shadowy path through New Brunswick to Boston searching in vain for some substance to the story, but perhaps not realizing that he already carried in him what she had to give: her gentleness and her fortitude.

Sometime in 1901 or 1902, she met a fellow Maritimer, a journeyman machinist, Stanley Ernest Knowles, at one of the regular church or prayer meetings of the Methodist church in Boston. "Times have changed," remarked their son many years later, "there aren't as many romances that come out of prayer meetings today as there were in those days."[1] Nonetheless, he is rather pleased; the setting was somehow appropriate and continued to be so when his own romance blossomed in the 1930s in another church thousands of miles away in the Canadian west. At the turn of the century, the pair from the Maritimes were eyeing the American west. Stanley Ernest Knowles had been unhappily married; there had been a divorce and he was anxious to leave the east. San Francisco beckoned. Would this shy young girl from New Brunswick share the adventure? She would, and more. She would wait in Boston while he scouted the west, tested the employment opportunities, the living conditions, and the weather. He liked what he saw. By mail, the romance and the plans proceeded apace; he would fetch Margaret at his family home at Upper Woods Harbour, Nova Scotia and they would be married on 22 August 1904, the day after his thirtieth birthday.

In the early summer of 1904, Margaret journeyed by boat from Boston to Yarmouth and then by train to Barrington Passage where the first members of her new and large family welcomed her. There were her fiance's seven brothers and sisters, his parents, his cousins and second cousins, aunts, uncles, and great-relations thrice re-moved. They spread back in time and all over in space. Margaret was amazed and delighted. So too was the new family. Now their Stanley would have a good wife! If only they were not planning to settle so far away. Not that it was so unusual. One of Nova Scotia's main exports had always been the young people and the Knowles family was no different. One sister, Ida, had just taken up a farm in western Manitoba and another, Lois, was a missionary on the other side of the world. As for Stanley, he had never been interested in farming which was all the family had to offer, so perhaps San Francisco was a good idea. In the meantime, the family welcomed Margaret as a daughter and prepared to give her a proper wedding. It was to be in the family home at Upper Woods Harbour where so many Knowleses had come and gone that the early post office was named for them. The house is still there, on the east side of the main road, a yellow, rambling place still withholding secrets from the younger Stanley Knowles.

For the elder, the expedition to fetch his bride was a long and roundabout one. Instead of taking the direct and expensive American route, he took an indirect and cheaper trip through Canada. The Canadian Pacific Railway, hoping to lure passengers onto its lengthy transcontinental run, offered excursion rates which permitted Knowles to travel from San Francisco to Vancouver, across Canada to Montreal, then to New York and Boston, and finally Nova Scotia, all for less than the through rate on an American line. The itinerary permitted him to stop in Manitoba to see his sister Ida and her husband Tom Bailey on their new farm near Carberry. Twenty years later, his son took the same route, liking the family and the farm and Aunt Ida so much ("as near a mother to you as she could be," wrote his "glad and thankful" father)[2] that he subsequently decided to stay. For his father in the summer of 1904, the immediate not the distant future held his interest. In Nova Scotia he would find his new wife and his old family, friends, and relations. Many of them were also along the return route to the west. The young couple intended to do the right thing; they would visit the friends they had made in Boston and they would go to Niagara Falls, a spot both more romantic and more spectacular then than it is today. By late September or early October 1904, they were settled in San Francisco, Mr. Knowles working as a machinist, Mrs. Knowles mistress of her own house.

As in Boston the couple's first social contacts were made through the church. The religion was strict — what their son would later call "religion of the old school; an individual gospel"[3] — but the friendship was warm. Indeed, in the days before radio, cinema, and television, the church was the social centre of any community. It enveloped individuals and families, promised to save their souls, and organized most of their non-working hours, not just on Sundays when two services were the rule but through the week as well, with prayer meetings, study sessions, women's sewing circles and missionary societies, children's bible classes, missionary bands, and play groups. Religion was an inescapable part of everyone's life. The Knowleses in fact would have it no other way. Their children too were born, nurtured, and educated in a religious setting.

For a while, it seemed that there might not be any children. A first daughter, Irene Blanche, died soon after birth. She was frail like her mother, and simply wasted away. When another child was on the way in April 1906, the Knowleses experienced the terror of the San Francisco earthquake. Their son believes that was "one of the roughest experiences my mother ever went through."[4] Although the quake lasted less than a minute, she was convinced that the house shook and the family's belongings tumbled about for at least half an hour. Neither she nor her husband was injured but, along with others, they had to move to the hills to escape the fire. Dead bodies littered the town and Mr. Knowles was among the men drafted to help bury them. While engaged in that awesome task, he pondered his own family's circumstances. His place of work had been totally destroyed and with it all his tools. A machinist's tools represented not just his occupation but a major monetary investment. A skilled tradesman with no tools was a liability to his family and they would have to start anew. Should they perhaps leave San Francisco and begin again elsewhere? A move would not be costly since the Southern Pacific Railway was offering free transportation on any of its lines to those people wishing to leave. The Knowleses joined the exodus, packing all their belongings into two trunks, wavering in their decision at the last minute, only to be jostled into a hurried departure by the tail-end of the quake, a forgotten tremor that revived all the recent horror. They headed for Los Angeles and a new home. Perhaps there might be a family yet.

But the expected child, Margaret Ruth, did not live any longer than her sister the year before. Might there be a jinx upon the Knowleses? First an earthquake and now this oddly named street on which they lived. In a city that numbered all its streets with mathematical logic, Pico Street stood out between Twelfth and Fourteenth as an acknowledgement of superstition. The Knowleses also knew that many children died in infancy: it was a fact of North American life at the turn of the century. Infant mortality rates were, however, of little comfort and the couple counted on their new friends at First Methodist Church and their relatives in Nova Scotia to ease the hurt. The city itself provided some relief; it was an improvement on San Francisco since there was less fog and the Knowleses were able to rent a house with a front and back lawn. Mr.

Knowles earned a little less — $1.95 compared to $2.05 a day — but he did find work at his machinist's trade. Los Angeles was then a manageable city of three hundred thousand and the Knowleses made it their home.

There, on 18 June 1908, a boy was born, as frail as his sisters and showing every sign of following them to an early death. His mother could not nurse him and he refused or could not tolerate any sustenance. He was therefore simply referred to as "Baby," although he had a name. The relatives in Nova Scotia were anxious about him for by October 1908 he still had not gained any weight.[5] The parents, more anxious still, were willing to try anything. With equal hope they collected the advice of neighbours and solicitous friends. From the latter came the suggestion of goat's milk. Goat's milk? Well, why not? Almost instantly, "Baby" came alive. The terse, hardly-daring-to-hope messages filtered back to Nova Scotia: "Baby has gained six ounces more . . . weighs ten lbs. now"; "Baby weighs 13 lbs and 11 oz".[6] "Baby" was going to live. By April 1909 he could be safely baptized and have his name officially recognized. Named after his father and the close Boston friend who had originally suggested the American west as the ideal place, "Baby" was Stanley Howard Knowles. Only twenty years later did his father admit what was going through his mind at the time of baptism:

> I note how your soul is burning with the vision and zeal of youth to carry the message of good news to the peoples of the earth that will make this earth more heavenly and certainly a better place to live in. I understand from experience something of what you feel, only I did not get the preparation to carry on, and therefore I gave you my name with the hope that you might do something of what I intended or wanted to do. I never told anyone before why I gave you my name, but really that was what was back of it.[7]

How early did the child, plump and healthy by the first birthday, realize that he had his father's business to attend to in the world?

From the autumn of 1909, goats were a part of the Knowles family. Tethered in the vacant lot next door or down the street, they provided milk for young Stanley, for neighbour children to whom the word had spread, and eventually for a younger brother Warren, born in November 1913. Thanks to the goats, there was never any doubt about Warren's living; as a child and a young man, he was always more robust than his older brother. The goats even provided companionship; an early photograph captured baby Stanley and baby goat together in a wicker stroller. By the time the youngster was

"baby Stanley and baby goat together in a wicker stroller." Los Angeles 1909.

three he no longer needed goat's milk, but the goats remained with the family until about 1918. One of the chores was to milk them and part of any moving day was to walk them over to the new home. The goats' milk, along with the produce from a large vegetable garden, was a small source of supplementary income for a family that today would be classified as the working poor. Much later, in the 1930s, the elder Knowles took to keeping goats again, surmising perhaps that what had been good for his infant son so many years ago might now be good for him in late middle age. By then, however, a city by-law prohibited the keeping of goats in the back yard and so they were staked in a vacant industrial lot some distance from home.[8]

Like his parents, young Stanley was initiated into the church at a tender age. First Methodist had a Babies' Band, a Beginners' Department where he wailed when left,[9] a Sunday school, and innumerable groups and associations. The parental discipline and then his own meant that he never missed a church function; he was always present and always punctual. Indeed his later faithful presence in the House of Commons reflected that earlier training. During the walk back and forth to church he also became used to long, serious conversations with his parents. One that he remembers was his father telling him about the arrival of a new baby; he was just over five and was told the whole story, without the embellishment of storks or cabbage leaves. His father was like that.

"By the time the youngster was three he no longer needed goat's milk . . ." Los Angeles 1911.

And so was the young son. A precocious, serious lad, he could read and write and 'cipher' long before the schools were ready for him. His political consciousness began in 1912 when, at the age of four and a half, he followed the American presidential election that had Woodrow Wilson winning on a split vote. He remembers the change of year from 1912 to 1913, wondering as his father explained the calendar just how far the numbers would go.[10] There is no record of an early wit, but now he could ask why the new year was not called 19Pico.

By 1913, however, the family had moved out from the centre of Los Angeles to follow Mr. Knowles' job. He was then working for the Los Angeles Street Railway and the yards and machine shops were in the suburbs. Like other working people of the time, Knowles had to live near his place of employment so he could walk to work. His son remembers the family home on East 55th Street and the one across the road where he stayed the night of Warren's birth. He has been back to the area, never able to let go of the past, and always looking for clues to that elusive mother who left him so young. Now it is part of black Los Angeles; the people are friendly and interested in his story, but they will not let him into their houses. In 1914, by the time he was in school, the family owned a home for the first time. The five-room bungalow at 853 West 58th Place with a large garden seemed enormous to the boy and perhaps to his parents as well. There his first job was to sell vegetables from the family garden up and down the street.

He worked as hard as a young salesman as he did at everything else. He completed the eight grades of elementary school in six, skipping half years along the way. An enterprising principal at Budlong Avenue Public School established a print shop in the school but permitted only those students who could afford time away from their regular classes to learn the secrets of the printing trade. Young Knowles was first in line. Although he admits he would be lost now in a modern printshop, and that the printing practised in that small school shop was "closer to Gutenburg than to today's printing," at the time the experience gave him a skilled trade.[11] Later, as a young man, he earned his way across the continent and into college with his printer's skills and he has maintained his membership in the International Typographical Union. Out of his early experience editing and printing his public school paper, the *Budlong News,* developed his industrial and trade union ties and also his insistence on correctness and exactitude. For the ten-year-old Stanley Knowles, things had to be right.

But things were not right at home and all the boy's precision and precociousness could not make them so. His mother had been ailing

"For the ten year old . . . things had to be right." Los Angeles 1918.

for years and had been unable to shake a cold contracted in the summer of 1918 when she and the two boys were at a camp for poor families in the hills behind Los Angeles. By April 1919, tuberculosis was diagnosed and a death sentence pronounced. She could not last another two months. The family knew it and the boys knew it. How does an almost eleven year old react to such news? Did his natural solemnity increase? Did the large blue eyes take it all in and bury it down deep where no one would find the hurt? Did the quick mind confirm the injustice of it all? The doctor said that Arizona might help. What working man in 1919 could take his family to Arizona?

They could as easily go to the moon. But why should Mother die because Father could not afford to take her to Arizona? And why should Mother have had so few good years? Surely something was wrong with the way of the world.

It took the young Stanley Knowles many years to work through the hurt, to seek religious answers and then political answers to questions barely acknowledged that early morning in June 1919. In the meantime an unhappy father and two lonely boys had to be comforted. Ironically the consolation came through Mrs. Knowles' death; an insurance policy provided one thousand dollars, and a heartbroken father who only months before could not send his wife to Arizona now was reluctantly persuaded by friends and neighbours to take the boys home for a long visit — to Canada.

2
CANADA

He grew up fast. Within six and a half years of his first visit to Canada, Stanley Knowles had decided to come to stay. Like his parents, he set out, very young and very alone, for a new country. There were relatives sprinkled across the new land — and he was heading for them that day in June 1926 just before his eighteenth birthday — but still the decision had been made alone and the way would probably continue to be a lonely one. The border formalities were minimal. Questions asked of prospective immigrants, at least of those whose home was California, were few. He knew as he stepped into Canada at Emerson, Manitoba that this was to be his country.

It was not a particularly foreign place to him in 1926. Letters from Canada had been a highlight of his boyhood days in Los Angeles and his parents had always been fond of reminiscing. There was even a tinge of American romanticism about the great lone land to the north. Young Knowles absorbed it all. Then too, he had his own bittersweet memories of the trip to Nova Scotia in the summer of 1919 when Canada had eased the first great sorrow of his life.

He and his brother Warren, the first with all the seriousness of a bereaved eleven year old, the second a bouncing and wondering lad of five, had left Los Angeles one month after their mother's death. Accompanied by their father, they took a long train ride across the American south to Washington. There, everything seemed to belong to George Washington: the trees, the buildings, the monuments, even, wailed Warren, the kitty that scratched him. The trio absorbed their American heritage and also the sympathy of their Washington relatives. Stanley was particularly impressed by the young page-boys in Congress. That would be an interesting job. In New York and Boston they again combined tourism with family offerings of condolences before taking the ferry to Yarmouth (where an old lighthouse keeper many years later remembered the boat but not the boys) and finally the train to Upper Woods Harbour. There the grandparents, Benjamin and Elizabeth, aged seventy-six and seventy-two, kept open house for the Boston grandchildren and, now, in the summer of 1919, open hearts and arms for their son and his boys from the far west. The elder grandson remembers his first sleep in Canada; he also recalls that his father's recently acquired toupee aroused the most interest among the Nova Scotian relatives.[1]

The summer was long and splendid. Grandmother and aunts treated the boys like small princes and they revelled in it. Grandmother even suggested that they stay in Nova Scotia, to be mothered and properly cared for by her. The idea seemed too unreal to be taken seriously. Nova Scotia was marvellous for a summer, but home was on the other side of the continent. Perhaps young Stanley had already checked to find no print shop in the local school. Certainly he wanted to tell his Los Angeles school chums about his trip and he may already have been planning to do so while keeping a detailed chronicle of the summer. By October, the three were back in Los Angeles, the boys in school again, and Stanley's story in the school paper, no doubt edited and typeset by himself.

His printing interest and activity continued through secondary school. At Manual Arts High he followed the engineering programme and continued his scholastic record of excellent grades, skipping semesters as fast as he absorbed the material. What held his interest most, however, were the extra-curricular activities, all centred around the print shop. There he both wrote and printed much of the *Manual Arts Weekly* and the semi-annual class book, the *Artisan*, even introducing and physically printing the first colour issues of the paper. The teacher called him "Knowles" and he felt very grown up.

In fact he was. By fifteen he had a high school diploma as well as a printer's training and he was about to seek work before deciding on further education. His very first job, a linotype operator with a printing company, earned him more money than his father's meagre income. That sign of adulthood was also enhanced by the intellectual companionship and mutual devotion between father and son. The son thrived on it and continued to do so until his father's death in 1935. There never was, he claims, a generation gap during his teenage days.[2]

Nonetheless, he was only fifteen and there were truancy and

child labour laws in California. A youngster had to be in school until age sixteen and if for some legitimate reason he was in the labour force before that age, he could not be working later than certain daytime hours. There, however, was young Stanley Knowles, at fifteen and a half working the night shift in a composition company in downtown Los Angeles (about which he commented many years later: "I'd be scared stiff to walk there in the daytime now"[3]) and earning more than his father. What would this first encounter with bureaucracy make of that? The truant officer was easily satisfied that the boy had indeed completed high school; the law would not keep him there just because he was under age. But the job was another matter. The truant officer could supply a work permit, but the document revealed the birth date and his employer would see it. What then? It had never occurred to the boss that this assiduous young man could be any less than eighteen. Would this mean the end of the good job and the good pay? Moreover, the job was interesting, perhaps even a portend of the future for the company was printing election lists. What should he do? He dithered awhile and then hit upon the secret of bureaucracy — delay. He simply would not turn the work permit in until after his sixteenth birthday that June. What the employer did not know would not hurt him.

Being an adult in work and pay and paternal companionship also meant coping with the emotional power of adults and he was not quite ready for that. In the early 1920s his father had

"the emotional triangle that younger brother Warren seems to have missed by virtue of his age." Los Angeles c. 1924.

remarried. Anna Sanderman, a young widow who had moved west from Indianapolis, alternated between effusive affection and bitter hatred for this grown-up child of her husband. Jealousy no doubt played a role in the emotional triangle that younger brother Warren seems to have missed by virtue of his age. As for Stanley, Anna Knowles encouraged his longing for travel and the sooner the better. He had his own money and if he wanted to go, he should. She even added a threat to the encouragement; if he did not leave, she might well do so. In the late summer of 1924 the lad departed, just after his sixteenth birthday.

The break was sharp and perhaps because of it he carefully carried his past with him. He traced the same route his father had taken twenty years before, in 1904, north to Vancouver and across Canada to fetch a bride. For the younger Knowles in 1924 there was no bride waiting at the end of the route; he was both too young and too serious to think of such things. But there were relatives along the way, particularly the aunt and uncle, Ida and Tom Bailey, who had settled in Manitoba in 1904 and who now had six children ready to greet their American cousin. Might he recapture a family on the Canadian prairie? Certainly his printer's skill could be turned into quick cash whenever he needed it. He was adventurous, determined, and alone. More than fifty years later he was still able to capture the excitement in his typical, laconic fashion: "Canada was just . . . just wonderful" and he was "thrilled to bits"[4] to be travelling on the fast summer train of the CPR, the Trans-Canada Limited, east from Vancouver, through the spiral tunnels in the mountains, across the face of the prairie, and into Winnipeg. No time there to see visions of a political future but just enough to catch the local train back west to Carberry.

There the Bailey family "mesmerized" him. They opened their home and took him in, embraced him in their large farm family. He had never known anything quite like it. Aunt Ida thought nothing of adding another boy to her brood and he was more than willing to find a substitute mother. In a mere week's stay he was enchanted, with the family, with the farm, and with Manitoba in September. He even accompanied the family as they settled daughter Mary into her lodgings in Brandon for a year at Normal School. He saw Brandon College but did not yet think of weaving it and this wonderful family into his future plans. He still had the rest of Canada to see.

Before the east-bound train reached Winnipeg again, he was homesick for his Manitoba family. However, it was not yet time to turn back; he intended to complete his planned trip and then see.

By mid-September, he was in Ottawa, noting the British flags and the horse-drawn wagons and the incomplete peace tower on the parliament buildings. Fifty years later, when Ottawa had become familiar and parliament home and church in one to him, he took his old photos to the CBC. There, both the pictures and their source inspired the production of a half-hour televised interview of Knowles by Mary Lou Finlay to mark the fiftieth anniversary of his first visit to Ottawa. Entitled *The Man Who Came to Dinner* after his domestic arrangements as a new MP in Ottawa in the 1940s, the programme recounted the familial and religious impulse of Knowles' political career and outlined some of the social changes that have taken place since his first coming to parliament. In 1924, however, all that was totally unknown: the man, the dinner, and the setting were all twenty years in the future. In the meantime, Ottawa compared favourably with Washington, he thought, recalling his visit there in 1919. The House of Commons, however, was not in session so he could not see if the page-boys were as impressive as he had found their American counterparts.

The rest of the trip was less inspiring. From Ottawa he went to Montreal and New York where he visited relatives and worked in a print shop. It was late autumn, he was unhappy, lonely and pining for Manitoba. He did not like the job in New York; perhaps the relatives in Boston could cheer him up. Instead, they gave him a dose of fundamentalist religion and set him wondering whether he ought not go into mission work. After all, his father's sister Lois was in India, and the whole family was deeply imbued with religion. The elder Knowles admitted to having been similarly swayed in his youth by the certainty of a literal interpretation of the Bible. Once on that path the way seemed easy: one need merely go out and spread the Word in order to justify one's existence. The younger Knowles needed another year and a half to sense that the path was too simple and too dogmatic for him. But in the early winter of 1924 it seemed like such a sure and safe thing to a boy far from a California home which he was not sure wanted him any longer.

He did know, however, that the family in Carberry would always greet him warmly. Moreover, he wanted to see snow. Perhaps he could go west in time for Christmas and stay for a while. An initial disappointment on arrival was that there was so little snow, a mere dusting among the wheat stubble. This was not the Canadian winter he had imagined. But if there was not enough snow, there certainly was enough cold. Even the warmth of the Bailey family could not soften this Californian's initiation into a

Canadian winter. One day, while helping with the wood cutting in the timber limit some distance from the farm, he froze both feet. He knew they were cold but he would not complain and after a while he could not feel them at all. Only later when he and his cousins arrived back at the farm did he discover that his feet were like pebbles, frozen solid. He lost his toenails to a prairie winter and the new ones have reminded him of it ever since. He soon learned how to dress for the elements and how to run a farm. He followed the seasons of an agricultural year, helping with all the activities. By the end of the summer, he was ready to return to Los Angeles and to school. He had been away a year.

His father and stepmother were glad to see him, but the year proved difficult and at the end of it he decided to leave permanently. Before then, he had to settle his schooling. He was still attracted by missionary work and by the Bible school training necessary for it. Perhaps his father recognized the oddity of such a course for his boy; certainly when his son spoke of it many years later, he remarked: "I feel as though I'm talking about somebody else, not about myself."[5] At the time father and son went together to the Bible college that the young man was considering, chatted and weighed and discussed the issue with the result that he changed his mind. Instead he chose a small liberal arts college, California Christian College, affiliated with the southern branch of the University of California. To pay for his studies he also had to work. At least now there was no question of his age. He could easily get a night job as a printer, carry his schooling during the day, see his father and brother frequently, and his stepmother as little as possible. The law said he was old enough to carry such a load and family finances demanded it. But it was heavy and the strain told. He lived at home and the relationship with his stepmother was "not the best."[6] A girl friend also added to the tension since she was much like his zealous relatives in Boston, urging him to a fundamentalist religious future. In the midst of that emotional turmoil, he completed the academic year and the job at the printshop and decided to return to Manitoba. The family there would be more soothing.

Through the American west he went this time, knowing that he was going to Canada to stay. Emerson was the port of entry on 15 June 1926 and the officials, unlike the prospective new Canadian, were nonchalant. They waved him into Manitoba where the farm at Carberry worked its magic. By the autumn of 1926 he was ready emotionally and physically to think of further study. Perhaps nearby Brandon College would suit him. His cousins knew of it. One of them had in fact been offered a scholarship there but the amount was too small and the family unable to supplement it so he had had to turn it down. If Stanley wished to go there he would have to finance it himself but where would he get the money? His Carberry relatives more than welcomed him; he was by now quite part of the family. But his help around the farm could hardly enrich the Baileys enough to provide financial assistance for the education of a seventh child.

The Baileys did, however, know J. L. Cowie, editor of the Carberry *News Express*, a weekly paper published in town, six miles from the farm. Cowie had a linotype machine that did not work and a printer whom he did not much like either. Aunt Ida offered her nephew's services: he could probably fix the machine and next time he was in town he did so. A few days later Cowie was wondering if the young man could also print the paper better than his present employee. If so, he could earn twenty-five dollars a week. He could live at the hotel in Carberry and have many of his meals with whatever part of the Bailey family was then living in the tiny rented house in town where the younger Bailey children lived during the school year. For a few months then, he ran the local paper for businessman Cowie. In fact he had only to fill half of the four or six or eight-page paper because, like many weekly papers of the time, the news-sheets arrived from Toronto already printed on one side with stories and serials and recipes. The local paper merely filled the blank pages. Although the pay was less than the eighty cents an hour he had been able to earn in Los Angeles, the work was good. Soon, however, the pay did not compare at all as Cowie fell more and more behind in the weekly salary. How would the young man ever pay for his schooling? He had by now decided to attend Brandon in the autumn of 1927. Somehow he had to earn more money.

He could not go home to Los Angeles, but he could not break away completely from his family either. A cousin Emma was a monotype operator in Boston; she knew about wages and conditions for printers there. Perhaps he could earn enough in half a year in the States to pay for his initial year at Brandon. By Christmas of 1926 it was decided. Emma had assured him that he could earn a minimum of forty dollars a week and the various relatives in Boston were already squabbling over which family he should live with. Now all he had to do was get to Boston. Old Cowie certainly was tightfisted with his cash: he now owed his printer more than one hundred dollars. With that amount he could travel a long way. But the money was not forthcoming, so Stanley thought of a scheme. If Cowie would get him a ticket to Halifax, he would accept that in lieu of the back wages. His employer was unhappy to lose such a good printer (and such a cheap one!) but he was just as glad not to have to dip into his own pocket for cash. He therefore arranged, as Stanley knew he could, the same sort of payment-in-kind which he received from the railway companies as payment for advertising. He turned over a train pass to his employee, who could thereby have a 'free' ride to Halifax, as close as he could get to Boston on a Canadian line and also to his relatives in Nova Scotia. His aunt Lois was there on furlough from India; he would discuss the life of a missionary with her. Perhaps he could even arrange some way for Aunt Lois in Nova Scotia, his father in California, and Aunt Ida in Manitoba to get together. His passion for arranging things was in full flower at age eighteen.

Once in Boston it was easy enough to find a job. A skilled typesetter with experience simply went to the phone book and made a list of all the machine composition companies, those that did typesetting only under contract to publishers of small newspapers, year books, or election lists. Then he went to the company nearest Boston's South station to facilitate transportation and asked for a job. "What's your speed?" queried the foreman. "Oh ... four thousand," came the reply in printer's language, indicating that he could set four thousand ems an hour. "How much do you want?" "Forty dollars a week." "Can you come back at five-thirty?" "Yes." He had a job. If the entry was that easy he could probably add to the salary with overtime work. Soon he was making fifty to sixty dollars a week, working the night shift from five-thirty until four-thirty the next morning with a half-hour break. The ten and one-half hour shift, four nights a week, completed with a six hour shift on Friday evening, made up the recently acquired forty-eight hour work week. The work schedule then left the weekends free from Friday night at eleven-thirty until late Monday afternoon. "I couldn't stand that today, shifting from day to night every weekend, but I loved it. And one of the jokes was that my cousin Charlie and I kept our shared bed warm day and night — I'd come home and he'd get up."[7] From January until late summer he enjoyed his job, his relatives, the weekend excursions with cousins north to York Beach, Maine, or west and north through Massachusetts and into New Hampshire and Vermont. He also watched his bank account grow.

His plans remained unchanged: he intended to return to Manitoba in time for the beginning of the academic year at Brandon College. He also intended to knit his family together and take it with him. He persuaded Aunt Lois to join him in Boston and accompany him to Carberry and he persuaded his father to come from Los Angeles to meet them in Manitoba. That way they could all be together. He planned and organized and attended to all the details. He bought a second-hand car, a 1919 Essex Touring, packed Aunt Lois into it along with cots, tents, and coal-oil stove, and set out on a thirteen-day drive to western Canada, careful always to visit the places he had been before. He even crossed the border again in exactly the same place. No doubt he remarked to Aunt Lois about his sense of becoming a Canadian fourteen months earlier at Emerson on 15 June 1926. This time the formalities were more complex, not for the young man and the middle-aged missionary, but for the Essex Touring. What did Knowles expect to do with it? The officials gave him sixty days to take the car out of Canada or to pay duty on it. He sold it shortly and paid the duty but not before his new classmates at Brandon had had time to comment on this obviously rich young American coming to Canada on a bit of a lark.

The studies in fact were to be very serious while the real lark was the family reunion in Carberry. The new student had already decided to complete the arts programme at Brandon and then do three years of theology. Where it might lead after that was too far in the future; for the moment his plans were working and the dearest members of his family were together. How pleasant it was and how hard the leave-taking were reflected in a letter from his father just after the latter's departure from Carberry:

> I saved my tears until after the train started, and I didn't realize until then how much I wanted to take you along with me. I couldn't ask you for you had made your plans and it was useless. O why do I have to be separated from the boy I love so much? Well I must not give way to my feelings and write this way because it will make it harder for you.[8]

The leave-taking was heartrending, but the son was also looking forward to his studies. There were so many intellectually exciting things going on in the world and he had been too long away from them. Now he could wrestle with them and revel in them. He could argue the current debate over science and religion. He could start wondering about many aspects of his faith that he had taken for granted since childhood. He could think about the faith of that zealous aunt in Boston who had influenced him so greatly: could she really know God's plan for him? He could discuss endlessly with his fellow students who were as religiously conservative and conventional as he in his first year, and who became just as progressive, even radical by the end of three years. He would watch closely the careers of those professors who were considered too modern in their theological and philosophical outlook. University promised to be a stimulating place.

He shared the intellectual and religious excitement with his father in Los Angeles. The elder Knowles followed his son's progress with both yearning and delight and commented effusively on every detail of his son's weekly letters. In 1929 he wrote:

> I am glad you could go to college, get a new vision of life, hear old ideas and conceptions of religion exploded and not lose faith but adjust your faith to knowledge, without throwing away anything vital to a religious life, but also get an inspiration from a new conception of life and religion.[9]

By the end of his college years, the younger Knowles was almost completely committed to the social gospel.

There was of course more to college than religion. The younger Knowles enjoyed all the subjects, the professors, and the students. He was a quick student — "Give me a night and I could pass an exam."[10] History, English, Astronomy, and Economics, he lapped them all up. When the college refused to give a course in Socialism which had been announced in the calendar, he and a few of his fellow students, among them Tommy Douglas, protested, demanding their right to receive instruction in advertised courses. The college gave in and assigned the course to a conservative economics professor. The students followed it avidly, most of them already farther down the road to socialism than their professor would ever be.

Student politics also absorbed the energies and the interest of the new Canadian from Los Angeles. Tommy Douglas was a campus politician and what could be better than to have a cheer-leader who knew all the tricks of the Californian trade? That particular Californian had never done cheer-leading in the States but he knew how it was done. With a few adaptations, sporting yells became political yells, and Tommy won the election as president of the Brandon College student association. His friend continued to cheer for him for years. Indeed the two complemented each other. As Knowles remarked many years later: "He shone in some things that I didn't and I shone in some things that he didn't."[11] They were fast friends.

One aspect of student life seems to have passed him by — romance. He was too serious by nature, he never liked parties, and he had enough problems to wrestle with. The family and religion seem to have formed the boundaries of his emotional experience. Both were so far-reaching in the 1920s that there was little room for anything else. In that he was probably not very different from his fellow students. Among his classmates at Brandon in the graduating year, 1930, not one married another Brandon student. And yet the women students were fond of him, one of them even remarking at a class reunion in 1975 that she had waited forty-five years to kiss him. But in the 1920s such things passed right over the young man's head; if the twenties roared at all for him, they roared religiously.

Religion provided more than intellectual or emotional excitement; it could also be a paying occupation. Knowles financed most of his college education with weekly and summer jobs as a student preacher. One of the community services which Brandon as a Baptist college undertook to provide was student preachers for the surrounding area. The school raised no objections to the young student's professed Methodism and so for eight dollars a Sunday during the year, and fifteen dollars a week in summer, he followed the steps of many an earlier prairie preacher, as a circuit rider (though more often on foot) through the southern prairies. Although he had assisted at many religious services, the first one he had to conduct entirely on his own in the tiny Manitoba community of Rapid City made him very nervous. There was an immense congregation of eleven people — ten women and a man who was hard of hearing. He poured hours of preparation into writing his sermon: the first one had to be just right. When he got to the pulpit, however, he was so frightened that he did not even look at his notes. Concluding from that that he did not really need them, he has never used notes since. Only on one occasion in 1943 did he have a prepared manuscript and he was to be soundly chastised for that.

After a few Sundays' initiation, he was ready to take on an entire summer of student preaching. Although he was not yet a theology student, he knew that he was preparing for the ministry and such summer work seemed appropriate. Certainly the financial and physical strain were calculated to test the mettle of an aspiring preacher. His fifteen dollars a week during the summer of 1928 at Hairy Hill, Alberta, included neither expenses nor transportation[12] and Aunt Ida was worried that he would come home "looking thin and miserable" after all the miles of "circuit walking."[13] While the family fussed and advised — even to the extent of Aunt Ida's gently suggesting that he think about a word that he had spelled twice now as "paritioners"[14] — he continued the pace. The following summer, in 1929, he accepted a similar post at Reston, Manitoba. There he attempted to combine his pastoral duties with his own personal searchings and wonderings and studying. The family continued to worry about his health — and his handwriting. From Los Angeles his generally doting father admonished him about his writing and in an effort to have him change his ways, enclosed a comment of a pastor friend of his: "It takes not only a Greek philosopher but a Hindoo mystic to translate or transpose his heiroglyphics." "Everyone admires a good penman," added father somewhat more prosaically, but even while reproving him, he could not restrain his admiration for this precocious son. He allowed that Stanley's thoughts came so much faster than he could pen them that of course he had to scrawl.[15] When his son took to typewriting, the father admitted to the increased legibility, but mourned the lost personal touch.[16]

Of more importance to the younger Knowles was the fact that his father followed closely and sympathetically his religious evolution. Indeed the father seems to have believed that his son was expressing ideas which he had held for many years but had never been able to express. He agreed completely, for example, with his son's expression of Jesus' mission to the world: that He had come to build a better world and that the Kingdom of God is being built here and now. Both father in Los Angeles and son in Manitoba agreed that a life is successful to the extent that it contributes to such a better world.[17] Father was delighted that Stanley had caught a vision of a "grander and better gospel that links Christ and his life with every day affairs."[18] "I would not have you a narrow ranting fundamentalist splitting hairs over doctrines and neglecting justice, mercy and truth."[19] There was little danger of that. He had absorbed from his father, from his religious upbringing, from his studies, and from his own intellectual development the notion that the message of Christianity was that of an unselfish, sacrificing life — working tirelessly for the betterment of the human condition. Preaching such ideas, however, had him confronting accusations of heresy, deacons who speculated on the grain exchange[20] and, later, church boards who wanted to know how many souls he had saved. Believing such ideas eventually led him into politics.

Such a decision was, however, far in the future. At the moment, a more immediate one had to be made. Knowles had been associated with the Methodist Church in the United States. Now he was studying at a Baptist college and was preaching as a summer student from that college. Ought he to affiliate himself with the Baptists and the Canadian church? His father thought not. Through the summer of 1929 he referred again and again to the question:

> Of course you will have to choose for yourself, but I could wish that you would find it in God's plan for you to be affiliated with the church of your childhood and of your father and also of your native country. Perhaps Canada needs you, but the U.S. needs you too and I don't like to see you get weaned away from your own country.[21]

His son had heard that plea before and he chose to ignore those aspects of his father's letters. The decision for Canada had already been made back in 1926. Maybe Canada did need him, but he needed Canada even more. Nonetheless, the denominational question remained and his father kept at it: "You will find that the Baptist denomination pretty well lives up to the reputation of its nickname (Hardshell Baptist) and it will be hard for anyone with ideas of progress to break thru the shell."[22] And later still: "I think with you that the best place and the best agency to advance the Kingdom is in the Church, but possibly not the Baptist Church."[23] Whether the barrage of opinionated advice from his father or his own beliefs held sway, he never did join the Baptists but rather went on to a United Church theological school and into the United Church. Had he been a Canadian by birth he no doubt would have moved directly there with other Methodists at the time of Church Union in 1924. Once that affiliation with the United Church was made, he never broke it; he remains a licensed minister who marries, baptizes, and buries. But he seldom preaches, at least not within the walls of the church.

The 1920s presented an emotional, intellectual, and religious challenge to the young Stanley Knowles. He had come to terms with the death of his mother and the acquisition of a stepmother. He had been an under-aged child labourer, an industrial worker. He had travelled across North America three times and he had come to rest on the Manitoba plains. He had struggled with religion and had seen in the clear, bright, northern air the particular path he had to follow. In the spring of 1930 he had only to collect his B.A. — "the first Knowles to get a college degree," crowed his father happily.[24]

Actually it was not so easy. He had only one suit and it had gone to the cleaners the day of the graduation ceremony. Back it came in time, but with no pants! He hunted high and low but there were no pants to be found. With the ceremony only an hour or so away, what was he to do? In 1930 one could hardly wear a pair of grey flannel trousers with a blue serge jacket. Nor could he find an academic gown long enough to hide his nakedness. In desperation, he phoned the cleaners but the pants had been delivered. But where? The cleaner did offer to supply him with a more or less matching pair from the collection of oddments in the

"the first Knowles to get a college degree." Brandon 1930.

shop. None would fit the tall, lanky student, and the hour was getting closer. He would have to make do with a pair that was too short and too tight. By not buttoning the trousers he could let them hang down at his hips and the cuffs would reach the floor. With any luck the ceremony would be brief. In any case, his gown would cover most of the ill-fitting suit. He had to run to the church where convocation was already under way. In the line ahead of him, he spotted a tall friend with a long gown: "Gordon, can we trade gowns? It's terribly important and I'll explain it to you later."[25] Once enveloped in a bigger gown, he felt more secure and was able to hitch at his trousers without being too conspicuous. The individual degree granting went smoothly and quickly and he was relieved. Then, with no warning, he was called back to receive first one medal accompanied by an appropriate congratulatory speech from the college president, and then another with an even lengthier speech. The graduating student was pleased and from the gallery his Aunt Ida was beaming. But to himself he was muttering: "J.R., for heaven's sake, quit before my pants fall down!"[26]

The pants stayed, the degree stayed, the medals stayed, and Stanley Knowles stayed. He would be a Canadian and a minister . . . and what else? He voted in the federal election that July . . .

3
FATHER

2 September 1932

The morning's mail had just been delivered to the young student minister, completing his first summer with a United Church mission at Winnipeg Beach, Manitoba. He shuffled it quickly, looking for the familiar hand of his father, eager to carry on the weekly discussion that was by now a necessary part of both Stanley Knowles' lives. Little did the younger Knowles know when he had his father's letter in his hand that he held his own future as well. The year was 1932; both Canada and the United States were plummeting towards the depths of the depression. Father, at age fifty-seven, had been laid off.

The shock and the tears and the hows and whys overwhelmed him. His father was a skilled machinist and had years of steady employment with the Los Angeles Street Railway. He was a prized employee; he took an interest in his job; he had even made suggestions — and been recognized for them — about ways of improving the company's operations. He was serious and sober and honest: an employer could not ask for a better worker. But he was fifty-seven. And the company, in financial straits, had sought the advice of an efficiency expert who, without any consideration of seniority, skill, or length of service, had calmly pronounced that anyone over fifty-five was expendable. Mr. Knowles would have to go and he would have to go without a pension, without severance pay, without unemployment insurance, without any sickness benefits and without, except for one particular instance, ever having had a paid vacation. The scrapheap of the depression claimed him.

His son never forgot that day. He was about to enter the final year of theology at United College, Winnipeg, and his father, through his misfortune, had just shown him the path. The social gospel that he had awakened to during his years at Brandon would have to be the guiding principle of his preaching. He had never been comfortable with the notion of a minister's role as a preparer of souls for the after-life; now it would be impossible even to think, let alone speak that way. If the economic system wreaked such havoc as was visible every day in Winnipeg, if it discarded fifty-seven-year-old skilled workmen, if so few voices were protesting, the young student minister would have to take a stand. He had planned his life in and around one of the strongest social institutions man had created — the church. But now he intended to use that institution as a public platform. The feeble social conscience of the time would have to be strengthened and he would have to do his part. Through the church, he would urge a change in the social and economic system, for no society should mete out such treatment to any of its citizens, let alone the elderly. Hence the battle lines for Knowles' career were drawn. For the moment the setting would be the church — the political decision came later — but the nature of the battle was clear and it never changed.

His father had, of course, provided much more than the immediate occasion for a quick but long-lasting decision. All his adult life he had provided the surroundings, the ideas, the stimulation, and the affection to nurture such a son. The stunning letter in the late summer of 1932 was merely the occasion for the son to declare his colours. His father had been indicating the colours for years.

Stanley Ernest Knowles was born in Upper Woods Harbour, Shelburne County, Nova Scotia, on 21 August 1874. He could trace his ancestors back to a Richard Knowles on Cape Cod in the 1630s and further still to relatives on the *Mayflower* in 1620. The Knowles name appeared among colonial legislators, and sometime in the late 1750s, Nathaniel, great-grandfather to Stanley Ernest, migrated from Cape Cod to Nova Scotia, settling first in Liverpool and then in 1771 in Barrington Passage. He may have been one of the "neutral Yankees of Nova Scotia" during the revolutionary period for most of the Knowles family remained in Massachusetts to become some of the first Americans; Nathaniel's descendants were some of the first Canadians. A son Jonathan bought a farm at Upper Woods Harbour in the 1820s and his son Benjamin continued it. There Stanley Ernest was born and he remembered the combination house and barn that the family lived in until 1896 when a "real" house, was built closer down the slope of the hill toward the road. He knew at first hand and always cherished his own father's "uprightness of character and rugged honesty and devotion to the higher things of life."[1] Indeed that was perhaps all many Nova Scotians of the area had to cling to for the land was stingy. Before a potato could be planted a rock had to be moved; before a new mouth was added to a family, an elder offspring had to move out.

Benjamin Knowles' children departed in the order of their coming and eventually not one of them was left at Upper Woods Harbour. Daughter Lois, the seventh of the eight children who lived, provided a partial exception to the pattern although her experience was not unusual for the time and place. At infancy she was given to daughterless relatives across the bay and grew up calling them Pa and Ma and knowing her own parents as Uncle Bennie and Aunt Libbie. In adult life, she became a missionary to India. Before departing from a farm that simply could not support them all, the children acquired elementary schooling in the local one-room schoolhouse; some of them developed a passion for education that would only be satisfied by their children. And then they set out. Stanley Ernest's leave-taking was prepared by two summers, 1891 and 1892, working as a waiter on the boat running between St. John, New Brunswick and Halifax. Like his son after him, he maintained his family ties and always delighted in bad summer weather which forced the ship to take the inner passage around the tip of Nova Scotia. From there he could see the family home.

Sentimental attachment never did enrich a subsistence farm, and Stanley Ernest soon followed his elder brother to Boston. By 1900 he had acquired work and skill as a journeyman machinist. His job with the Holzer Cabot company was a good one and the young man was both interested and took pride in it. He was also known for his scrupulous honesty; fifty years later, a nephew, Samuel Knowles, began work with the same company and the name caught the attention of some old-timers in the plant. Was the newcomer related to "Honest Knowles," the man who refused to walk off with the merest nut or bolt from the company's scrapheap? Besides his honesty Knowles also had professional ambitions. For some years he took correspondence classes in drafting and engineering, possibly hoping to emulate his friend Howard Chandler, a mechanical engineer.

That particular ambition was never realized but Chandler did persuade Knowles to leave Boston for the Pacific coast. The friendship lasted through Knowles' marriage in 1904 and the young family's difficulties first in San Francisco and then in Los Angeles. The closeness was later reflected in son Stanley's being given Howard as a second name, even though the American west had not delivered all that Chandler had predicted. Many years later, Knowles wrote his son in Winnipeg and described his state of mind as the small family eked out a precarious existence in 1908:

> For five straight weeks before you were born I search[ed] in vain for employment, and only secured work the day before you were born. During those weeks the injustice of the social system was impressed upon me as I tramped the streets because of the lack of carfare to pay for rides, in a vain search for remunerative labor. I cut a few lawns and altogether made about $2.00 and I do not doubt that it was impressed upon your mother also, tho she said little about the deprivations we were enduring . . .[2]

The birth of Stanley Howard may have brought luck to his father; from 1908 he generally had steady employment as a machinist, mostly with the Los Angeles Street Railway.

His job was one of precision and accuracy and Knowles had satisfaction from it. Often, if he had overtime work to do, he would take his young son with him to see the huge planer that he operated. The boy could scarcely believe planing metal to within one thousandth of an inch, but his father showed him exactly how to measure such an amount and exactly how to accomplish the task. As a mere child, the younger Knowles learned about calipers and micrometers and subsequently never lost the fascination for precision instruments (and even for toys and puzzles with similar complexity). His father emphasized those same characteristics outside the workshop too. When Stanley had parts to play at school or church, his father would coach him in the accuracy of his facts and the precision of his delivery.

Although his father usually had regular work, the income remained low. There was no money for fancy expenditures, for cars, or for holidays. Supplemented by sales from the garden, the weekly income was just enough to keep the family. Over the years, some small savings were put into property: the family bought its first house in 1914 and thereafter gradually acquired a few other shabby properties. Mr. Knowles did the maintenance on the houses and the rent was intended to provide an income in his old age. In the meantime, any extra pennies went into the debts and the upkeep.

Son Stanley absorbed it all. As a very small boy he kept an account book similar to that of his father in which he recorded all his income and expenditures: .05 cents for delivering papers; .02 cents for selling vegetables; .03 cents borrowed from mother; .01

cent lost. Every penny counted and he kept track of them all. He still remembers the astonishment and anxiety he felt when his father offered the church minister an entire silver dollar to help pay for the gas when the minister had driven Aunt Lois, on a furlough visit from India in 1917, around Los Angeles.

By 1918, however, family finances were improving. Wartime wages had risen and his father had a new job with the booming shipbuilding industry in a dry docks at San Pedro, some twenty miles from home. He and some co-workers from the vicinity shared the expenses of a car pool and one day in 1918 young Knowles returned from school to find a "machine" in the shed out the back. With great excitement, he danced around, bellowing "We've got a machine! We've got a machine!"[3] as the 1913 Model T Ford sat there in all its splendour. The family had arrived. Now perhaps they could enjoy the "outings" so many others seemed to indulge in.

Outings, or in fact vacations of any sort, were a luxury for most working people. Paid vacations were not yet part of a worker's contract and Mr. Knowles only had one in his life. He did manage to send his son and wife to the seaside once by taking them out to Wadonda Beach, parking them in a tent there for a week, and returning to fetch them the following Sunday. The only other vacation was the ill-fated one in the mountains in 1918 when Mrs. Knowles took sick; there too Mr. Knowles did not accompany the family. Indeed a worker had only two ways of taking a vacation: he could have one forced upon him by the temporary closing of his place of work or he could quit his job and hope to locate another after the holiday.

Mr. Knowles took the second course in 1919. In order to accompany his boys to Nova Scotia after the death of their mother, he left his job with the dry docks and counted on being able to find another when the family returned to Los Angeles in the autumn. A different shipbuilding firm in San Pedro willingly took him on in the fall but by then he had an additional worry. The twenty-mile drive terrified his eleven-year-old son, now fearful that he might lose his one remaining parent in an automobile accident. Whenever his father was a few minutes late arriving home from work, Stanley was sure he was dead. For months the boy lived in daily terror and when the Los Angeles Street Railway indicated its desire to have Mr. Knowles back among its employees, Stanley pleaded with his father to take the job. The pay was less but he could walk to work and his son would be secure. He used all his budding reasoning powers and many of his small boy's tears. His father agreed.

Once back with the Street Railway, Mr. Knowles proved to be an even greater asset to his employer. During the 1920s the company was engaged in a political battle to have the city outlaw jitney buses, small vehicles that picked up fare-paying passengers anywhere along any route. The Street Railway thought the buses represented unfair competition. Knowing Mr. Knowles' argumentative and rhetorical skill, the company asked for his assistance, speaking and writing in defence of the company's interests. For that he could have time off, with pay. When the case was won, the Street Railway gave Mr. Knowles a week's vacation with pay.

In 1932, however, a financially strapped company chose to forget its prized employee, his skills, and his more than twenty years of cumulative service. Mr. Knowles was old, so Mr. Knowles would have to go. The blow struck deeply. Only a few weeks earlier he had been telling his father in Nova Scotia of the recent time and pay cuts which had reduced his wage by twenty-three percent in the last two years. He was also having difficulty collecting the rents on the houses he owned; one tenant owed more than one hundred dollars. Then there were medical expenses for himself and his wife Anna, his sons' stepmother. Nonetheless, he was able to add that ". . . I am thankful that I have a job and am well, when millions are idle and in need."[4] Within a few weeks he was to join those millions. His father's views had come earlier. Like some ancient prophet from the distant gloom of Nova Scotia, he saw in the depression the fulfilment of the scriptures, "for it sayes that in last dayes a time of troubel such as thare never was and I belive that time has come."[5]

The grandson in Winnipeg could no longer accept such answers. He had many of his grandfather's characteristics but not this one. The depression was a human and social disaster, not some Heaven-ordained infliction. The way out was not resignation to the inevitable, but immediate care for the victims and long-term action to change society so that such a disaster could not recur.

Neither the religious nor the political response to the depression was of much solace to Knowles in Los Angeles. He had to go begging to his former employer, knocking on all the doors he knew in the hope of finding a sympathetic response. When he did, the only job available was that of cleaning the street cars. He had to accept it, but his bitterness remained:

The more I think over it, the more I realize what a monstrous injustice the Corp. has done to me, putting me at my age to such hard and unskilled labor, when I am still in the prime of efficiency, after such a long period of faithful service. No excuse of the necessity of economy can justify such treatment, when they keep younger and less efficient men in their service in my place and then notify me that I will not be eligible to qualify for a pension. I can't get over it and only the dire necessity of an income makes me continue my connection with the Corp. I want to use my skill and experience at my trade, creating something, instead of uninteresting, unskilled and menial labour that only requires a strong back and a weak mind.[6]

Knowles never did have a weak mind and in his late fifties he no longer had a strong back. Within a few months, he was in hospital with ulcers. And in spite of a change to a less physically demanding task operating the transfer table that turned street cars around and placed them on different tracks, he was hospitalized again two years later. This time, the diagnosis was cancer and the doctors could do nothing. He was dead at sixty-one and his son remains convinced that the psychological blow of that firing in 1932 hastened the end.

Certainly it hastened the younger Knowles' decision about his future. He had already distanced himself intellectually and religiously from his Baptist surroundings at Brandon but the actual break came when the First Baptist Church in Winnipeg where he had been a student minister during his second year of theology at United College could no longer afford to pay him the ten dollars a week in winter and eighteen in summer. In the summer of 1932, therefore, he took his first mission field with the United Church. By the fall, he knew exactly what his role in the United Church had to be: one continuous effort to ensure that his father's experience would not be repeated. The father in Los Angeles became all the working people in Canada and the son in Winnipeg determined that they should have health, decent wages, vacations, pensions and job security. From then on, he saw his father in all the railway workers in Winnipeg and across the country; he sensed his mother in all old and ailing women. He would do their bidding.

Actually, he owed more of his life's work to his father than just that one fateful letter in 1932. His father had been a close friend, a fair disciplinarian, a keen discussant, a firm guide, and an avid enthusiast. He and his eldest son were emotional and intellectual companions and became even more so after the death of Margaret Knowles in 1919.

The family had been warm and close and affectionate. The

"so much more fun to go and play." Los Angeles c. 1916.

two boys were surrounded with all the love and devotion that only two parents who had lost their first two children can provide. Mother was gentle and caring; father was loving and guiding and ever so reasonable. He did not believe that a child should ever be chastised in anger. So his boys received appointments for their punishments for their childish misdeeds long after the action to ensure that father was meting out fair justice and not simply indulging his own anger. His son recalls more of what upset his father than the misdeeds themselves or the punishment. As a youngster he had once balked at his daily chore of watering the lawn and garden. It would be so much more fun to go and play. The garden hose already had a leak; supposing the leak turned into a torrent? Stanley helped it along and skipped off to play. Later his father wanted to know why the watering had not been done. "Well, the hose broke," came the reply. But his father's sense of precision was too good for that. He spotted the extended rip and knew the cause. He then discussed the matter with his son and revealed his concern, not for the damaged hose or even for the parched garden but rather for the fact that his son would deceive him. So an appointment was made and Stanley was duly punished. He does not remember the punishment but he does remember the cause of it.

His father's religious beliefs have stayed with him too. In fact,

"The two boys were surrounded with all the love and devotion . . ." Los Angeles 1916.

in many ways the younger Knowles followed a path similar to that of his father. Time and circumstance were to take him a step further, but until the early 1930s the two were companions on the same road. His own attraction to fundamentalist, revivalist religion in the mid-1920s had been foreshadowed by his father's similar interest in a Holiness Movement in Nova Scotia in the late

1880s and early 1890s. With no formal secondary schooling and no organized entertainment for young people religion had provided both intellectual and emotional excitement. But once Knowles left Nova Scotia his ideas changed. He remained an intensely religious person and considered himself a Christian all his life. But he came more and more to believe that the purpose of Christianity was not the preparation for a life after death, but rather the making of a better life on earth. Such a belief did not necessitate the discarding of notions of immortality or of life after death; indeed, Knowles had strong ideas on both, but he also felt that such matters were precisely the lot of the next world and could therefore take care of themselves. What mattered here and now was the betterment of present society. Putting his beliefs into practice, he wrote to newspapers and for church bulletins, he acted as a lay preacher, and he spoke at the endless round of prayer, class, and brotherhood meetings that the Methodist Church which he attended in Los Angeles continuously hosted. Although he was greatly respected and loved by his fellow church-goers, he was also considered just a little different. Where others would give witness to the faith and testify to the Lord's action upon their souls, he would speak of the need for a real brotherhood of man and of the creation of a Kingdom of God on earth. He was a social gospeller long before the term gained popular parlance let alone credibility. And he passed those beliefs on to his son.

The younger Knowles carried them two steps further, first religiously when he began querying the divinity of Christ, and then politically when he realized that changing the world meant public action. About the latter, his father was very excited. The former, however, left him dubious although never sufficiently to withdraw his tolerance and encouragement. As he remarked in a letter to his son:

> To come to the subject of the Divinity of Jesus, I can appreciate all of your arguments, and say as I said some time ago, I can tolerate and overlook anything except a betrayal of the spirit of Him who taught and spoke as never man taught or spoke; so I will not enter into any controversy with you on the subject but will say that if your interpretation of Jesus as a man gives you a greater inspiration, a more devoted life to the principles he taught and died for and leads you to devote your all to the spreading of the kingdom of love I have no word of condemnation or reproach; but rather of praise for one who will give his all for the truth as he sees it.[7]

Father may have been ever so slightly hesitant about his son's "modernism" but he would always support him and would always defend him from any detractors.[8]

In the early 1930s, the letters between father and son discussed economics to a greater extent and in that the father had also shown the way. Ever since his early days in Los Angeles, the elder Knowles had been pondering the economic system. In 1908 he had given up on prohibition as the social panacea of the day and had begun to contemplate the writings of Henry George, the advocate of the Single Tax. George's panacea developed out of his ideas about land values. In an era of massive speculation in land, George postulated that its value was created by a community, not by an individual. A piece of land two hundred miles from nowhere had no practical value until a community had developed around it and had given it some worth. Why then should someone who had simply held that piece of land from a distance until others had created its value reap the profit? The profit should go to the community that had created the wealth. A Single Tax on land values, on what the land was actually worth for use, would provide the community or the state with the necessary money for various social services. George believed his scheme would eliminate speculation and provide the community with necessary funds.

Knowles and his brother Charles became single-minded devotees of George's Single Tax. Both of them carried on a thirty-year campaign among relatives and friends to convince them of the appropriateness and accuracy of George's views. In the Knowles home in Los Angeles Single Tax literature abounded and the young Stanley was immersed in what his father called the "gospel of Henry George".[9] But he seems not to have accepted that particular gospel as readily as his father did, nor as readily as he accepted the religious gospel. Indeed, by the late 1920s he was arguing with his father about the lack of a religious or spiritual element in George's plan for reforming society. His father replied plaintively that he should give George's readings one more try.[10] How closely the elder Knowles had linked his own religious and economic beliefs was evident in a letter to his son in 1930:

> Of course I agree with you and any others who say that economic reform is not sufficient to lead us to God, nor any amount of material prosperity will satisfy the spiritual nature of man. Yet unjust and unnatural conditions under which we live are not conducive to developing the highest and best in man, and so I link the Single Tax reform as a part of the

message of Jesus toward building a better world, a world without war and misery, poverty and greed, a world where men are brothers, and all have an equal chance to the bounties of our Father God . . .[11]

The difference of opinion between father and son over George's economics began by being a religious one. It soon became political. From the George notion that land values were created by the community, it was not a long step to the idea that all wealth is created by the community. It was not individuals doing particular tasks, but rather society as a whole that created the wealth of a given community. Hence the impossibility of measuring the particular contribution of each person to a society's wealth whether it be in the form of buildings, railways, transportation, food, or clothing. The creation of wealth was a social process and its distribution should be the same: to society as a whole. Knowles maintained that belief for the rest of his life arguing that ideally wealth should be distributed equally among all members of society. Before that might be achieved, however, one should at least ensure that the wealth of a society benefit everyone and not just the individual who happened to own the land, the building, or the patent, or to have been there first. The step from George's notion of the Single Tax to socialism was an easy and natural one for him. The faith behind the step, however, remained a religious one even though the language became more and more secular. His father had a more difficult time releasing the economic belief that had comforted him for so long; only in 1935 would he grudgingly admit that the link from the Single Tax to socialism was a logical one.

The elder Knowles' emotional and intellectual attachment to his son in Winnipeg grew as his own family life deteriorated. His wife Anna had kept the household running and had mothered the younger son Warren through the 1920s but she had always wondered about her husband's affections. They seemed so centred on his sons and after Stanley's departure in 1924, even more drawn to him. The tension between husband and wife increased and by the early 1930s they were very bitter to and about each other, he wondering how a "sane person could have such a poisoned tongue."[12] and she complaining that her husband was always blaming her for Stanley's departure.[13] No wonder he buried himself in his son's letters on a Sunday afternoon and debated religion, the Single Tax, and socialism through the mail with his more compatible son.

By 1935, the son had taken a very exciting step indeed. He was to run in the federal election as a CCF candidate. Still clinging to his religious upbringing and training, he described the decision "as distinctly a call as anything I ever experienced,"[14] but his father was more prosaic about it. He thought the move was just great, exactly what his son had been preparing for, and indeed something he would have liked to do himself. In Los Angeles, Mr. Knowles had participated in a recent EPIC — End Poverty in California campaign — and he had always been drawn to a public crusade. Now another of his ambitions was to be fulfilled by this dear son. He was of course convinced that his son would win. The thought of defeat never entered his mind and he began making plans to come to Ottawa to see his son take his seat in the House of Commons.

But it was not to be. At least the father would not know of his son's defeat. By the summer of 1935 he was in hospital, spinning out an agonizing death from cancer. In mid-election campaign, his son took his first flight, from Winnipeg to Los Angeles, to see and say good-bye to his father. Mr. Knowles was in pain, but ever so pleased to have his son near again and present for his sixty-first birthday. When Stanley left to return to Canada he knew he would not see his friend and dear dad again. The telegram came on 3 October. He lost his father and eleven days later he lost his first election. There would always be another election to win but his father was irretrievable and the twenty-seven year old, alone in Winnipeg, was heartbroken.

But he had long since acquired his parents' fortitude and knew how to hide the hurt and keep them close even over the distance of death. To the relatives in Nova Scotia he reported his father's dying words at four A.M. on 3 October: "Nurse, I think there's something wrong," and went on to put his own words into his father's voice:

> A prophetic word out of a heart of vision and love — "Stanley, there are things in this world that are wrong; I leave you to carry on, pursuing the vision I have given you of a world set right through the application here in this world of the teachings of Jesus."[15]

Ever since then, Stanley Knowles, fully aware that he is Exhibit A of a person doing what his parents wish for him, has been doing his father's work.

4
HOW MANY SOULS?

16 April 1934

The board of Central United Church in downtown Winnipeg convened early that evening in April. It was concerned about its young minister, the Reverend Stanley Howard Knowles. What were his future plans for the church? Did he intend to continue his somewhat questionable behaviour of the past year? His radio sermons attracted attention to the church. Was that really what the board wanted? And what of the ferment of the year before that, with the Sunday night forums drawing people into the church who had not even attended the sermon but merely dropped in later to participate in the discussion? It was not quite proper. And where was all the money coming from to finance these radio services? The board knew that twice a year the provincial radio commission offered free Sunday-night air-time to each of the main downtown churches and it was flattered to be considered among them after the hard times of recent years. But Central United was heard from more than twice a year and its minister was urging social reform. The board was not amused. What was behind it all? Moreover, asked one board member, looking directly at the minister: "How many souls had Mr. Knowles saved by all this activity?"[1]

The minister was taken aback. After almost two years at Central United, he was used to the board, but he was not in the habit of counting souls. Indeed for some time, he had seriously been questioning the notion that the purpose of Christianity was to save souls. Through his schooling at Brandon and then during his theological training at United College and even more so in his weekly letters with his father in Los Angeles, he increasingly believed that the intent of Christianity was to incorporate ethical, moral, and religious principles into contemporary society. To do so would necessitate social change. But here he was, confronted with a church board whose members were mostly businessmen and who were not at all interested in dramatic changes in society even though many of them were suffering the economic effects of the depression. In response to the query about souls, he quietly explained what he believed were the two main messages of Christianity — one for the individual and one for society. Board members nodded at the first and frowned slightly at the second. As Rev. Knowles went on to acknowledge the first and grant it its due, the board thought it was to be mollified. Knowles, however, did not stop. His own mission as a Christian minister, he claimed, was to stress the second message, the social rather than the individual gospel, particularly in times such as the 1930s. And if the board was worried about the financing of the radio pro-grammes, it could relax; the minister had asked both his congregation and his radio audience for contributions to help pay the twenty-five dollar cost for each of the broadcasts. The money had come flowing in and was all duly recorded by the church secretary who also made the payments. Everything was quite proper. Nevertheless, the question of how many souls hung in the air of the meeting and lingered in the minister's mind. It raised all of the problems that he had experienced with Central United and that accompanied his continuing connection with the church until, in 1940, he took a paying job elsewhere and never returned.

Central United Church, formerly Central Congregational, was in fact one of the main churches in downtown Winnipeg. In terms of physical size, it was the biggest church with an enormous auditorium. Progressive ministers such as James L. Gordon just before the First World War and George Laughton in the 1920s had drawn huge congregations. But since then the church had declined. The congregation had even split in the late 1920s under the ministrations of one Campbell Morgan, a fiery evangelist and ultra-fundamentalist preacher. The man had so enraged one part of the congregation and delighted the other that it could no longer live as one; Morgan departed with his followers to form Zion Church and to continue the witness for fundamentalism. Having lost half its members and much of its zeal, Central United declined steadily. Preacher after preacher attempted to restore a large congregation, and with it some measure of prosperity, but none of them succeeded. By the early 1930s, with the depression deepening over Winnipeg, the church considered closing its doors. In 1932 the board took one final risk. Two student preachers, cheaper than one ordained minister, might perk things up. United College provided the names of two students who were just entering their final year of theology and who could probably handle the task: William Hughes and Stanley Knowles. Knowles in particular had much experience, having been a student minister ever since 1928; one of his latest jobs had been at First Baptist, the church just across the road. Everyone seemed to know the young man and everyone spoke highly of him. Since the ministerial task was to be divided between the two students, college officials were not unduly worried about the possibility of academic strain.

So Hughes and Knowles became the co-pastors of Central United Church with the awesome task of increasing the congregation, and, presumably, keeping the board happy. Hughes succeeded in the latter and Knowles in the former. The two alternated the two Sunday services and divided the weekly ones; they both received ten dollars a week. Knowles' Sunday evening services soon acquired a reputation and the attendance slowly began to climb.

Perhaps the sermons, always on a social gospel theme, attracted the newcomers but the discussions that followed seemed to arouse even more interest. Every two weeks, after his Sunday evening service, Knowles organized a series of public forums. He invited outside speakers such as J. S. Woodsworth, S. J. Farmer, John Queen, Beatrice Brigden, Ralph Maybank, and Ed Russenhold, most of them close to or already members of the recently formed Co-operative Commonwealth Federation. The labour speakers were more than willing to come and their topics matched their cause: "Has Capitalism Failed?" "The Essence of Socialism." "Does Christianity have a message for the depression?" The questions and the discussion aroused increasing interest and Knowles' congregation grew accordingly. The collection doubled and tripled and the numbers were easy to estimate: one simply divided the total receipts by the usual contribution of five cents. Only later did the young student minister realize that he had accidentally renewed a tradition that had been broken in the early 1920s in Winnipeg with the demise of the Labour Churches. They had fulfilled both a social and a religious role for many working class people who subsequently never renewed ties with the traditional churches. When Stanley Knowles' Sunday night forums at Central United began in 1932, the same people reappeared.

Board members were less enthusiastic. It was all very well for the congregation to increase, but surely Mr. Knowles could do so without engaging in so many political matters. Some of the members argued that the church could not afford to heat the building after the sermon. The church caretaker could only manage to stoke the seven wood-burning furnaces in the basement of the church long enough to heat the building for the duration of the evening church service but more than that he could not do. The forums would have to cease for lack of fuel. Neither the chairman of the board, a former president of the Manitoba Liberal Association and a prominent member of the National Liberal Convention held in 1919, nor most of his businessmen colleagues wished to know whether capitalism had failed. And the few unemployed workers on the board, although they sided with Knowles, were too impecunious to have much say. Only one member upheld the notion of freedom of speech, but since even he had serious reservations about the kind of speech the young Knowles was inclined to make, he did not sway the board. The forums would have to go.

The board, however, was quite content to keep the minister. It merely wanted to restrain his enthusiasm. Although the board members put a halt to the forums in the winter of 1933 and even hinted that the young theology student might not obtain a ministerial position after completing his year at Central,[2] they did in fact offer him the full ministry after his ordination into the United Church of Canada in June 1933. A salary of twelve hundred dollars a year went with the job; to it the women's auxiliary later added ten dollars a month to cover car expenses. It was good money for the 1930s.

The ordination was not in fact as straightforward as the graduating student had expected when he chose a religious career six years earlier. Not that the examinations were difficult; he had never had any problems there. But given his own evolution during his student days, and considering the conflict with the board of Central United over the forums, he did wonder whether he ought to proceed with ordination. In that he was not alone. Several fellow students shared his questioning: was the church moving the right way during those dark years? They were not sure but they suspected the examiners might not be either. Therefore they took the oral examination, answered the questions as their social consciences and six years of training prompted them, and waited to see what would happen. If the examiners chose to reject their views of Christianity and of the church's mission then they would simply have to find another outlet. The examiners, however, had also absorbed the social gospel that had spread through the Protestant and particularly the Methodist-United churches since the turn of the century. They had taught their courses stressing the social side of Christianity and for the ordination exam they asked about the relevance of Christianity to the people of 1933.

Knowles' answer must have sufficed for he was accepted for ordination. Thenceforth, he would be the Reverend Stanley Knowles — his father immediately began addressing his weekly letters in the correct manner — although he now admits that he prefers the simpler title Mr.

Once ordained, he continued at Central United, accepting the board's decision to suspend the forums but eager to find another outlet for the message he felt he had to spread. During the autumn and winter of 1933-1934, he tried radio. The medium was still something of a novelty in the early 1930s and attracted an eager audience particularly on Sundays, the traditional day of rest. Religious services therefore abounded on the airwaves even when the evening ones had to compete with comedian Jack Benny. Knowles himself admitted to catching a few minutes of Benny before heading for his pulpit. As for his own broadcast sermons, there he would preach, not engage in politics. Surely his board could not object. He did, however, design his sermons carefully. Those for broadcast always emphasized a social gospel theme; he saved his more philosophical discourses for the morning services or for those evenings when the radio microphone was absent. He also prepared his sermons meticulously, only to do as he had done ever since his first attempt at preaching — he ignored the notes entirely once he stepped into the pulpit.

The topics were numerous and the audience increasingly so. No one, least of all the church, argued the young minister, could ignore the ever-growing breadlines in Winnipeg, the people without cash, living on relief vouchers and 'paying' for their relief by working in the woodlots or digging ditches. No one could ignore the increasingly gloomy international scene. Hitler's name was known; where would it lead? And where would the church stand should the worst fears of the decade be realized and another world war break out? There were enough problems to fill years of radio broadcasts, but Knowles made do with a few. They were sufficient to gain him a wide audience, much larger than that of the forums the year before. Indeed, he began to receive letters from his listeners, almost all of them favourable. The few critics of the time have long since become supporters.

The members of the board, however, did not send supportive letters. Indeed, they tended to cringe when they knew that one of the Sunday night services was to be broadcast. By the early spring of 1934, they had had enough. When it came time to plan the coming church year, they hesitated. Presumably they would keep the minister but did they have to keep the radio broadcasts? The church and the minister were acquiring just a bit too much notoriety. How could he be so sure that the depression was a man-made thing? And how could he be so sure that he had the answers? Moreover, was this really the kind of thing an ordained minister ought to be doing? The board members, from a different religious generation, worried about souls not about society. And so came the question: how many souls did Mr. Knowles think he was saving with all his activities? The question was asked so seriously and the minister's activities so obviously distressed the board that he knew he would have to resolve the problem.

Through the late spring of 1934 he wrestled with the question. Could one in fact effectively combine church work with what was becoming so obviously political work? And could one really be effective if there was always a board — the minister's own employer — in the background wringing its hands in consternation? The board did of course have the right to decide the course for its church. Perhaps therefore he should try to separate his religious life from his political interests. Certainly there was a political home waiting for him in the CCF. He decided to join it and contribute what time and talent he could spare from his minister's job. He contacted some of the leaders, spoke at great length with J. S. Woodsworth about how the older man had resolved a similar problem a generation earlier. Woodsworth in fact could not understand how Stanley had been able to maintain his church affiliation this long. But he was different from Woodsworth in spite of certain similarities and the almost deliberate cultivating of a Woodsworth-Knowles mystique. He seldom broke with his past and he was not yet ready to do so now. Instead he would distinguish his religious from his political tasks. He would continue with both but he would not mix the two. He therefore suggested no unusual activities for the religious season 1934-1935. That way he hoped to keep the board at bay.

An interest in politics, however, meant an automatic interest in elections and the Reverend Stanley Knowles was becoming quite well known. His Sunday activities increased enormously as he attempted the dual task of working with the new CCF and carrying out his religious duties. He preached morning and evening, still insisting heavily upon the social gospel. In the afternoons, he spoke for the CCF wherever the occasion presented itself — at trade union meetings, in labour halls, at public forums. As a day of rest for working people, Sunday was the one day he could reach them. It was a heavy schedule but he loved it. Nor did the board seem to object.

With every intention of continuing to undertake both his religious and his political tasks, he was a bit surprised when people from Winnipeg South Centre approached him late in 1934. Would he stand at the nominating convention towards the end of January in preparation for a federal election sometime in 1935? The infant CCF was riding a crest of popular interest and enthusiasm and Winnipeg South Centre wanted a strong candidate. Knowles' surprise was less at the political "call" itself, but that it had come so soon. Both he and his friends had noticed the direction of his thinking, his preaching, and his speeches: he would have to be more than a CCF spokesman; he would have to be a CCF politician.

The nominating convention was held on a Tuesday night towards the end of January 1935. The Agnes Street Labour Hall was packed as the fledgling CCF showed every sign of being a serious contender on the federal political scene. With four names in the ring, the young minister had to count on his own speech and his growing reputation in the city. Both worked and he won the nomination on the first ballot. He would be the CCF candidate, something quite far from his mind less than year earlier when he had decided to separate his political activities from his ministerial duties. Now perhaps he would have to choose one or the other. Certainly his father, watching excitedly from Los Angeles, claimed he had seen it coming all along and knew exactly the direction in which his son was headed. Shortly after the nomination he wrote that it was "an agreeable surprise, and not entirely unlooked for, tho' I did not expect it quite so soon. Sometime ago I said to Warren, that what has happened, would come to pass, viz, that the pressure from the church would eventually send you to Ottawa."[3] Fortunately the nomination meeting was on a Tuesday night; the parishioners and board of Central United would have the rest of the week to ponder the somewhat startling action undertaken by their minister.

As the minister, one of his duties was to call and preside over meetings of the board. Most of the members already knew either directly from the minister or by talk in the town that he had taken the plunge into politics. They were therefore ready for his announcement at the Sunday service that there would be a meeting of the official board the next evening. They were also prepared for what they knew would be the main item of business at that meeting: the resignation of their minister. Indeed, if he did not offer his resignation, the board intended to demand it. Knowing this, the minister had his resignation ready. It was to take effect at the end of that church conference year on 30 June 1935. By a vote of twenty-five to two the board accepted the resignation, grateful to be spared the nastiness of forcing their minister to resign but somewhat uneasy about the publicity he might attract to the church in the remaining months of his tenure. They would be glad to see him go and even began casting their eyes about for a new minister at a higher salary.

The hostility of the board and of some of the congregation to Knowles' political activities was evident in a small incident that same Sunday when the board meeting was announced. Like most single ministers of the time, he was the recipient of numerous Sunday dinner invitations. On occasion they even piled up for weeks in advance and this Sunday he was to go to the home of a particular member of the congregation. The invitation had been extended at least two weeks earlier and the family could hardly rescind it as the minister greeted his parishioners at the exit of the church after the morning service. The Reverend Knowles would be along to their home shortly. But when he arrived, the greeting was glacial. "Mr. Knowles," remarked the host, "if we had known what was going to happen, I don't know whether we would have invited you."[4] At least the dinner was warm, but the family was worried about what Uncle "so and so," a prominent member of the board of the church, would say about their entertaining this young radical. It was an awkward situation but the minister could not blame the family. They and many in the church had a view of politicians as rather shady characters who engaged in underhand activities at popular expense. What was their young minister, who seemed so earnest and sincere — even if he did have some peculiar notions about the way of the world — doing getting mixed up with such an unsavoury lot? Over the next forty years those same people ceased worrying about their minister. Whether their view of politics and politicians has altered is unknown, but they are sure of Knowles and they are all proud of their connection with him. The chap who was so worried about the number of souls has long since been dead and perhaps in a better position to count them himself; what he now thinks of Stanley Knowles is anybody's guess.

Before the board could locate its preferred minister — an orator who would fill the congregation but not disturb anyone — the city engineers decreed Central United Church a dangerous edifice. This was not a commentary on the politics of the minister, although the board would readily have agreed with that; rather it was an engineer's assessment of the state of the roof. The rafters were rotting visibly and the roof could collapse at any time. The church would have to make the repairs or close. But where was the money for such extensive renovations in 1935? Even supposing the expenses could be met, how would the church accommodate its congregation while the repairs were being made? The board and the minister conferred at length.

The simplest solution was to commence the summer pattern somewhat earlier than usual. In order to permit a vacation for their ministers, whose regular duties entailed no holidays, two congregations frequently joined forces during the summer. Each minister took charge of the combined congregation for one month of the summer. In that way, not only the ministers but the church buildings and presumably their caretakers would also get a rest since the double congregation would go for a month to one church and a month to the other. Knowles was familiar with the practice and it had worked well in the past two summers when Central United and First Baptist, two churches so close the congregations could hear each other sing, had combined during July and August. And so it was easy enough to devise a similar arrangement for the coming summer; the only difference was that the summer would begin earlier and the two congregations would meet solely at First Baptist. The board even had the audacity to ask Reverend Knowles to stay on after his resignation at the end of June to see the two churches safely through the summer. He could have his holiday — to be spent electioneering — in July but then he would take the joint congregation in August. His parishioners at Central United knew what the move meant: Central United would close. The joint services with First Baptist were in fact continued for a year, after which the decision was formally made to wind up the affairs of Central United, to send its records to Fort Rouge United Church and to have the building demolished. The wags might say that with his decision to go into active politics, Stanley Knowles had brought the roof down on his church.

Certainly the roof was collapsing on a good portion of his own life. During that joint summer with First Baptist he received word about the seriousness of his father's illness. Having borrowed money to pay for the flight to Los Angeles and the two-week leave-taking of his father, he returned to Winnipeg without a job. His duties with Central United were completed and the election was still another six weeks away. Ministerial supply work filled in a few of the Sunday gaps during the autumn while the inevitable dinner invitations kept him fed and election work kept him enthusiastic.

By mid-October, however, he had lost the election as well. His church, his father, and his election; what was he to do? His printing career was in the past and so was his education. His political decision seemed to have put the church in the past and now the electoral verdict appeared to have put the political decision in the past. He was twenty-seven years old, despondent about the recent past, but not particularly frightened by the bleak prospects for the future. Aunt Ida in Carberry shared the tears of disappointment and loss, but the relatives in Nova Scotia were treated to another side of the young man. Four days after the election he reported on it and on the recent death of his father:

> I have concluded one of my first skirmishes in that which he [Stanley Ernest Knowles] brought me up to do — to give my life to the endeavour to release men and women from the bonds of economic slavery and to establish the Kingdom of heaven here on earth. . . . I wish he could be here to sense the esteem in which his son is held as one who fought a political battle on the highest possible level and as one who can be counted on to continue his efforts for the common people until victory is won.[3]

Over the years he gradually discarded the religious expression of his political beliefs (although never the religious drive behind them) but he never lost the need to find public approval for what he was doing. His parents had left him too soon.

But what was he to do in the autumn of 1935? He knew how church appointments were made; he had in fact served on several church settlement committees whose function was to select ministers, keep track of churches without a permanent minister, and attempt to match talents to "calls". One church that always had difficulty attracting and keeping a minister was MacLean Mission on Alexander Avenue in the poorer section of north central Winnipeg. Few ministers were willing to undertake the church and it was now looking for a single rather than a married minister who would accept a salary even lower than that offered by most of the downtown churches to their single ministers. The settlement committee offered the post at $83.33 a month to the Reverend Knowles and he went there as minister for 1935-1936. Before long, he had under his care three mission churches in the same area: St. Andrew's, Point Douglas, and MacLean Mission, all of them, as well as the downtown churches with which he had been associated, in Winnipeg North Centre, the electoral riding then represented by J. S. Woodsworth. During the year at MacLean Mission Knowles resumed the radio broadcasting of his sermons and began something for which he seldom had time or inclination before: a romance with one of the deaconesses at MacLean Mission — Vida Cruikshank.

The romance was to last but the post at MacLean Mission did not. Towards the end of the conference year, in June 1936, it was decided to reduce the status of the church even farther, from that of a single ordained minister to a single student. He could be had for even less than the $83.33. The Reverend Knowles would have to leave. By then, however, he had already decided to enhance his own status by becoming a married minister; the wedding was to take place in November 1936 and he needed a salary that would support a wife.

By the time of the wedding he had accepted a "call" to Kildonan United Church in the north end of Winnipeg and the newlyweds settled into a tiny house near the church. There they spent four years, the longest time Knowles had spent with any one church. For the first time he and his church suited each other. The parish was heavily working class and it matched the kind of preaching that the new minister brought to it. Neither parishioners nor board raised any objections to the political activities of its minister. He in fact curtailed those activities during 1936-37 and he did not run in the Manitoba provincial election of 1936. But he fully intended to do so in the next federal election, due in 1940, and he suspected that that decision too would wrench a few minds and attitudes in his new church.

When the time came for that decision it was his pacifism, not his socialism, that upset certain members of his church. For by the late 1930s the outside world had reached right into the north end of Winnipeg: another European war was in the offing. Knowles was a pacifist and was concerned lest the churches repeat what he considered to be a mistake during the First World War when they had given their religious sanction to one side in the war. He convinced many of his young parishioners and they participated enthusiastically in his radio sermons to shout a youthful "no" to what the politicians and warmongers were preparing for them. Ultimately their voices carried little weight and many of them had their lives cut short by a Second World War which Canada supported and the churches blessed.

By 1939 Knowles was increasingly active in the CCF. He resumed political broadcasts over the radio, made speeches all over Winnipeg, and assisted groups wishing to begin riding associations. He was chairman of the Manitoba CCF and a member of the national council of the party. At the end of July 1939 he was also an official CCF candidate again, this time for the Manitoba riding of Springfield which the CCF hoped to capture in the forthcoming federal election. The nomination necessitated a repeat performance with his church. Just as at Central United in 1935 so now at Kildonan: he called a meeting of the church board and submitted his resignation.

This time, however, the situation was somewhat complicated; there was a baby due at the Knowles household. And the baby decided to make his appearance the very day of the board meeting on 2 August. Mrs. Knowles urged the doctor to speed up the delivery; her husband had to get to a meeting to resign his job. Baby, mother, and doctor co-operated: David Stanley Knowles appeared just before seven and his father met the board at eight. Adding to the complicated familial situation was the fact that the board did not want to accept its minister's resignation. Indeed it voted in exactly the same proportion as the board of Central United back in 1935 — twenty-five to two — but this time to reject his offer to resign. Unlike the earlier occasion when the minister had had to foresee and plan for the board's obvious desire to get rid of him, this time he was in the strange position of having to convince the board that it really did not want him. An active politician, he argued, could not give his full time to his ministerial duties and that would be unfair to the congregation. The board persisted and so did the minister. When he finally succeeded in having his resignation accepted for the end of June 1940, he knew that he was terminating the most sympathetic relationship he had had with a church. Moreover, although he did not know it at the time, that August evening also decided the end of his active ministerial days.

For the rest of the church year, however, he continued the combination of religion and politics. An illustration of how it could be done — admittedly somewhat hectically — came early in September 1939. David Lewis, the national secretary of the CCF, had instructed Knowles to use the five hundred dollars the party had allotted for organizing in the province to ensure Manitoban presence at an emergency meeting of the party's national council. The CCF had to determine what stand it would take on the European war should Canada decide to enter, as everyone expected it to do. The party leader's views were well known: Woodsworth could not sanction war at all. But should the party follow his lead? S. J. Farmer, Beatrice Brigden, and Stanley Knowles headed for Ottawa, to speak for the Manitoba CCF. Knowles took the night train from Winnipeg after his Sunday evening service, to be in Ottawa for the meetings on Wednesday, Thursday, and Friday, 6, 7, and 8 September, and returned to Winnipeg in time for his next Sunday services, having prepared his sermons on the train.

The council meeting was long, strained, and difficult. Woodsworth made it clear that if the party chose to support the war, he would have to resign not only as leader but also as a member of the CCF. Knowles and the two other Manitobans agreed with Woodsworth in his utter rejection of war and of CCF support for it. But besides being in a minority they also knew that a formal split between the party and its pacifist leader could destroy the CCF. After three days of bitter debate, therefore, the council agreed to a compromise. Without resigning, Woodsworth would nonetheless speak only for himself in the House of Commons in reply to Prime Minister Mackenzie King's statement about Canadian participation in the war. He would voice his total opposition but then M. J. Coldwell would speak for the party. He would stress what Woodsworth and the party had in common but he would also indicate CCF support for the war albeit of a limited and conditional kind. Canada should mount a home defence, offer material support to Britain, but should not become involved in overseas military adventures. On the evening of 8 September, Knowles watched from the gallery of the Commons, his heart with Woodsworth but his mind absorbing one of his first lessons in party solidarity. Would he have a seat in the House soon so that he could help mould that solidarity?

In May 1940 the electorate said "No" and for Knowles it was a "heartbreaker to lose."[6] The riding had looked good; everything seemed to go well until the very last moment when he sensed, with that sharp electoral awareness that accompanied all his campaigns, that something had turned. The Conservative candidate took ten polls, the Liberal fifty, and the CCF forty-nine.

What was he to do now? Just as in 1935 he had no election and no church. This time he also had a wife and a baby. The church no longer seemed willing to have this unsuccessful young politician under its wing. The settlement committee arranged for some offers, some "calls," but changed the rules about the congregation's vote of acceptance on a prospective minister. For most cases, a mere majority of the congregation need approve and the aspiring minister would be hired; in this case, the congregation was to approve by a two-thirds majority. Knowles thereby lost two "calls." The committee then offered him two impossible charges and he began to recognize the strategy. The church wanted to place him where his voice would not be heard. He refused the offers.

At that point the CCF itself came to the rescue. It needed a provincial secretary and organizer for Manitoba and it was prepared to find a salary to equal the fifteen hundred dollars Knowles had received as minister at Kildonan. He therefore took the staff position and while there began the numerical, indexed, and cross-referenced filing system which has enabled him to keep

"still performs weddings . . . mostly for close friends." Laura Wright and Andrew Brewin, Victoria 1980.

track of himself during more than forty years of intense political life. He also organized the CCF at the constituency level and spoke all over the province. He helped select potential candidates for the Manitoba provincial election in 1941.

By then the trickle of supply preaching that he had been offered through the autumn of 1940 had dried up. But still he could not sever the connection with the church that had nurtured him, educated him, and provided him with his first notions of the ethical and moral needs of society. In the face of considerable provocation through the late 1930s and early 1940s he insisted on maintaining that connection. During the annual application necessary to stay on the presbytery rolls he frequently encountered opposition. Since presbytery actually voted on the applicants, it could, if it chose, eliminate certain people. But if Knowles had opponents within the church, he also had friends. And the friends insisted that if his name was to be dropped from the rolls of the United Church, then so should the names of all other ministers who were not actually performing ministerial duties. The Knowles' name therefore stayed on and now no longer presents a problem. The only concern of the list-maker is just how his name is to be recorded. Should he be among the retired? He is, he insists, by no means retired. The name therefore appears under the heading Ministers without Station . . . Stanley Knowles, MP.

As a minister of the United Church of Canada, Knowles still performs weddings, funerals, and baptisms, mostly for close friends. He maintains his connections with the past and is bemused by the fact that in his younger days the church held a formidable place in society but did not use its power to full advantage. Now, when its position has diminished considerably, it does not always use the allies it has in other walks of life. Knowles would have liked the church, for example, to join him in his battle against state lotteries in the late 1960s. To him lotteries are a regressive form of taxation making those who can least afford it pay for some of the state's more extravagant undertakings and encouraging the unethical notion that one can get something for nothing. The churches did not come to his assistance on that issue. But for all the disappointment, he never broke the tie. He still believes, as he did at the time it was asked, that the question about how many souls can best be answered through the more tangible ballot box and the subsequent political action it permits. In 1942 the numbers fell his way.

5

ELECTION

30 November 1942

With half an hour to go before the polls closed, the CCF candidate in the by-election in Winnipeg North Centre was seated at a lunch counter having his favourite sandwich — toasted salmon — with a cup of tea and telling himself to calm down and prepare for defeat. He would need comforting words for his campaign workers who included the party's national secretary, David Lewis, and the local women of the riding who had kept the committee room supplied with coffee and sandwiches for the weeks and months of the campaign. He would have to say the right thing to the press which was waiting to add a fourth electoral defeat to the Knowles record. So he munched his sandwich and planned a speech. If by any chance he won the words would come easily enough; defeat was the difficult thing to acknowledge in public. In all his subsequent election campaigns, he always had a defeat speech ready. Mostly they were not used. Only in 1958 did he have to utter the carefully planned words and by then they were so well rehearsed that few people knew what the defeat meant to him. That of course was far in the future. For the moment he had only to wait for the worst as the minutes ticked away the end of the election day.

Back in the committee room at the corner of Notre Dame and Isabel, there was a bustle of activity as campaign workers readied themselves to receive the calls from the first polls. Indeed, before the candidate returned from his frugal supper the advance polls had started to come in. The first six had all gone handily to him. His wife was excited, but he was cautious. "It's too soon to tell," he warned. By the time ten or twelve polls had called in their results, he was excited too. It looked like victory. If so, he had achieved the goal he had set himself seven years earlier, to take his particular crusade for social justice to the one body in the land where something might conceivably be done about it, to parliament in Ottawa. The remaining polls confirmed the hunch of the first dozen. Indeed he won all but three or four and his Liberal opponent who seemed to have everything on his side, failed to garner even half the number of votes of the winner and hence lost his deposit. Since then, Knowles has always been able to tell which way the election was going by the returns from the first few polls. Neither chance nor superstition explains his clairvoyance. Rather a careful assessment of the riding, weighing the good sections against the not-so-sure ones, allows him to know the outcome soon after the polls have closed. On occasion he may discount a particular poll in his first quick estimate of the likely result. In 1974, for example, the first poll to be heard from was in the Sharon Home, a senior citizen residence which Knowles refers to more affectionately as the Jewish Old Folk's home; the poll actually called in a few minutes before the official closing time: seventy votes for Knowles and fifteen for all the other candidates combined. "Does this count?" wondered his daughter Margaret, knowing of the weather-vane that was in the first few polls. "Hardly," remarked her father, recalling that he could always count on the senior citizen homes and that he had visited this particular one just the day before. The next three or four polls, however, told the same story and he knew that all was well. Even in the election for which he had to use his defeat speech, he knew within the first few minutes. The initial returns came from polls close to the committee room, polls that had always voted for him but on that particular occasion, in 1958, turned him down. That he did not know in November 1942; this time he was winning and as he remarked years later in the laconic fashion he reserves for things that touch him deeply: "It felt pretty good."[1]

It was also about time, for the string of defeats had ended only with his winning a fill-in-term as alderman for Ward Two on Winnipeg's City Council. He was a long way from the federal House of Commons where he wanted to be. He had lost in the federal election of 1935 and again in 1940. He lost once more in the Manitoba provincial election in 1941. Indeed the CCF itself appeared to be losing its initial enthusiasm. Knowles' defeats were perhaps no more than a sign of the end of the new party that had seemed so promising in the mid-1930s. In 1940 the provincial party had reluctantly agreed to Premier John Bracken's suggestion of a coalition government for the duration of the war. Bracken was able to arouse popular support for his idea and thus could easily brand opponents as unpatriotic. The issue was discussed at the provincial council of the CCF, of which Knowles was secretary, and subsequently at a provincial convention, and once again at the party's national convention held in Winnipeg late in 1940. Party leaders came from Ottawa to discuss the question with the Manitoba CCF leader, S. J. Farmer, and with Knowles. Party members did not like the idea of a coalition but the leaders liked even less the prospect of having the still fledgling CCF branded as unpatriotic. They agreed therefore to take part in Bracken's coalition but hoped to maintain a semblance of autonomy by having the CCF members and their leader, who was to be the labour minister in the combined cabinet, retain their seats on the left side of the speaker in the provincial assembly.

The experience was not a happy one for the CCF and it later shied away from any similar proposals. In the 1940s the experiment took its toll. In the provincial election of April 1941, party candidates ran as "CCF officially supporting the coalition" and took a beating at the polls. Knowles was one of the candidates and he was sure the party's proximity to the government damaged its chances. Certainly the electoral system was more than fair, its complexity guaranteeing a representative distribution of the votes. The city of Winnipeg, for example, elected ten members by proportional representation and although the rest of the province was divided into single-member constituencies, there too the voting was complex, based on an "alternate vote" system. Knowles delighted in the mathematical complexities, but they did not favour him. When the final count and calculation were made, he ranked thirteenth in Winnipeg. It was the third of his electoral defeats in so many tries.

Indirectly, however, the defeat in the provincial election paved the way for his first victory. One of Winnipeg's aldermen, Rhodes Smith, vacated his council seat in order to run as a Liberal in the provincial election. His victory necessitated the election of another alderman to complete his two year term. Knowles contested the election, held at the time of the other civic elections in October 1941, and this time he was successful. Unlike the other elected aldermen whose new terms would not begin until January 1942, Knowles took his seat on city council immediately. He also began receiving a city councillor's salary of one hundred dollars a month and was able to reduce by that amount his income from the CCF, in whose employ he continued to act as provincial secretary and organizer. While an alderman, he gained immediate experience on numerous committees filling in for a veteran but now ailing member of council. He thus busied himself with city finances, with the relief rolls, and with something which he considers his major contribution, the establishment of a committee to deal with post-war reconstruction. The committee continued after his departure from council at the end of December 1942 by which time he was a member of parliament.

Indeed it was known at the time of his civic election that there would be a federal by-election in the city in the not too distant future. The member for Winnipeg North Centre and leader of the CCF, J. S. Woodsworth, was ailing after a stroke and few people expected him to live long. He had only retained his federal seat by a handful of votes in the election of 1940. The Liberals expected an easy gain; the CCF thought it would be a tragedy to lose. Indeed the two parties' potential candidates in the riding whenever the by-election occurred — Liberal Halinquist and CCF Knowles — had taken a dry run during the civic campaign. With Knowles' victory, the Liberals dropped their favourite and cast about for a more likely federal winner. They found one with just the right qualifications for a wartime election in Connie Johannesson, an air veteran of the First World War whose son was now serving in the RCAF. Johannesson was also of Icelandic origin, a significant factor in a riding like Winnipeg North Centre. He operated a flying school at Winnipeg's Steveson Airport, was well known and well liked. "He had," as Knowles remarked many years later, "everything in his favour, except the fact that he was a Liberal."[2] That fact Johannesson kept well hidden from his posters and campaign literature. Only after his CCF opponents taunted him about his unwillingness to announce his Liberal party connections did the word Liberal start appearing in the signs.

Winnipeg North Centre had a labour mystique about it. People from the riding recalled the Winnipeg General Strike of 1919 and ever since the federal election following it, in 1921, they had sent J. S. Woodsworth to Ottawa as their representative. It was just the kind of riding Knowles would like to represent. Racially mixed and heavily industrial, the area harboured all the kinds of social problems that Knowles had known in his own family, that he had denounced from the pulpit and that he now thought he could alleviate from parliament. The railway shops employed most of the workers, with the CPR Weston shops largely located in the riding and the CNR shops east of the city at Transcona attracting many workers who lived in North Centre. There were also steel and rolling mills, companies with names that hit the history books because of their association with the Winnipeg Strike: Manitoba Bridge and Iron, Dominion Bridge, Vulcan Iron Works. Packing plants, clothing factories, knitting mills, hydro plants, the big downtown stores and offices, all of them together made it Knowles' kind of riding and the people his kind of people. He would have to win the nomination and then the election.

The nominating convention was held in April 1942, just a few weeks after Woodsworth's death on 21 March. Knowles was expected to seek the nomination but would there be opponents? A few people suggested that Mrs. Woodsworth attempt to hold the seat until the next federal election. She, however, was more interested in seeing Knowles succeed her husband but she kept her views to herself until his nomination was assured. That was

WIN WITH THE CCF
VOTE LABOR

ELECT
STANLEY H.
KNOWLES   **X**

MONDAY, NOV. 30 — 8 A.M TO 6 P.M.
(Over)

"the official CCF candidate." Winnipeg 1942.

"his infant daughter ushered in his first federal victory." Winnipeg 1942.

done by acclamation and he was the official CCF candidate for a by-election that had not yet been called. Then Mrs. Woodsworth let it be known, through a public letter to the Women Electors of North Centre, that "Alderman Stanley H. Knowles, . . . the CCF candidate . . . is the man my husband hoped to see chosen as he believed Stanley well prepared to carry on his work."[3] The mantle did fit and has done so for so long that in the 1970s people could be heard greeting him on the streets of Winnipeg as Mr. Woodsworth. While a candidate through the rest of 1942, he continued his two jobs as provincial secretary of the Manitoba CCF and alderman for Winnipeg's Ward Two. In June his family increased with the birth of a daughter, Margaret, named for his mother. Daughters have in fact always accompanied political good fortune for Knowles. In 1942 his infant daughter ushered in his first federal victory; in 1962 his daughter-in-law Shirley Nelson joined the family ten days before the come-back election after the defeat of 1958; and in 1965 granddaughter Susan Knowles was there for yet another election win. "There are a lot of women in my life," he remarked in 1982, somewhat surprised but obviously pleased.[4]

In 1942 the campaign was long and strenuous. Even the date for the by-election was not known until the autumn. Mackenzie King waited until the last minute and then announced three by-elections, all to be held on 30 November, one in Winnipeg North Centre and two others in Quebec. For CCFers all across the country the contest in Winnipeg was crucial. Woodsworth's seat simply had to be retained. A nation-wide appeal for funds was launched — something that cannot be done in a general election when each constituency needs whatever funds it can raise — and four thousand dollars was collected. In 1942 that was a large sum and it continued to be so for many subsequent CCF campaigns. In Knowles' own elections, only in the 1960s, did he begin to surpass that figure. By 1980 expenses had climbed to $15,000 but by then there were official spending limits on election campaigns and Knowles was under his by $10,000. To direct the campaign in 1942 David Lewis, national secretary of the CCF, let the party take care of itself for six to eight weeks and came to Winnipeg from Ottawa. It was, Knowles recalled later, "one of the best jobs of organizing a campaign that David ever did — not excluding some of his own."[5] He certainly had the job cut out for him. The riding had virtually no organization, something which Knowles knew but which shocked Lewis. The first thing was to establish local CCF groups in areas of the riding where there were none. In Weston, for example, where the votes came thick and heavy for the CCF, there was not one official party member. No sooner was Lewis in town than he established a group in Weston and began collecting memberships; the members were then set to work canvassing polls, distributing literature, and convincing former Woodsworth supporters that Knowles was their man. Where Woodsworth had run largely on his own reputation, even legend, Knowles required a solid, organized base. Only many years later would he be able to count on the electoral attraction of his own reputation.

Of course he made use of the Woodsworth name and of the now public knowledge that the older man had wanted him as a successor. His programme stressed the connection. Knowles would carry on where Woodsworth had left off. He would continue the battle for pensions for working people; he would champion the rights of railway workers; he would voice labour and trade union objections to the wartime wage controls. He would insist, in the months following the conscription plebiscite of April 1942, that there be no conscription of manpower without conscription of wealth as well. And he would urge equitable mothers' allowances for the wives of soldiers overseas. He and his campaigners stressed that not one labour vote should go to Mackenzie King; the CCF claimed that the Canadian war effort was being fought on the backs of the working people. Knowles also argued the need to start planning for the end of the war. When it did come, there would be two urgent problems: how to maintain international peace and how to ensure peace-time employment for former soldiers and war workers.

The candidate used various means to spread his message. He was used to radio since his evening sermons in the 1930s and used it extensively in the campaign. He was used to public forums since his student days and also since his ministerial experience with Sunday evening forums at Central United during the winter of 1932-1933. He knew the printing trade and was thus able to supervise the appropriate campaign material. The provincial CCF paper, the *Manitoba Commonwealth*, put out a special edition for the campaign; there were colours and comics and family pictures and articles written by Knowles' wife Vida. The campaign imported CCF stars — party leader M. J. Coldwell, Angus and Grace MacInnis, she the daughter of J. S. Woodsworth and he a federal M.P., and Joe Noseworthy, still basking in his startling victory over Conservative leader Arthur Meighen in the York South by-election in February that year. On hearing Noseworthy speak, Knowles wondered how he could ever have beaten Meighen, but he was a formidable organizer and campaigner. The imported talent was an attempt to offset that brought in by the Liberal opponent. The very names — C. D. Howe, T. A. Crerar, and Angus Macdonald among them — indicated the importance the Liberals attached to this particular by-election. They stressed the war effort at a time when the war was becoming close and serious. Knowles, on the contrary, was, as he described it years later, "almost a pacifist," maintaining a long-standing belief that wars do not solve anything.[6] The campaign was a two-way fight: the Conservatives, knowing they had no chance of winning, did not

Noon-hour shopgating. Transcona 1957.

even put up a candidate. The only other candidate was a "somewhat odd chap"[7] running under a newly-coined name, Labour Progressive. Only later did the Communist party of Canada, in an attempt to get round the Defence of Canada Regulations, adopt that name as its own.

In the campaign Knowles also inaugurated what would continue to be his major campaign activity — shopgating. He had watched Woodsworth use the technique to great advantage in the federal election in 1935; indeed his own initiation into shopgating had been to accompany Woodsworth to the CPR yards in Weston and to speak to the workers from a small platform across the road from the entrance. At that time the workers had an hour at lunch and would wander out to hear "their man" speak. The platform is still there, but the hour-long lunch breaks have gone. Sometimes too, Woodsworth, with Knowles trailing him, was able to enter the workers' lunchroom to speak to them; the foreman was either friendly or deliberately absent. Both of these practices Knowles has continued in all his campaigns. He can still be seen in the grey dawn, a gaunt figure, somberly dressed, standing a bit diffidently at the various shop gates in his riding, shaking hands, passing out literature, renewing acquaintances, greeting forty-five-year-olds who look seventy and assuring them that he is trying his best to reduce the retirement age to sixty. There are even sons and grandsons of one-time workers who know he will be there and who come up to him: sixteen year olds, shiny-eyed, excited to take the hand of a man who, like Woodsworth before him, has become something of a legend in the riding. Knowles always returns to the shop gates the day after the election to thank the men for their support. Throughout the parliamentary term as well he can be seen now at one gate, now at another. These are his people and he does not forget them. Even when they forgot him, in 1958, he returned the morning after the defeat to thank those who had supported him. There were many who could not look him straight in the eye that day.

In 1942 a variation on the shopgating was used. Many voters in North Centre worked in the cordite plant in Transcona and Knowles accompanied them on the daily rain run out to the plant from Winnipeg and discussed their complaints about wages and working conditions. While the Liberal opposition poured money

Campaigning for CPR diesel shop. Winnipeg 1965.

"a gaunt figure, somberly dressed . . . shaking hands, passing out
literature . . ." Winnipeg 1979.

into advertisements, campaign literature, and radio broadcasts, all
stressing the war effort and the need to support it wholeheartedly,
Knowles was talking to the men who made the war effort possible.
While not denying the war nor Canada's part in it, he insisted that
Canadian workers not be made the scapegoat of the war, without
decent wages, houses, pensions, or even fair labour contracts and
faced with the possibility of unemployment after the war.

Knowles won North Centre with seventy-one percent of the
vote. He has done so ever since, the percentage fluctuating but the
victory never, except for the year of the Diefenbaker sweep in
1958. He likes to think that his riding is maintaining a tradition
that goes back to 1919, a certain labour consciousness that has
been kept alive by two ministerial figures, Woodsworth and
Knowles, and by the fact that families tend to stay in the riding
and pass on their voting behaviour to their children. But he also

recognizes that voters often go with winners: when one corner of his riding which had always suppoted him was detached to become part of the riding to the south, voters there began supporting the incumbent Conservative. When a later redistribution reattached the section to Winnipeg North Centre again, the votes switched back to the CCF and to Knowles. He also is uncomfortably aware that his riding has one of the lowest turnouts of voters in Manitoba. This worries him and often excites his opponents but they too have been able to draw out the hidden voters only once, in 1958.

The victory in 1942 was celebrated with a dinner at the Marlborough Hotel. Knowles was determined that as many of his supporters should be there as possible, but the hotel could offer no meal price lower than a dollar fifty per person. Knowing that most of his constituents could not afford that amount, he persuaded his campaign organizers to use some of the remaining money in the campaign fund to subsidize the dinner and bring the price down to seventy-five cents. It was, he argued, a legitimate campaign expense. But in his concern for his supporters, he forgot his own tickets and had to hold up the entrance line to dig into his pocket for three dollars for himself and his wife.

If the head of a young politician could be turned, this dinner was the occasion. The acclaim came from near and far with telegrams pouring in from across the country and David Lewis making glowing speeches about how Knowles deserved to be in parliament. But he also reassured the audience — Stanley won't forget you. That was precisely what the new MP was saying to himself. He had not fought seven years for this victory simply to acquire the status, prestige, and perquisites of a member of parliament. He had known the first two as a minister, but they had not impressed him much; he was too much his father's son for that. Rather he had chosen the political arena in order to pursue his crusade for a better world for ordinary people. The victory gave him the right to come to Ottawa; the duty that went with it, a duty he hopes he has not forgotten, was to continue the crusade. Certainly the workers who still greet him at the shop gates do not believe he has forgotten.

The work the voters of Winnipeg sent Knowles to Ottawa to do in 1942 has, he admits, been the most interesting of all the jobs he has held since being an underaged printer in Los Angeles in the 1920s. He works longer hours than at any previous job; he deals with highly complex cases both in the Commons itself and across his office desk. Some of them are impossible; some he is able to solve; he worries away at all of them. His correspondence is

"he deals with highly complex cases . . . across his office desk." Ottawa 1972.

voluminous, the parliamentary work unceasing, and there are frequent trips for the party or for parliament. Once in a while he wonders about a slightly less hectic life but not for long. He enjoys being in parliament, the surroundings are beautiful, and the work is always interesting. Moreover, he considers himself lucky: where others have to put in eight hours at some dreary job in order to finance their real living in the remaining hours, he has work which is both his vocation and his avocation. He loves it. For him, seven hours of rest are sufficient to live at, even for his work.

The electorate could of course put an end to his work at any time. Perhaps for that reason he is tense and uneasy during election campaigns. For him they are much more strenuous than the parliamentary routine, although that is a gruelling round to anyone watching him. During elections he enjoys the friendly contacts and the shopgating, preferring it to door-to-door campaigning, but admits that campaigns can be exhausting. The early ones were fun and the excitement has never worn off, but ever since 1946 when a serious health problem first presented itself, he has been wary. The illness, later diagnosed as multiple sclerosis, something he kept secret for almost forty years, came on while he was speaking at a banquet in Ottawa and, always one to trail his past with him, he has been fearful of such gatherings since. During the 1950s when he had heavy financial responsibilities for a home and young family, he just had to win. What else could he have done? Both printing and the ministry were too far in the past to return to. Being a member of parliament was his occupation. And so the tension was always high during an election campaign. By the mid-1960s with his children educated and settled, the financial burden became less, just as, over his opposition, MPs' salaries and pensions became much greater. But the campaigns themselves remain long and difficult. He undertakes most of the work himself, in effect acting as his own campaign manager. He shopgates at the morning and evening shifts, supervises the campaign room, delivers material to printers, talks on radio, visits senior citizen homes, and does chores for little old ladies on the very day of the election. He visits home-ridden voters and arranges for proxy votes and transportation to the polls. He flits about the streets of his riding like the pastor he once was, caring, soothing, arranging, and doing for his people.

While carrying such a load in the election of 1963, he came down with a vestigial illness, fittingly enough for someone who does not make breaks with the past. Only one person in a hundred still has two appendices; evolution has sloughed the second one off. But Knowles retained his, a Meckel's diverticulum. With a lining similar to that of the stomach, a misbehaving diverticulum displays all the symptoms of stomach ulcers. He therefore bled internally for days without being aware of it. He knew that something was wrong but he could not and would not give in in the midst of a campaign. Eight days before voting day, however, he was increasingly feeble and began curtailing his activities. He called off one meeting, cancelled an out-of-town speaking engagement in Saskatchewan that would have had him on the train in the middle of the night, and planned to spend the next day in bed. In the meantime, he could just manage a drive to the printers to leave some material and perhaps a tea out in Brooklands in the far west end of his riding. But the effort was too much and he startled passers-by on the street when he simply had to sit down on the curb to regain enough energy to continue. The following morning his family found him in a dead faint in the bathroom.

It was April fool's day and he thought the end of the world had come. Alone in the ambulance on the way to hospital, he was exhausted and thoroughly dispirited. His iron will had conquered every other hurdle in his life, but even it seemed bone weary now.

"Better a sick candidate than a dead one." Winnipeg 1963.

He did not even have his medical cards for admission to the hospital. "That's all right, Mr. Knowles," the attendants remarked, "we know who you are."[8] But it took sixteen pints of blood before *he* knew quite who he was. The blood count had been dangerously low and the doctors marvelled at his stamina. They tested for ulcers and pondered an operation, but there were no ulcers and eventually no operation. Instead, the Meckel's diverticulum showed up as the source of the bleeding. It gradually healed itself and the doctors simply removed a few more items from Knowles' already frugal diet. From then on he approached election campaigns with even more trepidation.

As for that particular election, how was he to win it from a hospital bed? Well, as the doctors told him, he would have to count entirely on his campaign workers this time. Better a sick candidate than a dead one. Not only the local campaign workers but people from outside the riding came in to help. Party leader Tommy Douglas, Stanley's old friend from college days, came out to speak and convulsed his audience by commenting that he too would be in hospital with stomach trouble if he had to read the *Winnipeg Free Press* every day. By election day, Knowles had improved so much on donated blood that he persuaded the doctors to let him out for a while. Under the strict care of his sister-in-law, Dr. Donna Cruikshank Patton, he went out to cast his vote and to visit the committee room. Then he returned to the hospital under orders to stay there until the first returns were in. Only when it was sure they were favourable was he permitted a second sortie still accompanied by Dr. Donna. She later told him what an agonizing day it had been: if anything had happened to him the reputations of numerous Winnipeg doctors would have been badly tarnished. Nothing did happen except that Knowles won an election from a hospital bed, by 13,000 votes to 7,000.

The Meckel's diverticulum and Knowles' various other ailments were far in the future on that November evening in 1942. The strenuousness of a campaign had not yet told on the features or the emotions of the thirty-four year old former printer and former preacher. Rather there was the tension and the excitement of a fateful day. If he did not win this election after three previous tries, his attempts at a political career would have to cease. But this time he won and would not have to face the prospect of a non-political future until 1958. With the victory on 30 November he was about to begin the task that both he and his father had seen for him back in the mid-1930s. He would go to Ottawa and he would take with him his parents' woes, enlarged to include those of all the working poor from his new political home of Winnipeg North Centre and from his adopted country of Canada. He also took with him the zeal of his religious days.

6

PLAYING THE GAME MEANS KNOWING THE RULES

3 February 1943

Speaker James Glen could not know then that he was about to launch the career of a procedural expert. Indeed he was reluctant to interrupt the applause the new member for Winnipeg North Centre was receiving after his maiden speech in the House of Commons. But he was being nagged by the Clerk of the House, Arthur Beauchesne. Beauchesne knew the rules of the House inside out and backwards — indeed he had committed many of them to paper in a standard text. But he was also a bit of character. During Knowles first speech, Beauchesne kept popping up to the Speaker, muttering "You can't let these new fellows get away with it."[1] Speaker Glen let Knowles have his day but then he gathered his authority about him, rose from the chair, and ticked him off. "The honourable member has just delivered his maiden speech in the House and because he cannot be expected to be thoroughly familiar with the rules I did not call attention to the rule which forbids the reading of speeches. I should just like to say that I hope no other member will take this as a precedent when he is speaking."[2]

It had been such a splendid speech. He had only been in parliament one week and was taking part in the debate on the Address in Reply to the Speech from the Throne that accompanies the opening of every parliamentary session. His colleagues expected him to make a good speech, a "Royal George", in the parlance of the day. To ensure that, they insisted he have a prepared manuscript. He would not actually read it — everyone knew that was against House rules — but it would be there in front of him in case he were suddenly struck dumb by the awesome surroundings. The new member protested; he had not used notes let alone a full text for a speech since his far-off days as a student preacher. That was almost fifteen years ago and he had made many a speech since then. But his colleagues argued that this was an entirely different situation and he gave in.

Carefully he penned his opening remarks. The seat he represented had been that of J. S. Woodsworth and Knowles paid homage to the man he had loved and admired. He gave warning to the House that he would emulate Woodsworth by continuing to be a gadfly on the left. He put in his first parliamentary reference to pensions — there would be thousands more in the years to come — and indicated that he would not be content until older people across the country were too. Then he launched into an attack on Humphrey Mitchell, the minister of labour in the Liberal government of Mackenzie King, accusing him of deluding workers. He added his own defence of the rights of war workers. He commented upon recent recommendations about the pay scales and union rights of wartime workers; Mitchell had ignored the suggestions and labour groups across the country were unhappy. Knowles even tossed into his speech the suggestion that Mitchell resign. And he delivered it all with the assurance of a trained and experienced preacher. Nonetheless, the text was in front of him and he was following it closely enough to agitate the watchful Beauchesne.

It was a big occasion. Knowles was thirty-four years old and he was finally in parliament making his maiden speech. His family and friends were watching from the gallery. His colleagues in the CCF all pounded their desks enthusiastically and even the Liberals and Conservatives, who usually gave only half-hearted attention to anyone outside their ranks, were attentive, polite, and friendly. The new member glowed: this was going to be a good place to work. Then came the Speaker's quick cutting down to size. In two sentences, he deflated the aura around the new member and left him dejected, annoyed, and powerless to respond. Of course he knew the rule about not reading speeches and it had only been at the insistence of his colleagues that he had a prepared manuscript at all. He had been led to believe, and indeed he saw many instances of it in his subsequent years in parliament, that new members, especially those elected in the middle of a parliament, were treated with considerable leniency. Such was not his case in February 1943 and although Speaker Glen later apologized for being so severe, the damage was done.

At the time all Knowles could do was say to himself, "That's the last speech I'll ever read," and, "We'll find out whether I understand the rules of the House."[3] A procedural expert was born.

He had always been fascinated by the mechanics of things. Mathematics was one of his favourite subjects and at one point he had thought of a career in engineering. When he turned to politics in the 1930s, he found a vast realm for his intellectual passion for intricacy, detail, and process. From Woodsworth, he had received copies of Hansard, the record of the daily proceedings in the House of Commons, and he had carefully analyzed the whys and the hows of the debates, the questions and the manoeuvres. He knew that Woodsworth had had a political interest in procedure and he maintained that interest: when to get into a debate; how to get the party's position heard. But he also added his own keen sense of the particular and the mechanical. He had an intellectual, academic, and later, a reforming interest in the rules of the House. Speaker Glen's acid comment was as much a challenge as an insult. Over the next fourteen years, Knowles established such a reputation as an expert in the rules of the House that he was offered the Speakership itself. But that is another story.

In 1943 he set to work to learn as much and as quickly as he could about the mechanics of parliamentary procedure. Armed with pen and scribbler he noted everything from his seat in the back row — he was the ninth member of the nine-man CCF contingent. He observed the opening ritual; he scrutinized the question period to see just how questions were put onto the Order Paper and what happened to them after. He took in everything and when something puzzled him he sought enlightenment from the two CCF members nearest him, George Castleden and Joe Noseworthy. In both cases he ran into a blank wall: Joe was hard of hearing and 'Cass' did not know the answers. He would have to learn by himself and the scribblers attest to his assiduity.

Parliamentary procedure offers a triple interest to Knowles. First, there is the elementary matter of survival in the House of Commons: to be an effective member, he had to know his way around; had to feel at home. Some of his fellow MPs, in all parties, do not even know the hour for the weekday sittings of the House or what the order of business is to be. To Knowles, the rules of procedure are a wilderness guide for members, an intricate agenda to the day's or week's business, a detailed map through a maze.

The rules of procedure as political weapons are the second aspect of Knowles' interest in them. A member of parliament is in

"the rules of procedure are a wilderness guide for members." Ottawa c. 1949.

the House to express a point of view; collectively a political party does the same. Just as in an old-fashioned schoolroom, so too in parliament: drill and repetition are the only way to teach the legislators. The party system depends upon maximum exposure for the ideas of a given party and an MP has to use every occasion to express his point, reiterate it, and then repeat it once again, if he ever expects it to find its way into legislation. When therefore is the precise moment for a motion or an amendment? What should the exact wording be so that the Speaker will rule it in order and therefore acceptable for debate? On which motions should a recorded vote be demanded in order to catch the government publicly voting against an issue it had earlier said it supported? And how is all that done? The man from Winnipeg North Centre knows.

During his years in parliament, Knowles developed a third interest in the rules. After the individual MP's survival and the party's partisan advantage comes a concern for parliament itself. Like society, parliament will only work by rule of law. Unless those rules are clear, stated, known, and adhered to, parliament cannot function. Should the Speaker or the government or even the opposition take it upon itself to dictate the business of the House, the entire parliamentary system would collapse as indeed it was near doing in the spring of 1982 when the Conservatives, leaning on the practice that party whips must be present for votes, simply stayed out of the chamber to avoid voting on a government energy bill. The bells summoning MPs to vote rang for two weeks and parliament in effect was closed down. Knowles was not there at the time and some people wonder if he might not have hastened a solution. But over the years he has frequently been on his feet in procedural wrangles, insisting not just on his own rights or those of his party, but also on those of the official opposition and even, on occasion, on those of the government. Parliament itself has to work freely and fairly if the political system itself is to do so. Parliament must also work efficiently and that concern led Knowles to ponder changes and improvements in the rules. If a proposed change will make parliament function better, he is quite prepared to give up individual or party rights in the House. Thus, his interest in the mechanics of things has taken him a long way; neither he nor Speaker Glen foresaw much of it that day in 1943.

Not long after that chastisement Knowles' colleagues asked him to put his growing procedural knowledge to the test. Unlike some procedural questions which have the effect of prolonging debate interminably — and Knowles used that technique to great effect during the pipeline debate in 1956 — this one actually brought a seemingly interminable debate to a close.

The occasion was conscription and the House was meeting in special session in November 1944 to cope with it. The minister of defence, J. L. Ralston, had been unceremoniously dumped from the cabinet because Prime Minister King had refused his demand that conscription be implemented immediately. King then attempted to buy more time by replacing Ralston with retired army general A. G. McNaughton in the hope that he could muster some last-minute voluntary recruits. But McNaughton was no more successful than other recruiting officers across the land and King had had to give in and declare, by order-in-council, the conscription for overseas service of some sixteen thousand of the home defence conscripts. At that point C. G. Power, the associate minister of national defence, resigned from the cabinet to protest the implementation of conscription and King was reported to have remarked that since Ralston and Power were now sitting equidistant from him, he, precisely in the middle and between the two extremes, must be right.

Meanwhile, the Conservatives were crying for blood. If they could lure Ralston and a number of his followers away from the Liberals, they might together be able to form a 'National Government', similar to the Union government they had formed in 1917, and the country would be rid of King with all his pomposities and superstitions. The Conservatives were willing to try anything to defeat the King government and the tension ran high around Parliament Hill. The problem was that there was nothing on the floor of the House to debate. The order-in-council had been precisely that — a cabinet order that did not need a parliamentary vote of approval. But the House needed something to debate. The opposition was insisting that it be given a chance to express its opinion and King himself had always said that "Parliament will decide." So the prime minister himself presented a motion: "that this House will aid the government in its policy of maintaining a vigorous war effort."⁴ Then came the mêlée that went on day and night: members of the opposition, now the Conservatives, now the CCF, now the *Bloc populaire* presented contradictory amendments and subamendments. Most were declared out of order or effectively argued against by the government. Always the opposition was ready with another, and the debate, so hard to start, now seemed impossible to end. CCF members turned to Knowles. He knew the rules; surely he could draft an amendment that would cut through the chaos. He pondered a moment, scribbled a note to party leader M. J. Coldwell to propose amending the government motion by striking out the words "its policy of." The meaning was clear: the CCF would support the war effort but it would not acknowledge that that effort was the sole doing of the Liberal government.

King was on his feet in a minute to say he would accept Coldwell's amendment. Knowles and his colleagues were taken aback. Most of the previous amendments had been declared out of order — a usual governmental means of avoiding an issue — or simply voted down. Most of the votes during the entire fracas had in fact been votes on appeals of the Speaker's rulings, appeals which are now no longer permitted. All Knowles hoped for with the amendment was that it be declared in order by the Speaker. It would then be debated and probably defeated since the government was not likely to acknowledge that maintaining a vigorous war effort was not its own policy. But King accepted the amendment, seeing in it a way to get his main motion passed without too much alteration and to obtain thereby an indirect approval of his conscription policy. The amendment passed amid taunts from the Conservatives that the CCF had bedded down with the Liberals. Certainly that was the way the vote appeared as Liberals followed CCFers to vote for Coldwell's motion with the Conservatives sullenly voting against it. The main motion as amended then passed and the special session came to an end.

Speakers and Speakers' rulings could also be a source of procedural wrangling and sometimes even of procedural fun. Speaker Glen more often than not played into the government's hands and the opposition was constantly challenging his rulings. Frequently Knowles had to argue with his own colleagues who wanted to vote on the substance while he insisted that it was the ruling that was at issue. Not that the arguments served much purpose for government members always voted to support the Speaker and thereby rebuff the opposition's challenge to his ruling. The following Speaker, Gaspard Fauteux, provoked even more appeals. He was a dentist by profession and the word quickly spread that he pulled more boners while in the Speaker's chair than he had ever pulled teeth in his dentist's office. A "nice guy" to those who knew him, he was, Knowles claims, quite out of his depth as Speaker. On occasion, however, he could unwittingly provoke some fun. During one incident in 1947 Prime Minister King was clearly overstepping the rules of the House but Speaker Fauteux refrained from silencing him. Knowles raised a point of order but the Speaker ruled that all was well. Knowing himself to be right, Knowles then appealed the ruling, but the government was able to muster its tiny overall majority and declare the Speaker right by virtue of numbers. King could continue his speech uninterrupted. He did so but he also kept an eye on the procedural expert from Winnipeg North Centre who chose that moment to slip down the hall to the men's room. As Knowles rose from his seat behind Coldwell and began moving towards the back of the chamber, the House was suddenly silent; he sensed it, paused, and turned around. "Oh," remarked King, "I thought my honourable friend was raising another point of order."[5]

That same year provided an illustration of the partisan use of procedure. As usual Knowles sought every nook and cranny in the rules to enable him to bring his concern for pensioners to the attention of parliament and the country. Sometimes a word, sometimes a question, sometimes an interjection, and on occasion, a major opportunity. In April 1947 the minister of health and welfare, Paul Martin, informed the House of a forthcoming increase in the Old Age Pension. According to the rules of the House at the time, a money bill had to be preceded by a resolution which stated the amount of money and its purpose. Martin's resolution did neither. It merely said there would be an increase.

Perhaps he thought the government could slip one by an inattentive opposition or perhaps he was just inattentive himself. All the more reason, Knowles argues, for having a few procedural experts around to protect parliament from the government or even the government from itself. In this case, since the government did not specify an amount in the resolution, the opposition was free to amend whatever amount the government did eventually indicate in the bill itself. What better opportunity for someone who had had a passion for pensions ever since his father had lost his job, without a pension, in 1932?

S. H. KNOWLES, C.C.F. WINNIPEG

A cartoonist captured the eagerness and, on occasion the mischievousness of Knowles. Ottawa 1947. (Jack Boothe, *The Globe and Mail*, Toronto).

In fact, the CCF was ready and looking for just such an occasion. In the preceding months, the party, working with the Canadian Congress of Labour, one of the then existing union centrals in the country and the only one to endorse the CCF, had circulated a petition across the country praying the House of Commons to double the Old Age Pension to fifty dollars a month. The petition had more than a quarter of a million signatures and was an unusual sight in the parliament of that day. But was it in order? Knowles worked on the wording to ensure that it would be acceptable for presentation to parliament, but he was a bit worried about the specified amount. After all, only the government had the right to initiate money matters. Still, the organizing committee decided to take a chance. Knowles and fellow CCF MP, Sandy Nicholson, carried the mammoth petition to their Commons' desks and Coldwell presented it to the House in mid-May. They then waited a weekend while the Clerk of Committees decided on its acceptability. When he agreed to it, he even linked the petition more closely than Knowles had dared to hope to Martin's resolution. Because that resolution was already before the House with its proposal to alter the Old Age Pension, the petition, which normally would not be allowed because of its request for the "expenditure of public money," was acceptable.⁶

What the petition did in effect was imply an amendment to a bill that had not yet been produced. Martin was furious: he had no intention of raising the pension to fifty dollars and here was the pesky CCF not only stealing his publicity but showing up his niggardliness in advance. When he did finally outline the provisions of his bill in mid-June, he went to great lengths to argue that his increase was substantial but the net effect was to raise the pension from twenty-five to thirty dollars.⁷ Knowles subsequently proposed an amendment to the bill, to increase the amount to fifty dollars. He argued from House rules which clearly permitted such amendment when a money resolution did not specify an amount. He argued from the petition with its hundreds of thousands of backers and the Clerk's pronouncement that it was in order. Both arguments were impeccable and most MPs not only knew it but were awed by his exposition of them. He was, however, ruled out of order on the grounds that only ministers of the crown can propose increases in expenditure.⁸ The ruling was immediately challenged and although the subsequent vote was strictly on the ruling, Knowles' arguments for the amendment had been so clear and the ruling so obviously unfair that the meaning of the procedural vote itself was clear: the government was not interested in increasing the pensions as high as fifty dollars. He therefore lost the vote and the ruling and the fifty dollar pension; the fight itself he never gave up. Knowing the intricacies of procedure was one of his many weapons in that fight.

But he could also put his procedural knowledge to the defence of the opposition itself. In November 1949 he won what he considered a "major victory,"[9] although he will acknowledge that the huge sense of fairness that went with the huge new Speaker, Ross Macdonald, helped considerably. On that occasion, the opposition had finally succeeded, after months of querying the government, in having the minister of justice table the McGregor report, an investigation of the flour milling industry carried out under the Combines Investigation Act. The report had in fact been submitted to the government almost a year earlier and under the Act should have been made public by mid-January 1949 at the latest. But the government, it seems, was not at all anxious to reveal the report with its finding that a combine existed in the flour milling industry. It therefore simply kept the report secret. By doing so it was clearly acting illegally but as long as the opposition did not know the report existed, the government was not unduly concerned.

The opposition, however, did begin to know of the report and was not at all pleased. When the CCF asked questions, it was rebuffed. When the report itself was made public just a week before the government introduced changes to the Combines Investigation Act itself all opposition parties condemned the government's illegal behaviour in hiding the report. In a curious procedural move, the government allowed the opposition to let off a bit of steam and then, a week later, when George Drew, the Conservative leader, brought the subject up again during debate on the Combines Investigation Act itself, claimed that he was out of order. One cannot debate a topic that has already been debated.

Unless one has Stanley Knowles on one's side. Knowles suspected something like this might happen. The timing had been too precise and he had armed himself for the government's point of order. Not that he was so fond of the Conservatives; indeed he thought Drew was moving in on an issue first unearthed by the CCF. Nonetheless he would defend Drew and the opposition's right to reveal and denounce governmental misdemeanours. With enough supporting cases — all of which he read — to overwhelm the Speaker, he argued that the House had to have expressed some judgment on an issue before it could come under the 'no second debate' rule. In this case, no judgment had been expressed: the only votes in the House on the day the McGregor report was made public were on quite different matters. Drew therefore had every right to continue.[10]

In an unusual move for a Speaker, particularly a newly appointed one, Macdonald agreed with Knowles. He ruled against the government's point of order and declared that Drew could continue. Drew did so, followed by Coldwell, Solon Low for the Social Credit, and Joe Noseworthy of the CCF. All of them spoke less on the subject of the bill than on the evil intent and illegal activity of the government in hiding the McGregor report. Knowles considered it a personal victory; it was also a parliamentary and public one. The right to know is basic to parliamentary and public freedoms, and, Knowles would undoubtedly say, party advantage is decidedly secondary. By 1949, then, he was already revealing his third area of interest in rules and procedure: the protection of the rights of the opposition and of parliament in general.

Over the years Knowles became so adept at using certain procedures that he resisted their abolition. Such was the case with appeals of Speaker's rulings, which came to an end in the 1960s. Most Speakers had been so partisan — they were, after all, named by the government — that the opposition's only defence was to appeal their rulings. Gradually, however, he was persuaded that abolition would at least save some time in the House and once the change was made, provisionally in 1965 and permanently in 1968, Speakers have actually become more impartial. Before then, a ruling against the government was rare; since then, there have been many such rulings. The abolition of the appeals resolved another conflict, this time for Knowles himself. Frequently he had had to argue not only with his colleagues but also with himself to make sure they all voted on the ruling itself and not on the matter which had given rise to it. The subtleties of procedure sometimes evaded his colleagues and the pressures of politics sometimes caught him. Both problems vanished with the appeals.

Knowles has in fact been closely involved with changes in House rules. Those changes have come about because of a double pressure. Firstly, there are the parliamentarians themselves; no matter what side of the House they sit on they want to have more rights and more opportunities for themselves. Fairness, therefore, often necessitates changes in the rules. But secondly, parliamentary business has mushroomed since Knowles first came to parliament in 1942 and it became increasingly impossible to conduct business in the allotted time. In the early 1940s a six-month session was normal although some of the older members complained about the exaggerated time-table of the

House: in their day three or four months had sufficed. Now the House sits virtually throughout the year and sessions can continue for eighteen or twenty months. When Knowles arrived, the government had an annual budget of approximately five hundred million dollars; now it budgets for more than seventy-six billion and the number of its concerns has grown accordingly. In 1942, the Old Age Pension was a minuscule item in the estimates of the finance ministry (and always rushed through at the last minute, grumbled Knowles); there was no family allowance, no Old Age Security, no Guaranteed Income Supplement, no Canada Pension Plan, no manpower programmes, no health care, no hospital insurance, no educational assistance, not even any highways. In 1942, no one was worried about the cradle or the grave, much less the period in between. External affairs and trade have also grown since the 1930s when Woodsworth was virtually alone in raising such questions in the House. Then there were economic matters and immigration and problems of refugees. How were they all to be fitted into the parliamentary schedule?

Time is the answer and hence the necessary rule changes. Parliament can no longer cope with its huge programme in the leisurely manner which Knowles recalls from his early days when the Throne Speech debate consumed a month and there were no time limits on any debates. Closure was the only means of limiting members' right to speak and, in Canada, it has never been a popular measure since its introduction in 1913. Common sense, therefore, was the only means of restraint and that could not always be counted upon. Knowles has even argued that endless debate on a given topic is the best form of closure since it effectively eliminates other topics. He still growls over the flag debate in 1964 which delayed the legislating of medicare. He has little use for those people who claim that any limitation on an MP's right to speak is a denial of freedom of speech. Parliament may be a speaking place but if everyone exercises unlimited freedom of speech, it would be years behind in its legislative programme.

Parliamentary reform has taken two paths, one relatively simple, the other more difficult, and Knowles has marked them both. The first entailed tidying up certain procedures and Knowles has always been a compulsive tidier, from the kitchen sink to the rules of parliament. Placing the question period in a specific time of the parliamentary day was part of the tidying in the mid-1960s. Left-overs were then relegated to an evening "late show" with specific time limits on questions and answers. Recipes for ministerial statements were devised: who was to make them and who, from the opposition, would respond to them. Means for initiating special debates were invented. The appeals of Speakers' rulings were relegated to the ashcan.

Of greater difficulty was the second aspect of parliamentary reform — time. Inter-party committees, of which Knowles has been an assiduous member, have met over the years to design equitable time for debate. There is now an eight-day limit on the Throne Speech debate, six on that of the budget. The speeches of MPs during those debates are restricted to twenty or forty minutes, depending on the rank of the MP and the nature of the subject. The process by which bills are passed has now been shortened. Prior to the change in the late 1960s, when a bill had had second reading in the House and clause by clause scrutiny in a standing committee, it returned to the House which, as Committee of the Whole, would go over every clause of the bill again. A "report stage" of a bill now eliminates that last step. Members may still suggest amendments at the report stage but they are then under strict time limits. Frequently there are no amendments since the parties in the Commons are represented on standing committees and will have argued their changes there. Hence the report stage can be quite brief and the bill proceeds to the usually routine and quick third reading. Only tax bills escape the new route. Knowles was on the procedure committee in the 1960s that designed that particular pattern. It has his touch.

He is still trying to advance a pet scheme of his for proceeding even more quickly with bills. Debate on second reading has become the longest part, now that the Committee of the Whole stage has been dispensed with, and Knowles would like to see it streamlined too. The task is not easy. On the one hand, a time limit applying equally to all bills would give some more importance than others and more than they may merit: debate would merely stretch out to fill the allotted time. On the other hand, no limit at all leads to chaos. Knowles proposes that the government's legislative programme as revealed in the Throne Speech and in the subsequent tabling by the prime minister of a list of forthcoming bills, be divided into three categories. Minor or routine matters which require no debate in the House at all could go immediately to committees for study. Routine bills which nonetheless require some debate in the House would have time limits. Finally, the more contentious items which deserve full and unlimited debate would have it in the House. Knowles suggests five items from the third category, ten from the first for immediate committee consideration, and the remainder for two-day consideration in the House. Any bills that were introduced after the beginning of a session would be added to the list of five. Knowles is convinced that the government and the opposition, working perhaps through the House leaders of each party, could perfect such a system.

He also has a scheme for the most contentious and difficult topic — the estimates. Parliament is supposed to scrutinize the spending of money, but there is simply no way in which it can peruse the budget of every government department. Now that the government has a set date by which it must receive parliamentary approval of the estimates — towards the end of June every year — the debate has become even more perfunctory and the scrutiny even more lax. Knowles has quizzed parliamentarians in Britain about the matter only to have them admit that they gave up on the problem sixty years ago. They rely on a good civil service, a sharp Auditor-general, and the Public Accounts Committee of the House. Knowles is uneasy about the abdication of so much of parliament's responsibility. He suggests instead that the opposition pick, on very short notice, the estimates from three or four departments in any one given year. Those estimates would be subjected to the careful scrutiny that is the obligation of an MP; the others could be accepted as presented. A department would never know which estimates were to be selected for such examination and hence would always have to keep a close eye on its budget.

Knowles has advocated his ideas to anyone who will listen. He has written about them, spoken about them, presented them at committees on procedure and to meetings of House leaders and to fellow parliamentarians in Britain. Everyone acknowledges the intellectual merit of his plans but not much ever gets done. In Britain, proposed changes in the rules are treated more seriously than in Canada and Knowles thinks the difference can be attributed to the more frequent change of government; members realize that they may have to cope with the problems as government or opposition members in the near future.

In Canada, however, parliament stumbles on with the only time limitations — apart from the Throne Speech and the budget debates — being the seldom-used closure and the complex and cumbersome Rules 75a), b), and c) dating from 1969. Rule 75a) permits the House leaders to agree on a time limit for a debate and requires a government minister to present a motion to that effect which is not debatable. Rule 75b) allows a majority of the House leaders to decide upon a time limit and similarly to have a minister present such a motion to the House, this time for a two-hour debate. Rule 75c) presupposes no agreement at all among any of the House leaders and therefore permits the government to introduce a motion to limit debate, a motion which is debatable for two hours only and then must be decided upon. Although Knowles had a hand in drafting 75a) and b) he thinks b) and c) are useless. Indeed the entire Rule 75 tends to create ill will and animosity. For him, agreement on the correct division of parliamentary time has to come through compromise, not through confrontation.[11]

Knowles believes this to be a life and death struggle for parliament. If changes are not made, the entire institution will be under an intolerable strain. The changes he suggests will, he thinks, give parliament a fighting chance to keep up with the business which will always be increasing. The changes themselves may come faster now that the proceedings of the House are televised, something of which he approved. All Canadians should watch over their parliament and now that technology permits them to do so, parliament should respond by streamlining its activities.

Long before television, back in 1943, Speaker Glen was entirely unaware of the challenge he tossed to the new member for Winnipeg North Centre. Knowles took it seriously and although he was annoyed at the time, the incident has stayed in his memory as a decisive one in his life. He believes that an intricate knowledge of the rules and a passion for procedure are essential to the survival of parliament and vital to those crusaders, himself included, who have causes to advance.

7
COLONEL IN THE BRITISH ARMY

25 February 1946

After considerable delay the British army leave train was about to pull out of Berlin headed for Calais and London. The troops were anxious for a break although they knew London would not look much better than Berlin. Both cities had been heavily bombed during the war and, less than a year after the end of European hostilities, both still showed their scars. The British army of occupation had a sector of Berlin to police; it was hard work and the lucky ones due for leave were glad to be getting away. On the station plaform and on the train itself there was a general shuffle as the men made themselves comfortable. It would probably be a long ride; in the unsettled times trains frequently moved only at night and parked during the daytime. The travellers would simply have to make the best of it. Among them was Stanley Knowles who, in the general commotion, found the compartment assigned to him and offered to take the upper bunk. "No sir," came the reply, "You're the colonel; I'm only a lieutenant colonel, I'll take the upper bunk."[1]

What was Stanley Knowles — pacifist, minister, and socialist politician from Canada — doing as a member of the British army that day in late February 1946? He certainly did not know he would end up with military rank as part of the excitement and intrigue that accompanied his first trip outside North America. Since that occasion he has been all over the world taking part in international gatherings of parliamentarians and (during the four years that he was with the Canadian Labour Congress from 1958 to 1962) of union officials. Such opportunities have expanded greatly since he was first elected and he has been to Britain,

Scandinavia, Switzerland, Spain, and Germany, into South America, and to Israel, India, Russia, and China. All the trips have marked his sensibilities and his occupation as he grieves over the poverty of India, breathes the tension in Israel, separates government from people in Russia or China, and constantly compares legislative and political processes. But the first trip in the mid-1940s was undoubtedly the most adventurous.

It all began one day in the House of Commons in the early autumn of 1945. From his desk behind CCF leader M. J. Coldwell, Knowles saw the justice minister, Louis St. Laurent, coming over from the government side of the House to speak with Coldwell, and he could not help overhearing the conversation. St. Laurent wanted Coldwell to go to London in November as a member of the Canadian delegation to the preparatory commission of the new United Nations. The two men had both accompanied Prime Minister Mackenzie King to San Francisco in June 1945 for the founding of the United Nations and the next step was preparation for the first general assembly to be held in London early in 1946. The preparation was crucial: rules and regulations for the meetings had to be specified; the assets and responsibilities of the old League of Nations had to be transferred to the United Nations; suggestions for a permanent location had to be discussed; a detailed agenda for the general assembly had to be drawn up. Coldwell, however, could not go and Knowles heard his name suggested as a possibility. St. Laurent went back to the government side of the House and Coldwell turned to his colleague to tell him what he had already heard. Within a few days it was settled: Knowles, along with three other MPs, would go as part of the Canadian delegation to the preparatory commission.

Getting to Britain was only the first of the adventures. There was little commercial air travel at the time let alone six-hour transatlantic jet flights. The Canadian delegation was to fly from Montreal to Prestwick in a converted Lancaster, the huge bomber carrier of the war days. The conversion was incomplete and the plane could only accommodate ten passengers and none too comfortably at that. They were all aware that something was wrong with some if not all of the engines and their suspicions were confirmed when the plane made an unscheduled stop at Gander. Ushered to a nearby mess hall, the travellers were told to settle in and relax. They did so, for three days. Finally another plane was brought to Gander to fly them to Scotland. Because of bad weather conditions over the North Atlantic the Lancaster had to fly at twenty thousand feet and the cabin was not pressurized. The passengers had to sport oxygen masks and they crossed the

Atlantic looking, and no doubt feeling, rather ghoulish. The motley bunch eventually arrived at Prestwick to be greeted, before any customs or immigration formalities, with a cup of tea. Again the weather caused changes to their plans and the scheduled flight to London became an overnight train ride.

On arrival, the Canadian delegates plunged immediately into the work of the preparatory commission. Most of it was done through committees which meant that the various national delegations were divided. Frequently Knowles found himself the sole Canadian delegate on a given committee. The position could be awkward since the delegates, although representing Canada, were not all members of the Canadian government; Knowles, for example, came from an opposition party. What were the delegates to do if they could not support a particular stand of the Canadian government? The directions from Ottawa were clear: they were to keep quiet. If a delegate found that impossible, he was to inform the leader of the delegation, Dana Wilgress, the Canadian ambassador to Moscow, who would have another delegate temporarily replace the uneasy one. The system worked fairly well and indeed strong opposition seldom arose.

On two occasions, however, the system was put to the test. One concerned the location of the new United Nations. Ottawa's official preference was Geneva, with the new international body simply taking over from the old League of Nations. But one of the opposition MPs on the Canadian delegation did not agree. Conservative Gordon Graydon suggested Canada or perhaps a location spanning the border between Canada and the United States. Failing that, then the headquarters must definitely be in the United States, to ensure full American support. When Graydon, the Canadian delegate on the committee that was discussing location, said he really could not support the government's preference for Geneva, he was replaced by Wilgress. Not particularly keen himself on Geneva, Wilgress was more willing than Graydon to express the Canadian government's official view.

The other instance involved Knowles directly. He was the sole Canadian on a committee dealing with the problem of refugees and there was a suggestion that an international organization be established to provide funds, aid, and refuge to the thousands of political refugees that the war had thrown up. The word from Ottawa was to say nothing. So Knowles, suspecting that Mackenzie King was probably sensitive to the question and to the fact that Canada had done very little to assist war or even pre-war refugees, sat silent, listening. During one session of the committee he realized that the delegate from the Ukraine, Dimitro Manuilsky, speaking for the USSR, was gesturing at him, interspersing his Russian remarks with the word Canada and obviously becoming quite agitated. He was condemning the whole idea of an international refugee organization, claiming it would just be a front for anti-Soviet propaganda. He cited Canada where, he said, the newspapers were full of pious sentiments about refugees (traitors and war criminals to him) and vitriolic condemnation of the USSR. If the newspapers said such things, they must be reflecting Canadian government policy. Canada was surely an example of what the proposed international refugee organization would be doing; the Soviet Union, he stormed, would have nothing to do with it.

Catching the gist of the tirade, Knowles was taken aback. Should he sit silent, as he had been told to do, in the face of such an attack? Fortunately the system of translation gave him time to ponder the matter. When a speech was delivered, interpreters took notes and then delivered the speech again in whichever of the four conference languages — English, French, Russian, or Spanish — had not been originally used. While Manuilsky's speech was thus repeated in three other languages, Knowles had time to decide. He certainly wanted to speak, but he had better check with his external affairs adviser behind him first. "You're the delegate," came the response, "It's your decision."[2] So he spoke.

He was known to be the Canadian delegate but he identified himself immediately as a member of the opposition from Canada. He was under no obligation to defend the government and he did not intend to do so now. Indeed, as a socialist (he heard Manuilsky snort "some socialist"[3]), he was opposed to most of its policies at home. But he did wish to defend his country and Canadians from the attack that the delegate from the Ukraine had just made. He denied the charge that whatever anti-Soviet propaganda one saw in the Canadian papers was necessarily government policy, but he could see the disbelief on Manuilsky's face. He insisted that whatever government policy might be (in fact he did know what it was; he had simply been instructed to keep quiet) he was certain that the Canadian people would want to share the world's refugee problem and would want the country to support the proposed international organization.

There, he had said what he wanted but what would the reaction be? He expected to be reprimanded if not actually shipped back to Canada. But not a word was said. Only later when he was back in Canada did he get an inkling of the reaction to his untoward speech. In March 1946 as the House of Commons gathered for the opening session and the members were greeting each other, the prime minister made a point of coming over to him. Unlike subsequent prime ministers with whom Knowles has spoken freely and easily, King maintained an aloof distance. "Knowles," he said — he addressed everyone by his surname and Stanley mischievously suggests he may even have addressed his mother that way — "I've heard about the good work you did at the United Nations, especially that speech you made on refugees."[4] Startled but pleased, Knowles thanked the prime minister. Later in the year he encountered the two Canadians who were going to London for the founding meeting of the International Refugee Organization. They told him that in the files that were accompanying them was that speech he had made. Obviously one could maintain one's integrity as an opposition member while being an official Canadian delegate, speak out of turn, and come out unscathed.

When not at the sessions of the preparatory commission and later at those of the general assembly, for which he was asked by the Canadian government to stay as an alternate delegate, Knowles spent his time in the gallery of the British House of Commons. He saw the beginnings of the Labour government under Clement Attlee and spotted the people, notably Winston Churchill, whose voices had become familiar over wartime radio. Already enamoured of parliament after only three years in the Canadian House, he was tremendously impressed by the British parliament. He even popped into the House of Lords for a moment where he saw the former Canadian prime minister, R. B. Bennett, now a Viscount and comfortably asleep in his lordly surroundings. Knowles thought no more of the House of Lords than he did of the Canadian Senate.

During the break between the preparatory commission and the UN general assembly, Knowles and two of the other Canadian MPs went to the continent for Christmas and the New Year. For security reasons, two officers from the Canadian army accompanied Knowles, Gordon Graydon, and Howard Winkler. Crossing from England to the Hook of Holland, the party drove through Holland and into Northern Germany to the headquarters of the Canadian occupational force at Oldenburg. There Knowles talked with Canadian soldiers and registered their complaints; mostly they wanted to go home. From there the group headed east to Berlin with the intention of going on to Moscow where the Canadian ambassador, Dana Wilgress, had returned for Christmas and was expecting them. The arrangements seemed straightforward: the RCAF was flying a shuttle service between Berlin and Moscow for a forthcoming foreign ministers conference and there was to be no difficulty in getting the three Canadian MPs aboard one of the flights.

Just getting to Berlin was somewhat nervewracking. The officers accompanying the MPs were armed but because the party had to cross the Soviet zone to reach Berlin, British authorities at the checkpoint thought they should be more heavily protected. There was too much night time shooting, too many people trying to escape for it to be safe for stray MPs to be wandering about. Two British armoured vehicles therefore joined the small procession to Berlin. Even there no greater sense of security prevailed. The city was in a shambles, the destruction awesome. The visitors were warned not to leave their hotel at night when everything was in darkness and anything could happen. They carried the best kind of post-war currency — cigarettes — although Knowles learned later that he was spending it far too freely in tips in the hotel. A chambermaid had startled him by getting down on her knees to thank him for an entire package of cigarettes; two or three would have sufficed. The hotel people were friendly but the atmosphere was unpleasant.

As for the planned Moscow part of their trip, the MPs and their escorts made the necessary inquiries, but nobody knew anything about it. There were no visas, no travel plans, no information, nothing. Knowles was prepared to wait; surely they would be able to go within a few days. But the others, either knowing more about Soviet practices or perhaps just more anxious to be in Paris rather than Berlin or Moscow for New Year's eve, persuaded him to return to France with them. Moscow would have to wait.

New Year's Eve in Paris was part work and part play, with Knowles as usual preferring the former. He visited the French National Assembly and saw the members engage in an acrimonious debate over the budget. So prolonged was the debate that it went on all night and into New Year's Day. When Knowles returned that day to watch the continuation of the debate, what struck him most was the big sign over the assembly declaring that it was still yesterday. Obviously some unfinished business was supposed to have been legally completed before the end of 1945. Knowles recalled the scene years later in the midst of the pipeline debate in the Canadian parliament when the Speaker took it upon himself to turn the clock back. As for the New Year's Eve clock in Paris in 1945, it wound down at a party in the officers' mess. For Knowles any party longer than half an hour is endless, but this one really did go on far into the night. He was glad to encounter his fellow CCF MP Scotty Bryce who had just arrived from London and to whom he could pass the equally endless supply of drinks. When their army officer companions had had enough they suggested returning to the hotel in a velocipede, a bicycle-taxi that was then a common means of public transportation. The velocipede was easy enough to find but the hotel seemed to be constantly eluding the driver. Eventually it was found and the driver paid a fancy sum. The next morning, out the hotel window, what could be seen? The very officers' mess from which they had come the night before, right across the street.

Before returning to London, the group toured some of the battlefields of the recent war. One of the accompanying officers had taken part in the Normandy landing in June 1944 and gave the visitors a graphic description. Through Bayeux, Caen, Dieppe, and Dunkirk, the group went, passing by way of Vimy Ridge to see the commemorative monument to a Canadian battle of the First World War. Knowles' view of the terrain through which Canadian soldiers had fought, died, or survived, confirmed his distaste for war. Especially when the after affects were so visible all around: the north of France had borne the brunt of the allied invasion and the German retreat; it was poor, devastated country and the people were bitter. As he described it to a friend:

The destruction war has brought to everything — physical, political, moral, spiritual — especially in Germany and France — is stupendous. One sees before his eyes the end of a chapter. . . . The world we were born into is dead. There is no going back. Ahead there is either anarchy and more war (war not more terrible than the last for it wouldn't last so long — the weapons are worse and the stamina of whole races is shot) or a new order.[5]

Back in London for the opening of the United Nations general assembly on 10 January, Knowles was accosted by Ambassador Wilgress. Where had he got to? Wilgress was mystified by the complications that had been thrown in the way of the MPs trying to get to Moscow but he suggested that they try again. If they requested a visa now, it might just come through before the end of the month-long sessions of the UN. The others declined; they were anxious to return to Canada. Knowles, however, not knowing when he would have another chance to visit Moscow — in fact it would be almost thirty years later — said sure.

Just as the UN meetings were drawing to a close in

mid-February he received the necessary visa for entry into Russia and instructions to be at RAF headquarters at the crack of dawn the following morning. There was just time to borrow a heavier overcoat, to arrange finances — difficult because of restrictions on foreign exchange and on taking money out of the country — and to pack his belongings. With that done he could attend the evening reception the Royal Family was giving for some of the UN delegates. What surprised him most was the informality of the family and of the gathering. King George, Queen Elizabeth, and the two princesses mingled easily with their guests, willing and anxious to speak to them all. Knowles watched others introduce themselves and decided to do the same. To the king he mentioned his country, occupation, and party affiliation. "Oh," said King George, "Mr. Coldwell's party." Perhaps it was his business to know such things, but Knowles was nonetheless astonished. The King wanted to know about the UN sessions, in particular how was his foreign secretary, Ernie Bevin, getting along in the Security Council? Poor King, thought Knowles, Bevin is your minister but you can't even go observe him at work. He then passed through the crowd and stopped to speak to Princess Elizabeth. When he mentioned Canada where she had not yet been, she remarked "That's the place where you get a shock when you touch the doorknobs."[6] He explained the link between central heating, plush carpeting, and static electricity which the princess's relatives, the Athlones, had experienced as the vice-regal family at Rideau Hall since 1940. On every occasion that Knowles has met Queen Elizabeth since he has reminded her of the subject of their first conversation.

The next morning he was off to Moscow, complete with borrowed overcoat. The RAF would take no money for the flight. One was either on it or not and since Knowles was on, all was well. The plane flew to Berlin via Hamburg and because of flight disturbances, gave the passengers lengthy circular views of the latter city which had been heavily fire-bombed during the war. In Berlin, Knowles was under the wing of the Canadian military mission, in effect a diplomatic mission, but since Berlin had a military government at that time, the diplomats were military people. He was able to borrow some Russian rubles from British sources in Berlin and took a Soviet flight to Moscow. There too the Canadian embassy, where he was to stay during the third week of February, took charge of him.

It was all very exciting. Not just because Moscow was such a strange place and Knowles was being treated so royally, but because the one notorious spy case involving Canada became public knowledge while he was there. The Gouzenko affair, revealing the existence of a Soviet spy ring in Canada whose purpose was to discover atomic secrets, had been known to Canadian officials since early September 1945. Members of parliament recalled receiving no excuse for a delay in the opening of the House that autumn; they later learned that the prime minister was receiving the Gouzenko news at that very moment. Knowles also remembered hearing one of the Canadian cabinet ministers, in London for the UN general assembly, mutter during a speech by a Russian: "I wish I could tell you something we know about these people."[7] He did not press the matter but later realized that it was a reference to the Gouzenko affair. By 16 February the story was in the newspapers.

He and the other people about the embassy in Moscow were summoned into a drawing room to learn of the case from Jack Thurrott, the second secretary, since the ambassador was still in London. Thurrott had been entrusted months earlier with bringing the message from the Canadian government to the embassy in Moscow. Mackenzie King would trust neither the codes nor the courier; both, it seems, were too easily rifled. So Thurrott had been given a routine posting to Moscow with a special message committed to memory. No one knew and the message was safely delivered. Thurrott's own wife learned of the affair at the same time Knowles did.

No one knew what the Soviet reaction would be. Perhaps the visiting MP would be detained. Certainly he could only leave with the blessing of the foreign office since all foreign passports had to be surrendered on entry to Russia and were only returned on departure. Knowles thought it a great adventure and, unlike his wife in Winnipeg, was not at all anxious. Vida Knowles had had conflicting information about her husband's return from Europe and when she knew he was in Russia and that "people have been caught giving information to a foreign power," her "first thought was wouldn't something like that happen when he is there." She was, she said, "so upset about all this I am past tears."[8] In Moscow, however, Knowles took advantage of the cancellation by the Russians of a number of scheduled appointments with government officials. For two or three days he was free to wander about entirely on his own. Instead of the selected visits to schools, factories, a hospital, and a people's court, or the attendance at the ballet, the opera, and the Red Army choir, all of which had fascinated him,[9] he now poked about the streets and squares of the city, took the subway and tried out his few words of Russian — bolstered by university Greek — whenever he needed directions. At the end of each day, he returned to the embassy and chatted with the Russian guard at the gate, telling him where he had been, what he had seen, and how he liked Moscow. Embassy officials gently chastised him: the guard spent his days keeping his eyes and ears open for the whereabouts of these foreigners and there was Knowles spilling everything out without even being asked.

Not knowing whether he would be leaving or not, he attended a party for the new Canadian military attaché on the eve of his scheduled departure. He asked Brigadier Jean Allard just what a military attaché did. The job, it seemed, involved finding out as many secrets as possible about the military operations of the host country. And what will you do here, pursued Knowles, knowing full well that military information was not to be had just for the asking. Well, Allard would talk with the other military attachés and see what information they had gleaned in their stay in Moscow. At the party too were some Russian officials who, after speaking with Knowles, mentioned that they would see him the next day at Foreign Minister Molotov's party for the new ambassador from Iran. But he had received no invitation; moreover he was leaving the next day and he told them so. One of the Russians commented that he did not think there would be any planes flying in the morning. Knowles wondered vaguely how he could tell that through the dark windows of the embassy but the Canadian diplomats were more used to interpreting that kind of language and they translated the message for him: you won't be going in the morning. But at five the next morning there was a call and he was to leave. Weeks later when he was back in Canada he received an invitation to the Molotov party, forwarded from the Canadian embassy in Moscow. As he says, "Some cog in the Soviet wheel slipped."[10] As one section of the foreign office invited him to a party, another put him on a plane bound for Berlin.

Like the Canadian Lancasters flying the Atlantic in 1945, the Russian plane, an American built Dakota, was not intended for passengers. Knowles sat on the floor, among crates, or stood up hoping to catch a bit of the heat passing along the ceiling of the cabin. Seven long uncomfortable hours later, he landed at an unknown airport somewhere in the Soviet sector of Berlin. The airport itself was a shambles and no one was present to offer assistance or information. With his few words of Russian and none of German, how was he to get out? Surely someone would know of his arrival. Half excited and half fearful, he prowled the battered airport. A tiny, grubby office revealed a telephone and above it, on the wall, a scribbled message in pencil: "British

passengers from Moscow, phone this number. . . ." There was no
one around the airport in the gathering gloom of evening so he
called the number. The connections were long and laborious but a
few hours later someone did come for him. He was then put in a
hotel for a day or so while his exit from Berlin was arranged.

   Like all the travel arrangements that one too was complicated.
The weather interrupted an RAF flight to London and other
transportation was extremely haphazard. The Canadian military
mission in Berlin watched out for the Canadian MP and urged
their counterparts in the British delegation to see what they could
do. Finally the British suggested that Mr. Knowles could perhaps
go on a British army leave train that was scheduled to depart for
London soon. The problem was that only British army personnel
were permitted on the train. The solution was to issue Knowles a
booklet which indicated that he had the equivalent rank of colonel
in the British army. Thus elevated he could take the troop train to
London and enjoy the deference of junior officers especially the
one sharing his compartment. The lieutenant colonel who insisted
that lower rank relegated him to the upper bunk was badged and
braided and smartly uniformed and looked to the somewhat
scruffy Knowles as if he had been through all the wars of the
twentieth century. Nonetheless, he played his subaltern role
throughout the trip, insisting that "the colonel" precede him
through doors and have prior food service. At Calais, when all the
officers of the rank of full colonel and up were asked to step
forward, Knowles' lieutenant colonel gave him a shove. The
senior officers were to go through customs and currency checks
first. When the train arrived in London, there was no official
ceremony to strip him of his rank, but he believes his time as a
colonel in the British army ended then. He does not recall ever
being saluted.

8

FATHER WAS A RAILWAY WORKER TOO

17 June 1948

It was the day before his fortieth birthday and Knowles had been in parliament almost five and a half years. He was about to win one of the important victories in his political experience and, he feels, one of the important victories for workers in Canada. The victory would show that an opposition member of parliament, even a member of a third party, but a member with all his wits about him, could in fact change things.

The struggle went back to 1919 although as a lad in Los Angeles, Knowles hardly knew it at the time. When the workers in Winnipeg went on strike in May that year, the companies retaliated by revoking the pension rights of the strikers. Not that the pensions had been particularly widespread or even particularly generous. Where pensions did exist, they were non-contributory and dependent on the company's good graces. Indeed employers justified low wages on the grounds that they would later pay pensions to retired workers. The workers felt the force of the argument and most often accepted the low wages and refrained from striking for fear of losing their pension rights. If a strike were in the offing, the company could always count on division among its workers, the older ones fearful as they counted their years of service and their expected pension, the younger ones more willing to strike for better conditions now. The tactics continued until well into the 1930s; the fear of losing one's pension rights in the event of a strike continued until Knowles set it right in 1948.

In a sense, the issue was tailor-made for him. It went with his riding of Winnipeg North Centre where so many of the strike-bound companies from 1919 were located. His predecessor in the riding, J. S. Woodsworth, had brought the issue with him when he first came to parliament in 1921. Since then, some of the companies, such as the Canadian National Railways and the Manitoba Telephone System, had restored the pension rights of those of its workers who had been on strike during May and June of 1919 but the Canadian Pacific Railway never did. Indeed, it added a rider to its pension scheme: after 1919 only those workers under forty years of age could join the pension plan. Many of the strikers were over forty. They had regained their jobs after the strike but they were now barred from a company pension. Woodsworth had raised the issue in the Commons on numerous occasions, urged by the employees themselves and by the trade unions that represented the railway workers, but all to no avail. After 1942, therefore, the task fell to Knowles.

The issue also touched him personally. Since the early 1930s he had been aware of the vulnerability of older workers. The case of his own father — a railway worker too — had touched him deeply; the older man had no pension when he was fired and when he was taken on again, out of sympathy, at a menial task, had been told that he was then too old to participate in the company's pension plan. In the railway workers of Winnipeg Knowles saw his own father. Many of those workers were also his constituents and supporters. He had only been an MP a year or so when a delegation of workers came to his home in Winnipeg to urge him to revive Woodsworth's plea and their own: that something be done for those former strikers of 1919 who had been deprived of their pensions. It was then almost twenty-five years since the strike; a number of retired workers received no pension at all and some who did received less than their due because the credits built up before the strike had been cancelled.

To raise the matter in the Commons, Knowles used every occasion that the rule book permitted. When the estimates of the Department of Labour were under debate in 1944, for example, he was on his feet with the question, only to be challenged by the labour minister, Humphrey Mitchell, that he was out of order. He then put his growing procedural knowledge to the test and argued the point. If the Speaker acknowledged that he was in fact in order with his intervention, Mitchell would grumpily snap, "Oh go ahead anyway," never admitting that the point had been won, and reserving stronger language for the corridors outside the Commons chamber.[1] During question period Knowles peppered the government with queries. Always he demanded one of two possibilities: that the government urge — perhaps even order — the CPR to restore full pension rights to those workers who had been involved in the strike or, since the government invariably replied that the CPR as a private company was not under its jurisdiction, then he urged that a royal commission investigate the problem.

Early in April 1945, his pestering finally evoked a reply from the prime minister. Mackenzie King told the House that although he had not yet received a request for a royal commission from the heads of certain railroad unions — the matter to which Knowles had referred in his question — when he did so he would certainly give it consideration.[2] Knowing full well that such a reply was frequently a means of silencing a pesky questioner, Knowles refused to let go of the matter. He immediately wrote the prime minister to express the hope that the "consideration" he had promised would in fact materialize. It did. From the train carrying King and other Canadian delegates to San Francisco for the founding of the United Nations that spring came a letter to Knowles. The "consideration" had become not quite a royal commission but at least an enquiry to be conducted by Harris S. Johnstone, an industrial relations officer with the federal Department of Labour. It wasn't the commission Knowles had wanted and he knew that government enquiries sometimes found what the government wanted them to find but still it was better than nothing. Indeed it could be considered a feather in the cap of a fledgling MP.

Johnstone completed his enquiry by early December 1945 but the labour minister managed to conceal the report for some time. Knowles only learned of it well into the next year and at his insistence it was tabled in the House of Commons and thus became public property on 20 August 1946. The seventeen-page report, bolstered by fifty pages of appendices and documents, upheld Knowles' contentions entirely:

> It is the opinion of the undersigned that the employees have established strong claims for consideration. The nature and extent for adjustments if any cannot be determined except by a more exhaustive analysis than was possible or even contemplated in this preliminary investigation. I would therefore recommend that a royal commission be established to examine into the whole question to determine what if any consideration should be granted and if so then to whom and in what manner pension adjustments should be made.[3]

Knowles had won the first round.

Armed with the Johnstone report he then continued his battle. By 1946 the question had taken on another dimension. There was still the matter of justice for the retired workers left from the Winnipeg strike. But time was running out on most of them so now there was the broader principle. Knowles had to make sure that this kind of thing could not happen again. Workers should not be under the threat of losing their pensions every time they contemplated a strike. Employers should not have that kind of power over their workers and should not be able thereby to exploit the age differences among workers. Knowles hoped to resolve both the practical case and the principle but he began stressing the latter.

Now he used the technique of the private member's bill. Such bills, one of the ways that an ordinary MP can propose a law, were almost invariably talked out — the debate simply continuing until the time ran out — and thus rarely came to a vote let alone found their way into legislation. They were nonetheless means of attracting attention to an issue. During the war they had largely disappeared under an annual government motion, to which the House agreed, that government business take precedence. MPs therefore became unused to them and few were proposed in the immediate post-war years. Knowles was thus always assured of a hearing. His bill was very specific: an act to amend the Railway Act. The wording varied from year to year as he persisted, but the intent remained the same: to add a clause to the section of the Railway Act that gave authority to directors of railway companies to deal with certain business matters. In 1947, for example, the clause stipulated that "absence due to an industrial dispute, strike or lock-out, shall not disqualify any railway employee from any retirement or pension rights or benefits to which he would otherwise be entitled."[4] Knowles' hope was that once the federal government had established standards in such a major industry as railways, other governments and other industries would follow suit. As often as he presented his bill, however, it would be talked out. Once, he did manage to have a colleague propose an amendment, which actually passed, to have the subject of the bill sent to a standing committee. There too the subject received more public airing but its public opponents could also appear to express their objection. Among the opponents was a lawyer for the CPR who "fought it like the mischief."[5]

In 1948, Knowles spotted another opening he might just slip his pet reform through. In the spring of that year, the House of Commons was debating a new bill, eventually enacted as the

Industrial Relations and Disputes Investigation Act and which is now known by the simpler title, the Canada Labour Code. The purpose of the bill was to replace wartime labour provisions which had never been debated in parliament, but simply imposed under the auspices of the War Measures Act. Once passed, the legislation would affect all those workers who worked under federal labour jurisdiction in industries such as banking, commerce, transportation, communications — approximately ten percent of the industrial work force. Any extension of such legislation to more workers required similar legislation by the various provinces, something which is an ongoing process. But in the meantime, if Knowles succeeded in amending the bill to protect the pension rights of striking workers, his reform would affect all those under federal labour legislation, not just the railway workers specified in his private member's bills.

If he could just get the amendment in at the right time and in an appropriate form, he might be able to muster enough support to have it passed. His private member's bills had always aroused support in the Commons, particularly from members representing railway towns, although there had never been a vote to test the size of that strength. The mail coming in from across the country certainly indicated public support for his reform. So he attempted first to have his amendment attached to the bill while it was being discussed clause by clause in a standing committee. But the committee was small and the support was not there; moreover Labour Minister Humphrey Mitchell was opposed. The bill therefore returned to the Commons unadorned by a Knowles' amendment. There was, however, still a chance in the House when the members engaged in what the rules then allowed — a second round of clause by clause study of the bill. An amendment might be possible there. But supposing he was ruled out of order? His private member's bill, dealing with precisely the same subject although in a different format, was once again on the Order Paper and an amendment to the present bill might well be judged unacceptable because it dealt with the same matter. Foreseeing that, Knowles arose one evening during private member's hour and, without giving any explanation, quietly asked that his bill be withdrawn. The way was now clear for an unchallengeable amendment to the Industrial Relations bill.

Assistance also came from an unexpected quarter. At the Press Gallery dinner that spring, an occasion by tradition closed to the public with the guests virtually sworn to silence, Prime Minister Mackenzie King announced his intention to resign. As he did so he praised himself and the various benefits that he, as leader of the Liberals and prime minister, had bestowed upon the Canadian people. He also spoke of the need for "tidying up" a few things before he actually passed his job on to someone else. Fellow dinner guest Stanley Knowles wondered how long the news could be kept secret but he also thought he might attach his reform to King's resignation. He knew King to be a vain old man and here he was wishing to tidy things up. . . . Perhaps Knowles could play on the vanity and the wish and obtain King's support for his own desired reform.

A letter to King began taking shape in his mind. He had been successful three years earlier in writing to King; the Johnstone report had resulted. Perhaps he could be successful again. In his missive he therefore referred to King's imminent retirement and to his expressed interest in tidying things up. He reminded the prime minister that the year 1919 which had occasioned the problem of pension benefits was also the year that King had become leader of the Liberal party with a well-publicized reform platform. He recalled King's earlier career as labour minister from 1909 to 1911 in the Liberal government of Sir Wilfrid Laurier and his attempts to arrange amicable settlements of some of the railway strikes in that period. He reiterated King's claim to be a friend of labour. And he ended with his own plea: wouldn't King support the amendment that he intended to raise on the floor of the House? Wouldn't that be an appropriate capping of the prime minister's career?[6] The plea was as genuine as King's vanity. Knowles' secretary typed the letter twice because she knew the prime minister could not abide erasures or corrections.

Meanwhile, the debate on the Industrial Relations bill proceeded in the Commons. Knowles had given notice of his forthcoming amendment and the time was drawing near. King's reply to his letter was not very promising but then one day Knowles received a call from the transport minister, Lionel Chevrier. Would he come over for a chat? Chevrier informed him that the prime minister had agreed to Knowles' suggestion — that this anomaly about pension rights for striking workers should be rectified — and he asked Chevrier to undertake the necessary negotiations. He was to consult with the CNR and the justice minister, James Ilsley. He did not mention Labour Minister Humphrey Mitchell whose bill it was. Knowles found that odd but he had what he wanted: King would support his amendment and that meant it would pass.

The details, however, had still to be worked out. The amendment was to be attached to that section of the Industrial Relations bill that dealt with unfair labour practices and it was to add, as an unfair practice and therefore subject to all the penalties the law imposed, any interference with pension rights in cases of strikes or lockouts. Chevrier broached the topic with the CNR; the company was agreeable but it wanted the specification that all the steps required by law had been taken and that the strike was a legal one. Knowles had no quarrel with that — indeed he felt that proviso was implicit in his own wording — and Chevrier was ready to give the Liberals' consent: they would accept and support Knowles' amendment provided the CNR's words were added.

Once that was agreed upon, there remained the question of how it was all to be presented in the Commons. Chevrier suggested that Knowles withdraw his present amendment and submit a new one incorporating the added words. It was a tempting offer: the amendment would be solely in his name and he had never had qualms about taking credit where credit was due. But there might also be a trap in such a procedure. Supposing the Liberals changed their mind at the last minute and left him high and dry with an amendment they would not support? That would permit his opponents to have an easy time with him. No, if this reform was really to go through, it would have to have government sanction all the way even if it meant that the Liberals would subsequently take credit for the change. So he suggested another possibility. His amendment would stand and Chevrier would introduce a sub-amendment with the CNR wording. The Chevrier name on the sub-amendment would ensure Liberal support and then the Knowles' amendment, as amended, would pass. The Liberals could hardly support the sub-amendment and then refuse to support the amendment. He was now sure, Chevrier was convinced, and the agreement made.

While these negotiations were under way in the offices and corridors of the parliament buildings, the bill itself was being debated in the House. Knowles even had to request that the consideration of his amendment be delayed while the negotiations continued. Even when making that request, however, he carefully drew the government to his side by remarking that "the Minister of Transport intimated to me this morning that he might like to move a sub-amendment, and it happens to be a sub-amendment I would be prepared to accept."[7] Only at that point did he realize that Labour Minister Mitchell knew nothing of what had been going on. He had been kept completely in the dark and he was furious. He stomped across to Knowles as the House rose for a lunch break and in no uncertain, but quite unparliamentary terms, let him know of his anger. He then stormed off with the parting shot: "Oh, it isn't worth the paper it's written on. You can have it."[8] And so he did, later that day, 17 June 1948. He spoke to his amendment and then quite happily accepted Chevrier's revised wording.[9] Later he had a leaflet printed for distribution which spelled out the change to the bill. And in subsequent revisions to the statutes of Canada he has always checked to make sure his amendment is still there in the Labour Code. It is, and to him it is worth infinitely more than the paper it is written on.

During the evening of 17 June, as was Knowles' practice, he went to the Hansard office to ensure that the House stenographers had recorded everything accurately and that the debate was being prepared for publication in precisely the manner it had been given in the House. Someone else was there carefully copying down the text of Hansard. Knowles recognized the lawyer for the CPR, a man who had often come to protest the reform that had just passed. CPR workers, among others under federal labour legislation, were now protected from loss of pension rights in the event of a strike and the company would have to conform. Knowles thinks that may have been one of the few occasions in Canadian history when something affecting the CPR was not released to the company in advance. "After all," he remarked with his tongue only partly in his cheek, "the CPR has been the government of this country since the late nineteenth century."[10]

The next day was his fortieth birthday and the messages poured in from across the country. Some said Happy Birthday, not knowing what an accomplishment it was for an infant fed on goat's milk to survive to his fortieth birthday. Some said congratulations, little knowing the intricacies of the battle, but happy in the results. In fact, it was a major accomplishment for an MP who had not yet reached the sixth anniversary of his election to parliament and had only been in the House just over five years. Very early in his parliamentary career, he had learned that an MP could not win a point the day he raises it in the House. If this particular victory did nothing for the veterans of the strike of 1919 — there were fewer of them every year — at least it would ensure that such an issue would not arise again. Knowles was glad.

Circumstances thus permitted Knowles to start from a particular case — that of striking railway workers in 1919 — and end with a general principle enacted in law. Both have continued to interest him and his victory in 1948 encouraged him to pursue both. With a riding full of railway workers he was not likely to forget the particular. In his various efforts to improve pension benefits, therefore, he has paid close attention to railway pensions and to those of the CNR in particular, for there an MP can expect to have some impact. Over the years he has argued for the escalation of CNR pensions, for improvements in their survivors' benefits, and for changes in their very calculation. All along he has known that what the CNR initiates the CPR will have to emulate even if, as has often been the case, the CPR tends to tell the CNR which of the various parliamentary proposals it should accept.

Knowles' preoccupation with pensions goes deep into his past and people who wonder about the single (sometimes even narrow) mindedness of it all neither understand his background nor the parliamentary process. The socialist, the egalitarian, the builder of better worlds, the son of a railway worker pushed into his political profession by the spectre of an old man tossed pensionless onto the heap of the depression cannot let go of the pension issue. His mathematical mind delights in the ever-increasing complexities of pension formulae. His constituents and their look-alikes across the land acknowledge him; they know someone in Ottawa is fighting for them. He cannot let them go either. Besides, there was that sweet taste of victory in June 1948 after the years of amendments, bills, and debates, after the chance inspiration, and the intricate manoeuvring. That's the way parliament works and that's the way Stanley Knowles works. The two were meant to get along.

9

A MEANS TEST IS MEAN

8 November 1951

The Old Age Security Act was about to be given third and final reading in the House of Commons. Knowles watched the proceedings contentedly. For a battle that had coincided with his lifetime, this particular bill was taking its course smoothly and quickly. It had only been introduced into the Commons two weeks earlier; there was hardly any debate and the final reading would be approved unanimously. The bill would take effect on 1 January 1952 and thereafter there would be no means test imposed on people seeking the old age pension. Everyone over the age of seventy would receive the pension as a right. Knowles considers it one of the most important pieces of social legislation in Canadian history and he is proud to have been part of it.

Smooth passage of the bill in the Commons in the late autumn of 1951 was not, however, an accurate reflection of the pension story in Canada. It all began the day Knowles was born although neither the Canadian government in Ottawa, nor his anxious parents in Los Angeles knew of it at the time. On 18 June 1908, the House of Commons gave second reading to the first Canadian legislation dealing with the financial situation of older people. A government-administered plan of annuities permitted people to buy in their younger years a series of payments for their old age. Such a plan was obviously limited to those people, by no means everyone in Canada in 1908, who could afford to purchase a pension. While Knowles realizes there were objections at the time to the annuities scheme on the grounds that the government should not be involved in such matters, he also likes to think that he may have howled with his feeble newborn voice that it was not enough. He has, in fact, been howling ever since.

In the years just before the First World War and during the war itself, the trade union movement took up the plea for some form of public pensions. Many of the trade unions had in fact originated as mutual benefit societies, providing sickness and death benefits for their members. In the nineteenth century, however, few of those members actually survived into old age and the question of pensions did not arise. Later when the issue was confronted, it was often met on a fraternal basis: the working members of a union would pay a small sum to provide pensions for their retired colleagues on the assumption that they too would be cared for in a similar manner by their younger working companions. The trade union of which Knowles remains a member, the International Typographical Union, initiated such a scheme in the 1900s. It was fine then and during the 1920s and 1930s but it did not take into account the technological changes in the printing trade. Automation and the computer have largely done away with skilled typesetters; there were fewer and fewer workers to pay the pensions of the growing number of retired printers. The fund dried up because the source dried up. That example is Knowles' argument against a limited — one trade or one profession — type of pension; pensions have to be under the aegis of the state to ensure that they do not vanish. The trade union movement was advocating just such public pensions for older people in the early twentieth century. Aware of western European, Australian, and New Zealand schemes, union members in Canada urged that similar plans be adopted here.

By the 1920s the labour movement had a tiny group in parliament to express its view. Two members — J. S. Woodsworth and A. A. Heaps — urged a state programme of old age pensions, but they had to wait until the Liberal government under Mackenzie King was in a minority position before they could exercise any leverage. When that occurred after the election of 1925, the two indicated the price of their support for any of the other parties. Whichever party would undertake to introduce old age pensions and unemployment insurance would be assured of the continuing support of the two labour members from the west. Robert Forke and the Progressives, holding the balance of power but usually supporting the Liberals, were in no position to promise such legislation. Arthur Meighen, the blunt leader of the Conservatives and holding the greatest number of seats in the House, was not at all interested. Mackenzie King's Liberals, however, trailing the Conservatives with one hundred and one seats to one hundred and sixteen, thought they saw a way of clinging to power. King would, he told Woodsworth, consider the matter. At a subsequent dinner meeting between the two, King offered Woodsworth the labour ministry. Maybe that would buy him off and shut him up. But Woodsworth was not to be bought. He had not, he said, come to Ottawa to acquire benefits for himself, but rather to be of service to his constituents and their counterparts across the country. He would not take the cabinet position, but he would continue to support the Liberals if King undertook to introduce old age pensions and unemployment insurance.

King was caught. Every vote in the House counted in the winter and spring of 1926. But he would not accept all of Woodsworth's demands. Unemployment insurance was quite impractical (indeed it would take a world wide depression, a massive royal commission and an amendment to the British North America Act before Canada would have unemployment insurance in 1940) but King did agree to some form of old age pension. Woodsworth insisted on having King's commitment in writing. Unwilling to hand free publicity to this disturbing member from Winnipeg, King refrained from writing him until after he had announced forthcoming old age pension legislation in the House. He then wrote the letter that was subsequently distributed widely as one of Woodsworth's major victories.

King not only kept his word but fought strenuously for his Old Age Pension bill in 1926. The bill proposed the establishment of a joint federal-provincial programme to administer a monthly pension of twenty dollars to those residents of Canada over seventy years of age who could prove that their total annual income was no more than one hundred and twenty-five dollars. The federal government would pay half and those provinces wishing to join the plan had to indicate their willingness to do so and agree to pay the other fifty percent of the pension. In the House of Commons, the Conservatives fought the bill ferociously. King, they claimed, was just bribing the member for Winnipeg North Centre who, in turn, had blackmailed the prime minister and, through him, the country. Moreover, such activity was not the business of the state; people should look after themselves. It would be unseemly for old people to be receiving handouts from the state. Whether the Conservative argument did in fact reflect public sentiment or whether the problem was the means test that accompanied the pension, many old people did feel the stigma, one which Knowles spent years trying to remove. In 1926, however, with Progressive and Labour support, the bill passed the

House of Commons only to be defeated in the senate. There some of Canada's most well-to-do senior citizens informed anyone who was listening that it was not good for old people to receive gratuities from the state and that moreover the budget of the country could never afford it. But King was now insistent. In the election campaign of 1926 he promised, if re-elected, to reintroduce the bill in the Commons and to ensure that it became law. It did so in 1927.

As Knowles remarked almost fifty years later, the Old Age Pension Act was a "meagre beginning."[1] It was also mean. The means test entailed considerable snooping on the part of the provinces which undertook to administer the test, since people requesting the pension had to prove that they had no other income above the permitted maximum. Their bank accounts were scrutinized, their goods assessed, a value placed upon any free accommodation they had if they were living with their children, and a lien was even put upon their homes. In the event of death, the home would be sold, with the government as first creditor. It was an extraordinary system only to be matched by the snooping and investigation of the relief officers during the dark days of the depression in the 1930s.

Knowles inherited this issue too, personally from his father and politically from Woodsworth, and took it with him to parliament. Part of his election campaign in 1942 centred on old age pensions: he wanted to see the amounts increased, the means test removed, and the age lowered. In the fifteen years since the pensions were first introduced in 1927, there had in fact been no changes. A slight administrative adjustment had been made during the 1930s when the Conservative prime minister, R. B. Bennett, first promised that the federal government would take over the total pension payments but then instituted a seventy-five/twenty-five percent federal-provincial division of the costs. Everything else remained the same. In 1942 when Knowles was first elected, the amount was still twenty dollars a month; the extra income one could have and still receive a pension remained at one hundred and twenty five dollars a year (for a total of one dollar a day — Knowles' calculation of the mathematical meanness); the means testers were still snooping; and one still had to be seventy years old to qualify. Knowles set to work.

He may have thought he was making no headway but it seems his voice was heard. When in 1944, for example, he complained to Finance Minister James Ilsley that there was so little time for the discussion of the old age pension, tucked as it was into the final pages of the estimates of the finance department, Ilsley retorted that there had been ample opportunity for such discussion at other times.[2] Indeed Knowles knew full well how to bring up the topic, adept as he was becoming at introducing his favourite ideas at every possible occasion. The next year he was nagging Ilsley again wanting to know why changes were so slow, only to be chided by the minister for his obvious inexperience with adminstrative matters.[3] But Knowles kept it up.

The needling may have helped, for the pension started inching upwards. During the war years, under the auspices of the War Measures Act, the government added five dollars to the monthly pension. But it did not raise the amount of other income a recipient could have. That was done by establishing a ceiling of six hundred dollars, including the pension, in 1947 at the same time that the government put the wartime increase in the pension on a regular legislative basis and added another five dollars to it.[4] Just before the election of 1949 the pension itself was raised again to forty dollars but the ceiling remained. Some administrative changes also occurred, by which the citizenship requirement was removed but that of residency maintained, and coverage was extended to missionaries returning to Canada after spending all their adult years abroad. But the other aspects of the old age pension to which Knowles and the CCF objected remained: the low basic amount; the low amount of extra income permitted; the seventy year age limit; and the means test.

The CCF tackled them all but increasingly the emphasis came to be placed upon the means test. The government could perhaps be shamed or cajoled into increasing the amount of the pension by albeit niggardly amounts, but it had shown no inclination to tinker with the means test. For Knowles, the principle of universality had to be won. A pension was as much a right of everyone over a certain age as was education for children, police protection for everyone, or postal service for all. Before the days of universal hospital and health care, the idea was a very radical one.

When the House of Commons met in February 1950, the CCF had done just about all an opposition party could do. Its candidates in the election of June 1949 had all spoken on the issue. They reiterated the demands of a petition that the party had circulated and presented to parliament in the spring of 1949. The Canadian Congress of Labour had also organized a massive post-card campaign: members of parliament and government members in particular were deluged with cards demanding the elimination of the means test and an increase in the pension. Press coverage increased the campaign. By 1950 the question had become a national issue with Knowles in the thick of it. And yet the Speech from the Throne in February made no mention whatsoever of the old age pension. For its negligence the government was subjected to a barrage of criticism from the CCF. The campaign and the criticism were voluble enough to evoke a response from the sixty-eight-year-old prime minister, Louis St. Laurent. Speaking in the debate on the Address in Reply to the Speech from the Throne, St. Laurent gave his personal objection to any change in the means test. "Why should I, within the next two years, get a pension of forty dollars per month. . . . Is that required in the interests of the Canadian nation?"[5] In other words only the needy should receive a state pension. Knowles was thoroughly annoyed. He believed that the means test was demeaning and its complexities exasperating. Where for example did one set the line for the needy? And why should old people have to bare their indigence to some nosy official? Surely a fair and just taxation scheme could easily recover the money from those in high income brackets who did not actually "need" the pension. St. Laurent had a lesson or two to learn.

The public and parliamentary pressure continued and on 10 March the government indicated some action. Paul Martin, the minister of health and welfare was going to have a joint committee of the House and Senate study the whole question of pensions and means tests. The terms of reference were, as Knowles later put it, "a half mile long"[6] and he was convinced that the entire purpose was to stall the question and eventually produce a report that would prove the impossibility of removing the means test without at the same time introducing some kind of contributory scheme, something the government had been arguing for years. He was opposed to both and since he was named to the committee, he had another chance to say so.

If the committee had any preconceived ideas, the amount of work it did soon dispelled them. Between its establishment in March and its report in June, it held fifty-two sessions, thirty-eight of them open to the public for presentation of briefs, and fourteen in private where the members thrashed out the issue. They spoke with deputy ministers, with financial experts, with trade unions, and with the Canadian Manufacturers' Association, with opponents and proponents from all walks of life. The deputy minister of health and welfare, George Davidson, was attached to the committee and supported Knowles' objections to the means test. But the finance department was dubious and sent along one of its officers, Mitchell Sharp, to argue against any elimination. The evidence amassed: there were briefs from the various delegations appearing before the committee; there were reports on all the countries in the world that had social security plans; there were graphs and tables and figures; there were the plans that the committee itself began drafting, amending, debating, and scrapping. The chief spokesman for the three parties represented on the committee — David Croll for the Liberals, David Fleming for the Conservatives, and Knowles for the CCF — argued and pleaded and chatted and pondered among themselves. It went on day and night and Knowles loved it. It was the best committee he had yet served on in terms of coming to terms with an issue and working incessantly at it. Perhaps another reason for his liking the committee was that it gradually began to swing to his point of view.

The committee itself recognized the change. After months of work it became evident that a system of universal old-age pensions without a means test, without the vast cumbersome machinery that a contributory scheme would entail, without the outmoded system of annuities, was indeed possible. The committee was, however, a government committee; it was not about to admit that Knowles had been right all along. The report really had to show Liberal initiative. David Croll was therefore assigned his task. He should approach Knowles to see if he would back a particular government proposal. He need not bother speaking directly with David Fleming; it was CCF support that the Liberals wanted to ensure.

Croll made his offer. Would Knowles agree to a thirty-dollar monthly pension to be paid entirely by the federal government and not subject to a means test? The provincial governments could pay the remaining ten dollars to bring the amount to what it had been for the last year. If he agreed, the Liberals would draw up the legislation and see that it passed in the House. But Knowles would not agree. He wanted a fifty-dollar pension and, moreover, he had never liked the divided responsibility between the federal and the provincial governments; this particular suggestion seemed to entrench the division and might even result in some people who lived in recalcitrant provinces not even receiving the ten dollars. Not only would they receive no increase but they might even have their pension cut.

So he countered. What he could support was a forty-dollar pension without a means test if the government would also devise some assistance for those people aged between sixty-five and sixty-nine. Negotiating that took time. Croll consulted with his Liberal colleagues while Knowles did the same in the CCF. Eventually Croll indicated the government's agreement. It would ensure a forty-dollar monthly pension to everyone over seventy without a means test and the federal and provincial governments would jointly split a programme of pensions for those between sixty-five and seventy who could prove their need. What the Liberals wanted in return was the promise that Knowles would support the agreement when it came before the committee as a proposal and subsequently before the House as legislation. They knew only too well how easily he could poke fun at the niggardliness of the government. Knowles agreed: the important thing was to have the means test removed and some recognition of people in their late sixties. He did, however, warn Croll that once the bill was passed he would start to work for increases in the amount of the pension, but during its passage he would support it. Croll thought the government could live with that since Knowles had been making speeches like that for years.

The commitee then prepared to draft its final report. The members were asked, one by one, in alphabetical order, what each thought the committee should recommend. The first to speak was Thomas Ashbourne, a Liberal from Newfoundland and a nice old fellow, according to Knowles, but one who had barely opened his mouth during the entire lengthy round of committee meetings. Now he blurted out that the committee should recommend three things: old age security of forty dollars a month to be paid by the federal government to everyone over seventy; old age assistance to be paid half and half by the federal and provincial governments to those people between sixty-five and seventy who had "passed" a means test; and a monthly pension for the blind of forty dollars, three-quarters of which to be paid by the federal government and one quarter by the provincial governments. It was the longest speech Ashbourne had made in all the committee meetings put together and it was word-for-word what Knowles and Croll had agreed upon. Other committee members then gave their views with Liberals merely saying that they supported the Ashbourne plan. The Conservatives, realizing they were caught, muttered that they would go along with the plan but that it was not enough. Knowles added his support and the committee drew up its recommendations, adding constitutional provisos and details on how the pensions were to be paid for: a two percent increase in corporation taxes; a two percent slice of personal income tax; and two percent of the federal sales tax. It then presented its hundred-page report to parliament on 28 June 1950. The government, having expected just the opposite when it established the committee in March but aware of the changing views within the committee, would now consider its recommendations.

By early 1951 the government had done its considering,

arranged for an amendment to the British North America Act, and drafted the legislation. The report of the committee was divided into two parts and those sections of its recommendations requiring matching provincial legislation — the old age assistance for the sixty-five to sixty-nine year olds and the pensions for the blind — were passed into law before the end of June. The section of the report eliminating the means test entirely and giving a forty-dollar federal pension to all people over seventy came before the House in October and was passed on 8 November 1951. Both bills were to take effect 1 January 1952. No sooner had they done so than Prime Minister St. Laurent announced that since he would soon be seventy, he would be applying for the pension. "I want it to be clear," he said, "that this is the right of everyone, that no one should feel any stigma because he applied for the old age security."[7] It was less than two years since St. Laurent had spoken against the very idea of universal old age pensions. Knowles had done his job well.

But for him the job was never done. Although the means test for the sixty-five to sixty-nine-year-olds was administered much more humanely than the earlier one, it was still there and he continued to believe it was demeaning. Moreover, the amount of the pension remained at forty dollars well into the 1950s. As usual, he and the CCF raised the issue in parliament and across the country. By 1957 the Liberal government, on very shaky last legs after the pipeline debate of the year before, tried to stave off some of the inevitable by offering an increase in the pension just before the election that year. The fifteen percent increase sounded reasonable enough but the actual amount — six dollars — looked strange. Knowles thinks the Liberals would have done better to offer a forty-five dollar pension than to suffer the Conservatives' ridicule (stealing the CCF's interest in pensions, according to Knowles) as the "six buck boys." The Liberals, somewhat surprised that no one seemed to appreciate their generosity, faced severe criticism during the election. They were branded as tyrants for their treatment of parliament during the pipeline debate — the result of which was millions of dollars to "Texas bucaneers" — and as tightwads for their treatment of pensioners. The criticism told and the Conservatives were elected albeit with a minority government. They then raised the pension another nine dollars to bring it to fifty-five. Some of the pensioners in Winnipeg North Centre who helped to defeat Knowles in the next election in 1958 told him brokenly the following day that they had merely wanted to say thank you to John Diefenbaker, but they had not intended that Knowles should lose. Pensions counted and the Conservatives knew it. Prior to the election of June 1962 they raised it again to sixty-five dollars a month.

After the Liberals returned to power in 1963, a new kind of pension was designed: the Canada Pension Plan. As a plan into which one would contribute during one's entire working life, the CPP would permit a retired worker to receive considerably more than the fixed amount of the Old Age Security. Although Knowles is a self-styled "unrepentant advocate of universal pensions just as high as we can possibly get them,"[8] he is not unhappy with the Canada Pension Plan, geared as it is to the salary one made while working. But he was not willing to have the Old Age Security eliminated and he fought Liberal attempts to do so or to limit it to a base amount of seventy-five dollars and have the CPP provide the real pension. There were far too many people whom the CPP did not cover. He fought the initial Canada Pension Plan bill because of its promise to add ten dollars to the old age pension when the CPP began. But that was much too far in the future to suit Knowles since it might be years before the plan was implemented and people drew benefits. And since the Liberal government was in a minority position, it bowed to the pressure and added the ten dollars then, in 1963. It also named Knowles to the committee that would work through 1964 and 1965 on the details of the new Canada Pension Plan.

That committee too, like the earlier one that dealt with the means test for the old age pension, was a delight to Knowles. It worked while the House was not in session, hard and long, and without interruptions. It insisted on something for the new plan which Knowles had long been hoping to see attached to the old age pension: indexing. The CPP was in fact to be indexed two ways. It was adjusted according to the wage rate of the individual worker during his years in the labour market: the contributions early in a working career were to be computed at a higher wage level by the end of a thirty or thirty-five year period in the labour force. And the pension itself was to be indexed to the cost of living. As the latter went up, so too would the pension. Since that indexing was to be part of the Canada Pension Plan from the beginning, Knowles found it easy to argue that the Old Age Security should also be indexed. That in fact began in 1966 but a ceiling of two percent was put on the index. "Some index," he grumbled, as he watched the seventy-five dollar pension rise by a dollar fifty. The Liberals were content to let the pension inch its way up; Knowles and his colleagues wanted a basic rate of one hundred dollars, indexed without a ceiling to the cost of living.

Before they could win that, however, Knowles was arguing for a lowering of the age for the universal pension to sixty-five. He was, in effect, fighting the battle of the means test again. People over sixty-five should receive Old Age Security, not assistance, and they should receive it as a right rather than a mark of their indigence. On the committee dealing with the Canada Pension Plan he argued and won the starting age of sixty-five for both the CPP and the OAS. But it would have to be a separate recommendation since the committee was not prepared to amend the CPP provisions itself. Prime Minister Pearson acted upon the recommendation: the CPP itself would begin at sixty-five while the OAS would gradually be lowered to that age, the means test being removed one year at a time until, by 1970, universal old age pensions were available to everyone at age sixty-five. The means test was gone.

But it returned in another format. In response to the problem of what to do for those people who were either not eligible for the Canada Pension Plan or who needed assistance now, before it became fully operative, the government instituted in 1967 a Guaranteed Income Supplement. It was to have a life of ten years, coming to an end as the CPP gradually produced maximum benefits. It provided an extra thirty dollars a month to the basic seventy-five of the Old Age Security. Of course, one could only receive the thirty dollars if one could show need. Knowles admits that the means test in this case is less severe than in the bad old days — it is now merely a matter of checking income tax returns — but he is still unhappy about it. He was even more unhappy about the proposed termination of the Guaranteed Income Supplement: once it was instituted it was hardly fair to take it away again, particularly since the CPP did not cover everyone. By the early 1970s the GIS had become a permanent feature of the federal pension programme.

Politics more than principle accounted for subsequent pension changes. Just before the federal election of 1972, the Liberal government which had already increased the basic Old Age Pension to eighty dollars, removed the two percent ceiling on the indexing of both the Old Age Security and the Guaranteed Income Supplement. Knowles accused the government of electioneering but he could hardly object to the change. After the election, however, the Liberals were in a minority, and with the NDP by then urging an increase in the OAS to one hundred and twenty-five dollars, there was room for dickering. With Knowles as the emissary, the NDP let it be known that it would support the government if the pension were increased. The Liberals countered with an offer to increase the Guaranteed Income Supplement.

Knowles said no: the pension itself would have to go to at least one hundred dollars. The Trudeau government, anxious to conciliate supporters, agreed in the spring of 1973. Since then, with occasional additions to the GIS, and both OAS and GIS indexed to the Consumer Price Index and calculated on a quarterly basis, the amounts have risen to $232.97 for the OAS in June 1982 and, if one has nothing else, the GIS adds another $233.89. In 1981 the total yearly amount was five hundred dollars short of the poverty line. Knowles is still uncomfortable with the qualification 'if nothing else' of the GIS for it keeps the means test alive but he does admit that it is all so much better than thirty or forty years ago when old people were kept in the back room, poorly housed, poorly clothed, creeping out in shame to cash their pension cheques and merely tolerated by society. Now senior citizen apartments mushroom across Canada's cities and senior citizens flash gold plated cards from the government admonishing observers to extend all privileges to the bearer. Knowles shaped many of those changes and he is pleased.

Now he would like to see the pension available at sixty. So too would many of his constituents, particularly those who work in heavy industry. All the Liberals would offer in the middle of the election campaign of 1974 and then implement in 1975 was a spouse's allowance available at sixty. A legally married spouse, living with a recipient of the OAS could — if she proved her need — receive a pension starting at age sixty. Once more a means test was required and once more Knowles objected as he had been doing since the 1940s. But this spouse's allowance was even worse for it discriminated against the really poor women between the ages of sixty and sixty-five: the single and the widows. One could only have a pension before age sixty-five if one had a man and a legal one at that. Then, to make matters worse, the spouse's allowance disappeared with the death of the pensioner. At the time of the legislation in 1975 Knowles predicted that it would not last long and he was on his feet in the House protesting it until it was changed. Late in 1979 the shortlived Conservative government of Joe Clark removed the worst aspect of the spouse's allowance and it now continues after the death of the pensioner until the survivor reaches age sixty-five and is eligible for the OAS. Even so, spouses receiving an allowance constitute barely one-tenth of the million or so people in the sixty to sixty-five age bracket and Knowles would like to see the entire group gradually included in the Old Age Security, perhaps by extending its coverage one year at a time as was done in the late 1960s for those between sixty-five and seventy and perhaps attaching an employment gauge. If one is out of the paid labour market, one would be entitled to the pension. On the same grounds, Knowles would like to see the Canada Pension Plan available on a voluntary basis from the age of sixty.

The struggle for a decent life and a decent income for older people has been with Knowles if not all his life — although he is amused by the coincidence of dates between his birth and the first Canadian legislation in the pension field — then at least all his political life. The speeches have been innumerable; the campaigns arduous; the victories few. Nevertheless it was Knowles himself who selected three victories in the pension field as days of great significance to him: the prohibition in 1948 of interference in pension rights because of a strike, the elimination in 1951 of the means test on the old age pension, and the escalation of civil servants' pensions in 1969.[9] Indeed, as he says, "I sometimes think that if our party, or if I, had done nothing else in this country but play a part in getting this kind of improvement, it's been worth all the effort and all the struggle." He recognizes that older people today have a much more secure place in society than they did when he was a young preacher or a young politician. "So we've done well and I'm proud of having been involved in it, but . . . we're just getting started."[10]

10

PIPELINE REVISITED

25 February 1957

It was Monday and Knowles had already put in a week's work. He was sure he had unearthed something to show that the indomitable minister of trade and commerce, the Right Honourable C. D. Howe, had lied to the House of Commons the week before. More than that, if he could prove the lie, he could also revive the whole pipeline case of the previous year. It needed a rehashing; there was an election coming sometime that spring and the public needed to be reminded of the dastardly deeds of the government.

The preceding Tuesday, 19 February, C. D. Howe had been under close questioning from the opposition. Was it true, the Conservatives wanted to know, that two or three of the top executives of Trans-Canada Pipe Lines Limited, the company with which the Liberal government had made its notorious deal the year before, had recently exercised their stock options to buy company stock at the original low price offered by the company when it was first formed? Yes, that seemed to be the case. Howe could hardly deny it; the Monday papers had all the information and were spreading it around the country. The directors, it was to be assumed, had purchased the stock cheaply, and then sold it at the current price and realized a handsome profit. Since the Conservatives had no philosophical quarrel with such transactions, normal to private enterprise, they did not pursue the matter beyond the confirmation of the newspaper reports.

But the CCF was both opposed to that kind of economic practice and deeply suspicious of C. D. Howe's connections with big businessmen. Nor had CCF MPs been aware that stock options existed in the original agreement that had caused so much furor in parliament the year before. So they pursued the matter.

Had the minister known in 1956 that these top company directors held such stock options? No, came Howe's categorical reply; he even doubted that those options had existed at the time when the government and the company had come to their agreement.

Knowles was immediately suspicious. Howe's reply seemed to contradict the press reports that had sparked the parliamentary questioning. And how could the directors now be buying stock at lower than market value unless they held options from some earlier date that permitted them to do so? Moreover, Howe had been so closely involved with the entire arrangement with Trans-Canada Pipe Lines over the preceding years and he was known and admired for his tremendous capacity for detail. The stock options must have been in the initial contract and Howe must have known about them. Knowles set to work.

Never one to raise a matter which he had not thoroughly mastered, he spent the next few days digging back into the record. He went through his own files in and around the pipeline issue of 1956; he dug into the Sessional Papers of the same time; he made discreet telephone inquiries to people in the Privy Council and in Howe's own ministry. And he found what he was looking for: a copy of a document that had been available to the public but not apparently known, clearly indicated the existence of stock options. It also specified that only the two or three officials whose names had so recently hit the press held such options. Howe's statement doubting the existence of such options was clearly in error. But what about his denial of any knowledge? At the bottom of the document that Knowles had unearthed were spaces for signatures of the various people involved. Among the spaces was one for C. D. Howe but there was no signature. Knowles still had to be sure of his facts before he raised the question in the Commons. He therefore continued his sleuthing through all the offices and corridors of Parliament Hill. Eventually he had what he needed: the assurance that Howe's signature had indeed been on the original document. Armed with his knowledge and that assurance, he was ready by the weekend to raise the matter when the House met on Monday. He would accuse the minister of "misleading the House" — parliamentary language for lying — and he would launch into a condemnation of a government that had provided eighty million dollars of public funds to a private company, certain directors of which were now making a killing. He would ask rhetorically if the purpose of government was simply to smooth the path for millionaires. Oh, it would be a great day.

But his nosing about during the week had hardly been secret

and the Liberals knew he was up to something. For them, the question was how to put a stop to him. They knew, as did Knowles, that the coming Monday, 25 February, had been set aside as a private members' day; only private members' resolutions could be debated. The Liberals therefore could not deflect any attacks by reverting to government business, but nor could Knowles bring up whatever was on his mind because the private members' resolutions for that day were already on the Order Paper and were known. He must be going to try the trick permitted by Standing Order 26: a motion to adjourn the House in order to discuss a matter of urgent public importance. If the Speaker allowed the motion, then, according to the rule and unlike normal motions to adjourn, it would be debated and Knowles would have a field day, no doubt dragging out all the skeletons in the Liberals' pipeline closet. They would have to prevent it.

The Liberals had in fact guessed the strategy precisely. Knowles was indeed ready to make use of Standing Order 26 and he had his motion typed out in front of him: he would ask for an adjournment in order to discuss the urgent matter that Howe had misled the House, that the country had been robbed by the deal between the government and Trans-Canada Pipe Lines, and that no one had been told of the stock options in the original contract. He was sure of his facts but a bit uneasy. The Speaker would decide whether his motion was allowable and in the meantime there was anxiety within the CCF caucus where just that morning, after Knowles had revealed his plan, M. J. Coldwell, the party leader, had suffered a mild heart attack. It was a tense day.

The House met early in the afternoon. The Speaker called the members to order and Knowles was about to rise when C. D. Howe himself got up to speak on a point of privilege. He had, he announced, inadvertently misled the House the preceding Tuesday in his response to questioning. "I now find that my memory was at fault, and that in fact . . . I was aware of the fact there were options outstanding."[1] Howe's cabinet colleagues leered across at Knowles; they had stolen his thunder and there would be an end of it. But they ought to have known better. While Knowles thought fast about what he could do, Howe lectured the opposition on its inattention of the previous year; with any scrutiny at all it could have known the details of the contract and this one about stock options was there for anyone to see. Knowles kept only half an ear on the lecture while he studied his motion. Within minutes he realized that he need only strike out the reference to Howe's having misled the House, leave all the rest, and still try to have the matter debated under Standing Order 26. To the Liberals' consternation, he was on his feet urging precisely that. He accepted Howe's apology but still argued for the special adjournment motion so that the House could discuss the government's misleading of parliament and the country about the extent of private gain that had resulted from public financial support to Trans-Canada Pipe Lines. He sensed the excitement among opposition members behind him and saw the dismay on Liberal faces across the floor.

Now it was the Speaker's turn. He could decide whether the motion was allowable or not, or, if he had any doubts, he could ask the House if it thought the matter important enough to set aside government business. But there was no government business that day since it was entirely reserved for private members. So Speaker René Beaudoin said nothing. In parliamentary terms that indicated he thought the motion allowable. Procedure then dictated that if there were any objections to having the motion debated, the Speaker called upon those who advocated the motion to show their strength, strength which could be as few as twenty MPs. Needless to say, there were a great many objections from Liberal ranks, but Knowles and his CCF colleagues, with some support from the Conservatives, were easily able to muster twenty people. The debate would be held and it continued all day.

As mover of the motion, Knowles made the first speech. He reviewed the entire pipeline issue and debate of May and June 1956. He stormed at the government about the insidiousness of its deal with Trans-Canada Pipe Lines. The government had known all along that insiders stood to make a healthy profit; yet it was willing to facilitate that with public money. It had then concealed that aspect of the deal, but now that the existence of stock options was public knowledge the whole thing was even more despicable than it had been the year before. And that had been abominable. Knowles was in fine form and the Conservatives joined heartily in the debate. Everyone knew an election was in the offing and here was a superb chance to revive the whole pipeline scandal with its dictatorial muzzling of parliament. It was open season on the government and the opposition had an entire day at its disposal.

But how was it all to end? The motion being debated was the special one to adjourn and the debate would continue until there were no more speakers, at which point a vote would be held on the motion, or until there was no more time. The CCF wished to have a vote on the motion; simply to have the clock bring down

the curtain on such a vital matter would be a rather flat ending. So
when Prime Minister St. Laurent finished speaking ten minutes
before the normal close of the parliamentary day, the CCF did not
put up another speaker. Knowles' motion to adjourn had
therefore to be voted upon. It was of course defeated as the
government majority roundly voted that the House not adjourn.
By the time the vote was counted, however, it was ten o'clock, the
evening closing time. So the Liberals then proceeded to vote in
favour of another motion, this time from the prime minister that
the House now adjourn. There was no record of the hoots of
laughter from the opposition and, as Knowles admits, it was one
of the games that are regularly played in the House of Commons.[3]
But games are all part of the political warfare for if an opponent
can be made to look silly in the House, he may just appear so to
the electorate. On 25 February 1957 the vote on the special motion
to adjourn came as close as the opposition ever had to a vote of
confidence in the government for its handling of the pipeline affair.

That affair had rocked parliament and the country just nine
months earlier.[4] In May 1956 the government added an eighty-
million dollar loan to Trans-Canada Pipe Lines for the prairie
construction of its natural gas line from Alberta to the east to a bill
that had been before the House since March to create a crown
corporation to undertake the construction of the line north of
Lake Superior. Like earlier transportation projects in Canada, this
one too had run afoul of the geographic nightmare that was the
terrain of north-western Ontario and the Canadian government
had agreed to build that section itself and lease it to the company.
Now Trans-Canada, like earlier transportation companies, wanted
assistance for the construction on the prairies as well. The Liberal
government in 1956, like earlier Canadian governments, lent a
receptive ear. Indeed, in Trade and Commerce Minister C. D.
Howe, the pipeline company found a willing ally.

Howe was determined to have his way with his Liberal
colleagues and with parliament in 1956. He had been miffed over
the pipeline issue twice before and he did not intend to take that
treatment again. On the first occasion in 1955 Howe had tried to
get the government to guarantee the bonds of the Trans-Canada
company. Such a guarantee would facilitate the marketing of the
bonds and hence the financing of the company and therefore the
construction of the pipeline from the Alberta gas fields to eastern
Canadian markets and to American export markets. But a
government guarantee of bonds was more than Howe's cabinet
colleagues would accept in 1955. In spite of his dominant position

and personality in the government, Howe was unable to sway them. They balked and he sulked.

Later in 1955, Howe was given another opportunity to nurse a grievance. He was then seeking parliamentary approval for an extension of his powers in his double capacity as minister of defence production. He had exercised such powers under emergency powers bills during the Korean War between 1950 and 1953. Now he wished those powers to be continued by means of an amendment to the Defence Production Act. The Conservatives fought the bill strenuously, objecting in particular to the unlimited time permitted by the amendment. They argued interminably for a three-year limit and they gave every indication that they might continue the debate for just as long. During one weekend a weary St. Laurent took advantage of Howe's being away on a fishing trip to arrange a cease fire with the Conservative leader George Drew. If he would call off the Conservative filibuster of the bill, the government would write the three-year limit into it. The agreement was made, the change specified, the filibuster terminated, and the bill passed before Howe returned from his fishing trip. He was furious.

He was also determined there would be no repeat performance. He was, after all, the senior minister in the cabinet and in terms of parliamentary service he was also senior to the prime minister. Indeed on many occasions St. Laurent had seemed subservient to Howe. He certainly permitted him more latitude than the previous prime minister Mackenzie King ever had. Used to that, but now slighted on two occasions, Howe was more determined than ever to have his way.

He therefore drew up the pipeline bill in the spring of 1956 and presented it to cabinet as a *fait accompli*. It was a package deal and the cabinet would have to accept it or Howe's resignation. The cabinet session was unusually tumultuous for there had been no preliminary discussion as was normal with most bills and in particular those entailing huge sums of money. Howe informed his colleagues that the pipeline company had already agreed to the terms of the bill. And what was more, the company needed the money by 7 June. Cabinet had better proceed expeditiously so that he could have the necessary legislation presented to and passed by parliament. Reluctantly, it seems, the cabinet agreed, with people like Louis St. Laurent and Lester Pearson barely aware of the treacherous path Howe was leading them down. Armed with cabinet approval, Howe informed the Liberal caucus only a few hours before the matter was to be introduced to the House. If he could make parliament behave as obediently as his cabinet and caucus colleagues, all would be well and the company would have its money in record time.

But parliament would not behave. The CCF and the Conservatives combined their respective objections to the bill and worked closely together to try to delay it; given the government's large majority they could not expect to defeat it. Knowles and the CCF had three objections to the bill. First, they believed the pipeline should be publicly owned; perhaps, the CNR could undertake the construction but certainly a private company with massive public assistance should not be doing it. The eighty million dollars might well just be the loan the bill said it was but supposing the company failed? There would be eighty million dollars of public money down the drain. And even if the company did succeed, thanks to government largesse, how would the people of Canada profit from their massive investment? They had no shares in the company. The second thing that infuriated the CCF was the fact that the private company that was to undertake the construction of the pipeline was largely American owned. Should the government really be financing foreign firms to such an extent? The third objection of the CCF was the very insult to parliament that the bill represented. Howe had given a guarantee to a private company that parliament would do his bidding. Knowles' passion as a socialist and a parliamentarian was aroused: he condemned the entire scheme as an illustration of capitalism at its worst and a sure means of destroying parliament.

In spite of the intense opposition from the CCF, the pipeline debate probably would have been even shorter than it was had the Conservatives not added their voice to the twenty-three CCFers. Certainly the fifteen Social Credit members, mostly from Alberta, did not utter a word of opposition. And the Conservatives, for all their support in the debate, did not share the CCF's philosophical hostility to capitalist economic practices. They merely wanted to see what Knowles called "Canadian bucaneers" replacing the Texan ones behind Trans-Canada. But they were also appalled by the way Howe seemed to be treating parliament. Thus in the ensuing weeks Conservatives George Drew and Davie Fulton conferred frequently with Knowles of the CCF. Together they devised strategy and planned the attack: the Canadian public had to see that parliament was not in the pocket of the minister of trade and commerce.

To delay the bill necessitated the use of every procedural trick that the rule book permitted and Knowles knew them all. Indeed he was on his feet with objections before Howe could even support his own bill on 14 May. And he stayed on his feet virtually non-stop for the rest of the sixteen-day debate. When he was not speaking, he was prompting other opposition speakers. As both critics and partisans, then and since, have acknowledged — although Knowles does not admit to it himself — he was the "architect" and the "mastermind" of the debate. Most of it indeed was more on procedure than the substance of the bill. There were motions to adjourn the House, motions to adjourn the debate, points of order, and points of privilege. And when the Speaker ruled against the various procedural points of the opposition, as he invariably did, there were appeals of the Speaker's rulings which took up more time. Delay was the point.

The government, however, had a major weapon against delay in its arsenal. Closure, a weapon seldom used in Canadian parliamentary history since its introduction in 1913, and not at all since 1932, permits a government to apply strict time limits to a debate — in effect to close it off. The limited usage closure had had in Canada suggested that it ought only to be invoked after extended, perhaps unduly extended, debate. What was certain was that there had to have been some debate. Closure could not apply before debate had even begun.

And yet that is what the Liberal government did on two of the four occasions that closure was used during the pipeline debate. Two instances did follow what the rule seemed to require although the debate on the resolution stage of the bill and later on third reading had hardly been extended, let alone unduly extended. But the other two occasions were worse and empha-sized the very point Knowles and the opposition were trying to make: that Howe and the Liberals were riding roughshod over the rights of parliament all to give millions of dollars to a private, American-backed company. The two instances occurred during the committee stage of consideration of the bill. There, with the House acting as Committee of the Whole, members study a bill clause by clause. During such study there is no limit on the number of speeches, and the opposition undoubtedly saw this as the ideal occasion to use all their delaying tactics. No one had ever heard of closure being applied in Committee of the Whole.

But Howe did it. He was not at all interested in careful clause by clause scrutiny of his bill with the delays the opposition was sure to devise. He had to meet his deadline of 7 June. He had promised the company. As the promoter of the bill, he therefore introduced each clause, one by one. As he did so, giving the barest outline of each and before anyone had a chance to say a word, he moved adjournment of the debate, in effect giving notice that closure would then apply to the clause. Through the bill he went, clause by clause, reading only the marginal notes rather than the entire clause, and again moving adjournment of the debate after each. Parliament was effectively gagged. It could not say a word. Having dealt thus with each clause and assuming that the "some debate" aspect of the closure rule had been fulfilled by his own minimal reading, Howe then moved closure for the final consideration of all the clauses. The result was to limit debate on the essentials of the pipeline bill to two days.

Knowles was aghast. There was no time to ask questions of the various clauses of the bill since Howe had cut off the debate. There was no time to consider the bill as a whole because it too came under the closure rule. And that rule was invoked before there had been any debate at all on any of the clauses. The opposition tried to argue that the use of closure in such an instance was not sanctioned by parliamentary precedent and Knowles and his colleagues flung every illustration they could find at the government including the speeches of Liberal Sir Wilfrid Laurier who had opposed closure with wonderful words back in 1913. The opposition kept the House sitting all night on four occasions and kept the public's attention on parliament as it had not been before or since. There were line-ups inside and outside the buildings as people waited their turn for a seat in the gallery. Parliament was an exciting place, a dramatic place, that spring of 1956. But Knowles was very ill at ease. He would gladly have exchanged all his procedural knowledge for the chance not to be using it for this purpose — to save parliament itself.

He could not even count on the assistance of the chief officer of the House, the Speaker. René Beaudoin, instead of being an impartial arbiter of debate, appeared to be doing just what the government wanted. He ruled against every one of the opposition's interjections or points of order and was always sustained by the government on the subsequent appeal. He even seemed to enjoy the sport. When Knowles dug up from the parliamentary debates of 1913 an ancient Liberal MP by the name of William Knowles who had also objected to the improper use of closure in committee, Speaker Beaudoin coyly asked what his counterpart had decided in 1913. Since the Conservative Speaker had decided against Knowles in 1913, the Liberal Speaker intended to do the same thing now. Beaudoin always seemed to know precisely what was forthcoming, particularly from the government side. If Finance Minister Walter Harris raised a procedural point which had not been used in half a century and which sent his opponents scurrying to the books of rules and precedents, Beaudoin always had the intricacies at his fingertips. Admittedly he was an able man; indeed until the pipeline fiasco, Beaudoin's name had been mentioned as a possible permanent Speaker. But his ability was not as great as the display he was giving. Obviously he had been primed. Ministers' cars had in fact been seen outside Beaudoin's home and they could not all be accounted for by social obligations. And ministers had been seen going into Beaudoin's office in the parliament buildings. Knowles knew of the latter very quickly, since the elder daughter of the family he had boarded with in Ottawa since 1944 was in Beaudoin's office with some high school friends one evening; when Finance Minister Harris came along, the young people were told to depart . . . Knowles explains Beaudoin's behaviour by his ambition; he knew very well that his bread, now and in the future, was buttered by C. D. Howe and he was not about to cross him. But by persisting in his ways, he brought the Speaker's chair into terrible disrepute. Across the country, and in Liberal papers too, cartoons and editorials displayed a crumbling Speaker's chair and lamented the fate of parliament.

All of that was before the Speaker created "Black Friday" on 1 June 1956. In the late afternoon of the preceding day, the opposition was again using every stalling technique it could find and even inventing some as Howe's deadline of 7 June fast approached. Colin Cameron of the CCF tried a point of privilege, expecting the Speaker to reject it. He referred to two letters to the editor which had appeared in the Ottawa *Journal* and which criticized Mr. Speaker Beaudoin severely for the way he had been handling parliament throughout the pipeline debate. Surely, Cameron suggested, the letters were an insult to the Speaker and he would like to make a motion that the writers be brought before the bar of the House to explain themselves and be chastised. Much to everyone's surprise, Beaudoin thought Cameron's point was well taken but that his motion was not worded in quite the proper manner. So the Speaker proceeded to dictate to Cameron how his motion should read. Cameron meekly accepted the wording, moved the motion, had it seconded by one of his colleagues, and began to debate it. Here was a splendid stalling tactic and provided by the Speaker himself.

Luck continued to play into the opposition's hands. No sooner had Cameron finished his speech than Conservative leader George Drew was on his feet ready to continue the debate, and as opposition leader, according to the existing rules, he could speak forever. While he went on for the rest of the evening, the CCF planned the strategy. Drew should continue speaking all the next day and the CCF would provide him with enough material to do so. The question of privilege which was being debated and to which he was addressing himself took precedence over all other business. The day would be his. But if he should cease speaking before the end of the day, a Liberal would undoubtedly jump into the fray, move that the debate be adjourned, and have what is an undebatable motion passed immediately by the Liberal majority. Once such a motion passed, the House would then return to the debate on the pipeline bill. So Drew was told to rest his vocal chords overnight while the CCF amassed material for him.

During the night, however, some Liberal cabinet ministers must have got to Beaudoin. For in the morning, just as Drew was about to rise and launch into his day-long speech, the Speaker himself rose to make an announcement. He had made a mistake the day before. The Cameron motion (which Beaudoin himself had drafted) was not in fact in order and therefore he intended to restore the business of the House to the point at which it had been at five o'clock the afternoon before. The Speaker was going to turn back the clock! As a spectator in the French National Assembly at New Years 1946, Knowles had seen that happen before but then it had been merely an amusing incident; now the Speaker in the Canadian House of Commons was interrupting proper procedure, wiping everything out, and returning to an hour that pleased him — and no doubt his ministerial prompters — better. Knowles was horrified; the Speaker seemed to be acquiring Howe's dictatorial temper. Knowles raised a point of order, only to be rebuffed by the Speaker. Beaudoin then said he would put the matter of turning back the clock to a vote of the House. Again Knowles protested. There was no motion to that effect before the House and the Speaker could not make one himself. But it was hopeless. The Speaker persisted and the Liberals, in a massive vote, declared that in spite of the June day outside, within the House, it was five fifteen on 31 May. The opposition, in protest against the highly suspect nature of the proceedings, did not vote at all.

Not that it much mattered for by this time the House was in an uproar. The normally sedate chamber was approaching bedlam. Members shouted and hurled insults at one another. The staid and gentlemanly M. J. Coldwell went to the centre of the chamber and shook his fist at the Speaker, calling him a tyrant, a Hitler. The House stenographers gave up even their usual device for registering chaos in decorous language — SOME HONOURABLE MEMBERS: Oh! Oh! — and merely recorded the Speaker's vain requests for order. Knowles stood by his desk the whole time, motionless but miserable, unhappy about the Speaker's behaviour, unhappy about his own colleagues' response, unhappy about the almost physical violence that was so evident. It was ghastly. A Black Friday indeed.

Despite the chaos, closure triumphed. The pipeline bill cleared the House of Commons in the early morning of 6 June and received Senate approval and royal assent in the nick of C. D. Howe's time on 7 June. The company received its eighty million dollars and prepared the way for certain of its directors to reap a great profit on the unknown stock options the following February.

In the meantime, George Drew missed an opportunity to bring on an election. By doing so, he may also have missed his opportunity of becoming prime minister. It all happened within a few days of the end of the pipeline debate. The government needed money to pay its own bills and therefore needed the required parliamentary approval. It had already had a series of interim supply bills passed — temporary financing until the main estimates of the government departments were approved. Now, in early June, it needed another interim supply bill; indeed if it did not have it within two days it would not be able to pay certain of its employees, among them the armed forces. It had not dared introduce the supply bill any earlier for the unlimited speeches permitted during a debate on supply would have interfered with the passage of the pipeline bill. Once that was passed, however, and as mid-June paydays approached, the government was anxious. How co-operative was the opposition likely to be? It was still very angry over the pipeline. What would it do in a supply debate where speeches were unlimited?

Both the government and the opposition prepared themselves accordingly. Prime Minister St. Laurent confided to his cabinet colleagues that if the opposition showed any signs of prolonging the debate on the supply bill, he would put an end to it by calling an election. He could then meet the government's current expenditures with governor-general's warrants, designed precisely for times when the House of Commons was not in session. As for the opposition, Knowles and Drew spoke together on Friday 8 June knowing the supply bill was to be introduced the following Monday and knowing that the government needed it passed within a few days. Would the two parties join forces again, stall the bill, and bring on an election? Knowles was willing, even though a number of CCF members had left Ottawa once the pipeline debate was over to help their Saskatchewan colleagues in a provincial election. Drew said he too was ready. He then went off to Toronto for the weekend and Knowles prepared for the fun of the following week.

Twenty minutes before the House was to meet on Monday, the Conservatives backed out. Howard Greene came to Knowles' office to announce that the Conservative caucus had decided not to debate the supply bill. Neither Drew nor Davie Fulton, the two Conservatives with whom he had had most contact during the planning of the pipeline strategy, had dared bring the news themselves. Behind Greene's message and what Knowles later learned was the fact that the financial backers of the Conservative party with whom Drew had spoken over the weekend were not at all interested in an election on the issue of the government's chummy relationship with private business. Drew therefore desisted. A disappointed Knowles took the news to his own CCF caucus and although some of the members thought they should attempt a filibuster of the supply bill themselves, they decided that with so many of their colleagues away, they really could not manage it alone. So the great plan fell through and the supply bill passed easily. "The Tories copped out completely," Knowles remarked, and Drew, he is sure, missed his chance to become prime minister. Indeed within a few months the ailing Drew was no longer even an MP let alone leader of the Conservative party and of the opposition. "One of the non-results of the pipeline debate," shrugged Knowles.[5]

As a result there was no election immediately after the pipeline debate. Had there been, the numbers of voters might have skyrocketed, so central had parliament become in the popular eye that spring. With no election, the issue might have gone the way of other scandals, creating a lot of heat, but little light, had it not been for that day in February nine months later. Thanks to Knowles, the whole question was revived. Parliament relived, and may even have digested for the first time — so enshrouded in procedural wrangles had the original pipeline debate been — the essence of the CCF's opposition. The government, insisted Knowles, had dealt most improvidently with a major aspect of the Canadian economy; that improvidence was revealed by the disclosure about profitable stock options. And the improvidence was clothed in the most blatant disregard for the rights of parliament, all in the name of Liberalism.

Knowles therefore dusted off the issue and exposed it once again to public scrutiny. Indeed, he would like to have written a book around the day 25 February 1957. It revealed so much about the pipeline itself, the workings of parliament, the philosophic differences between Liberals, Conservatives, and the CCF, the ways parties pair off for parliamentary advantage, and perhaps too how St. Laurent behaved as prime minister. Indeed that was one of the things that saddened Knowles most during the pipeline debate in 1956: St. Laurent had sat there, brooding, silent, and unhappy. He had been totally taken in by Howe, claims Knowles. And after many years of digesting the pipeline experience he concluded: "I'm more convinced that we were right than he was convinced that he was right."[6]

11
SPEAKER OF THE HOUSE?

19 August 1957

During the summer of 1957 the member for Winnipeg North Centre, re-elected in June, came to Ottawa for a few days. He had been startled by the election results for he had expected St. Laurent and the Liberals to be returned to power. But no; there was now a minority Conservative government with a leader probably as surprised as anyone else — John Diefenbaker. Perhaps all the fussing of the pipeline debate of 1956 and the re-run of it in February 1957 had in fact done the trick. The CCF had even picked up two seats, increasing its deputation from twenty-three to twenty-five. The session would be interesting and Knowles as House leader for the CCF had come to make the arrangements for office space, staff, and the seating of the members in the House. It was routine work for him; he could see to it all within a few days and return west.

The press, however, spotted his presence in the capital and assumed other reasons for it. Rumour had it, indeed, that Knowles was to be named Speaker of the next House of Commons. He would certainly grace the Chair and perhaps raise it from the low esteem in which it had fallen because of the pipeline fracas. There was no doubt that he knew the rules inside out and backwards. He would make the ideal Speaker. The rumours had arisen even before the election and were revived once the verdict of a minority government was pronounced by the electorate. Knowles was aware of the rumours and had pondered the possibility. He knew what his answer would be should the question ever arise in a formal manner. By mid-August, however, it had not arisen at all and he assumed it was buried along with so many other rumours that float about Ottawa when parliament is not in session. But the press, noting his mid-summer appearance in town, jumped immediately: "We know what you're here for! When are you getting it?"[1]

He denied it all. He was, he insisted, in town on party business. Moreover, he was not interested in the position and he doubted if Diefenbaker was either, given the late date. The press pointed out that Diefenbaker was still putting his cabinet together: anything could happen. Knowles left them to their speculating and went on about his business.

Later in the day he was walking from the Centre Block of the parliament buildings to the old Union Station (now the Conference Centre) to locate and organize some of his baggage. Passing the East Block which houses the office of the prime minister, he thought of dropping in to congratulate Diefenbaker on his surprising election victory. It was the proper thing to do. He therefore started into the building and up the stairs, only to see a crowd of reporters and television cameras waiting for the prime minister to appear and announce cabinet appointments. Knowles ducked out of the way as quickly as possible; if members of the press spied him here they would think he had been misleading them earlier. He vanished.

Nonetheless, the niceties had to be observed. Later in the day he returned to the East Block. This time there was no press hanging about and none of the security that has since come to surround the prime minister's office. It was therefore easy enough to gain access. Diefenbaker himself was out in the hall and saw Knowles coming. "Glad to see you, Stanley. I've just written you a letter. Come on in."[2] Once in the office the prime minister started to hand him a letter but then glanced at it, muttered something about the secretaries, and sent if off to be re-typed. The words personal and confidential were not to be on the letter; would the secretaries please redo it. Meanwhile Diefenbaker told his visitor the contents of the letter. Just as the press expected, the letter contained a proposal from Diefenbaker that Knowles take the position of Speaker of the forthcoming parliament.

The rumour had become reality. It was not, in fact, the first time such a suggestion had been made. Nor would it be the last. But it was the most official. The earlier occasion had been on 2 June 1956, the day after the notorious Black Friday of the pipeline debate. That day Finance Minister Walter Harris had asked Knowles to come to his office. In the middle of a very ordinary chat and without the least hint of what was coming, Harris suggested that perhaps the solution to the crisis in parliament was to have the Winnipeg member in the Speaker's chair. Knowles treated the remark in the manner it was given — lightly and in passing. He never mentioned the incident to anyone because it was so very unofficial. Harris could well have been merely making conversation. In fact, all of Harris' conversation, except for the comment about the Speakership, had been just chat. Reflecting later, Knowles realized that there had been no other reason for the summons to Harris' office on a Saturday afternoon. But if the conversation had little point except for that remark, the remark itself made no sense at all, coming as it did in the middle of one of the worst storms in Canadian parliamentary history. Indeed it was ridiculous. The only possible reason for changing the Speaker in mid-parliament was to ease the burden on the existing one and thereby ease the burden on the government. And the only purpose of that would be to speed the passage of the pipeline bill. Knowles' purpose, however, was to defeat that bill, or at least delay its passage. If Harris meant his remark seriously, and if Knowles treated it as such, then the situation was even worse than he had imagined for what could he think but that the government was attempting to buy him off? Knowles, a person of no cynicism and less guile, simply let the remark go in one ear and out the other.

Here, however, in the summer of 1957, the suggestion was being made again, in a much more formal manner. The letter offering the Speakership was being typed in the next office and he had to give some reply. The offer was, he recognized, a great honour. His own fascination and love for parliament centre as much on the workings as on the accomplishments of the institution and those workings only run smoothly under a master's touch; it is the Speaker who has, or should have, that touch. That other people thought he might have the required talent was high praise indeed. Moreover, as he mentioned to the prime minister, rumours about such an offer had already spread and he had given the matter some thought. Now, however, he had the prime minister's letter; he would give it serious consideration and tell Diefenbaker within a week. His answer, he added, might be yes or might be no.

Diefenbaker was shocked. Here he was, the prime minister, handing out plums; indeed, he had been spending weeks at the task, all the while listening to importunate demands for those very plums. He also enjoyed the look of delight on the face of the chosen recipient. But here was that sombre member from an opposition party being offered the most prestigious plum there was — with a commensurate salary — and blandly remarking that the answer might be yes or might be no. Diefenbaker let his annoyance show. "You'll never get another offer like this."³ Then it was Knowles' turn to be shocked. He was tempted to give the letter back immediately, so appalled was he by the crudity of the remark. But Diefenbaker quickly regained the manner of his office and the two men continued their discussion. Knowles even suggested other possible nominees, Conservative and Liberal. Among them was Lester Pearson, but even then Diefenbaker had no use for the man. He continued to persuade Knowles. One of the reasons for suggesting his name now, long before parliament was to reconvene in mid-October, was to permit him to "go away and beat up enough French to be able to handle the job."⁴ The entire discussion was, Knowles now thinks in retrospect, a commentary on the very brief history of bilingualism in Canada. In 1957 the Speakership could be offered to an English-speaking Canadian with the mere proviso that he "beat up" a bit of French. Knowles remains convinced, however, that Diefenbaker's offer was genuine. Here was a new prime minister who wanted parliament to function smoothly and who thought that someone from the opposition rather than from the government might ensure it.

The fact that the new Conservative government was in a minority may also have coloured the offer. Knowles, however, did not let that thought cross his mind, let alone his lips. But the suggestion lingered and embittered his relationship with Diefenbaker for years. In the meantime, he put the prime minister's letter, no longer marked personal and confidential, into his pocket and recrossed Parliament Hill to his own office in the Centre Block. On the way he noticed the same reporters who had told him with such certainty earlier in the day why he was in town. What could he say to them now that he had the actual offer in his pocket? And what would they think of him after his remarks that morning? The reporters, however, were already on to the scent of some other rumour and they were no longer interested in him.

Knowles was therefore left to ponder. His CCF colleagues were all out of town; leader M. J. Coldwell was vacationing north of Ottawa at Blue Sea Lake. His Winnipeg family was far away, and so was the Ottawa family that had housed him since 1944. Only one of the teenaged daughters of that family was at home; she would listen as Knowles pondered the offer aloud. In fact he was just confirming what he already thought. Much as he loved parliament and much as he was honoured by the suggestion of his being Speaker, he was also committed to the CCF and to his role as an MP. For all his love for the institution, he knew it was just a means to an end; for him that end was social justice. To that he had been committed long before he even thought of politics or parliament. Besides, he had just come through an election campaign in which he had made precise commitments not only to his own electors in Winnipeg North Centre, but also to people all across the country where he had campaigned for the ailing Coldwell. To turn around only a few months after the election and forget those commitments was more than he could do. He also knew that he was not indispensable to the smooth workings of the House; there were others who could handle the task as well and perhaps even better than he. Indeed the man eventually chosen to be Speaker, Roland Michener, was, Knowles says, one of the best there has been. He also claims to have thought at the time, although he admits it may be partly hindsight, that the job could have some very awkward moments. Supposing the government were not happy with his rulings? Things could become quite unpleasant. A Speaker chosen from the government ranks might weather such storms; a Speaker chosen from the ranks of the opposition would probably have to resign. He was not at all sure that the relationship with Diefenbaker could be a happy one. It was therefore decided: he would say no.

Before leaving Ottawa for home in Winnipeg and before writing an official reply, he borrowed a friend's car and drove north to see Coldwell. The older man knew immediately the reason for Knowles' sudden appearance at the lake. And he was uneasy. Was Stanley expecting his advice? If so, what would he say? He might even suggest that he accept the post. But he was spared the worry. Knowles had come to tell M.J. of his decision, not to ask his advice. And then he went west to write the letter from home:

359 Elm Street,
Winnipeg, August 24, 1957

Dear Mr. Diefenbaker:
  Thank you for your letter of August 19th. I am deeply appreciative of the very high honour you have conferred upon me by suggesting that you would be prepared to place my name in nomination for the office of Speaker of the House of Commons for the 23rd Parliament. You know of my keen interest in the rights and traditions of Parliament, and I assure you that I have given your suggestion most thorough consideration.

However, during the recent election campaign I placed emphasis not only on the need to restore the supremacy of Parliament, which I dare to hope will now be achieved, but also on certain measures of legislation which I promised I would continue to do my best to win for the people of this country. I made this commitment not only to the electors of Winnipeg North Centre but to my fellow Canadians generally, campaigning as I did in various parts of Canada. Important as is the office of Speaker, I feel that if I were to accept your offer I would be overlooking the firm commitments which I made during the election campaign. This I cannot do.

I am most grateful to you for the suggestion that in your view I would be able to perform a service if I were chosen to fill the office of Speaker, but I believe I can render greater service to my constituents and to the people of Canada generally by remaining on the floor of the House of Commons, and thus retaining the right to participate in the deliberations of this important 23rd Parliament.

Thank you again for the honour you have done me. I am sure you will appreciate the reasons on the basis of which I must decline the nomination you were prepared to make.

> Sincerely yours,
> (Sgd) Stanley H. Knowles

He never received a reply. In fact, all subsequent interchanges between the two men were marked by a studied coolness on the part of Diefenbaker. There the question remained for two months while the press, sensing that something had transpired between the two men, kept needling Knowles for information. He even wrote the prime minister suggesting that it was his place, as initiator of the correspondence, to release it to the press; he certainly had no objections. Again there was no reply and Knowles continued to evade press questions on the matter.

By October, however, when the House was sitting, the question had aroused enough interest for a Liberal MP from Saskatchewan to ask the prime minister directly about it. Irving Studer wanted to know if it were true that an offer of the permanent Speakership had been made to the member for Winnipeg North Centre. Studer usually amused himself by referring to Knowles as the member for Winnipeg-off-centre but on this occasion he was proper. Diefenbaker replied in a roundabout manner. Since there was no such thing as a permanent Speaker, no such offer had been made. But the prime minister did admit that he had offered to nominate the member for Winnipeg North Centre for the position of Speaker in this parliament. Studer next wanted to know if there was correspondence to that effect and if so, whether it could be made public by being tabled in the House. Diefenbaker, with an innocent glance across at Knowles, indicated that he had no objections if his honourable friend had none. Knowles, whose vocabulary of off-coloured epithets is limited to "You so and so," applied them under his breath to the prime minister who had known all along he did not object. He indicated his agreement and the two letters of 19 August and 24 August became public documents on 17 October 1957.[6]

For reasons having nothing to do with the Speakership, that minority parliament did not last long. After the subsequent election in March 1958, Knowles was neither the Speaker nor even a member of the House of Commons. Some people even attributed part of his defeat to the fact that certain voters considered he had snubbed the prime minister by rejecting Diefenbaker's offer. Diefenbaker himself appeared to consider it a snub and he maintained his distance from Knowles for years. While Knowles was executive vice-president of the Canadian Labour Congress between 1958 and 1962, he had many occasions to meet formally with the prime minister. Always it was "Good day, John," met with "Hello, Mr. Knowles." The executive of the CLC was unhappy about the coolness, President Claude Jodoin wondering why a relatively minor event back in the summer of 1957 should continue to rankle so with the prime minister. He determined to find out, and there were cabinet ministers willing to supply information. Diefenbaker apparently believed press reports during the election campaign of 1958 to the effect that Knowles had not considered the offer of the Speakership genuine. He was reported to have seen it merely as a trick on the part of Diefenbaker to remove one more opposition member — and a strong one at that — from the floor of the House, thus rendering his precarious minority position slightly more stable. Stung by those reports, Diefenbaker decided to give Knowles the cold shoulder.

But Knowles had never made such a statement. Even when press people attempted to put such words in his mouth he refused to do so. His only public — and indeed private — references to the matter always stressed the genuineness of the offer. But a reporter had been able to put such words into the mouth of the CCF leader M. J. Coldwell. By asking a peculiar question and receiving a vaguely affirmative reply, the reporter was able to "quote" Coldwell to the effect that Diefenbaker's offer to Knowles had not been genuine. The prime minister had seen the press account, attributed it to Knowles, and had been deeply offended.

The CLC executive therefore planned a means of breaking the ice. At the next meeting between the executive and the prime minister, the other three members would arrange to leave early and Knowles could have a few minutes alone with Diefenbaker. The plan worked, but the ice was merely cracked. Knowles explained that the story did not originate with him, that although he did not mind people disliking him for something he had said or done, he did not appreciate this coolness for something he had not done and had deliberately avoided doing. Diefenbaker was only half convinced; he accepted the explanation but added "Still it was a pretty mean thing to do."[7] With his elephantine memory for hurts, Diefenbaker remaind slightly stiff in Knowles' company.

"early in 1975 when he objected so strenuously to a pay raise for MPs
..." (Reprinted with permission, *The Toronto Star*)

With just as much doggedness, Knowles persisted in attempting to break Diefenbaker's reserve. He attended all possible occasions where the prime minister was speaking. He never missed an opportunity to solicit his attention, to make him know that he was determined not to let the matter drag on. Once in 1961 when Senator John Kennedy from Massachusetts was being greeted in Ottawa, the prime minister remarked that his wife Olive could trace her relatives not just to Massachusetts, but also to Cape Cod, and further still to the *Mayflower* in 1620. Brewster and Bradford were their names. Kennedy's reaction is unknown but Knowles started. His own family could be traced to those same people. He would use that as the final wedge in the door of Diefenbaker's affections. But Diefenbaker was not giving up lightly. When Knowles told him that his ancestors too had been on the *Mayflower*, the gruff reply came: "It must have been an awfully big boat."[8] But Knowles' persistence turned out to be more durable than Diefenbaker's sense of hurt, and he eventually prevailed. By 1975 he was one of the honoured guests at Diefenbaker's eightieth birthday party in Saskatoon and Diefenbaker said in public how pleased he was that Knowles was there. Diefenbaker supported Knowles early in 1975 when he objected so strenuously to a pay raise for MPs and praised him highly. For the rest of Diefenbaker's life the two were good friends, both being the senior MPs in terms of length of service. Diefenbaker had a slight edge on Knowles, having been elected first in 1940 and re-elected continuously thereafter. Knowles refers to his own position as that of the Avis rent-a-car firm which in its advertisements of the 1960s stated that it was number two and therefore tried harder.

For all the length of the Diefenbaker story, the question of the Speakership for Knowles did not end in 1957. In 1964, during another minority government, this time led by Liberal Prime Minister Lester Pearson, the Commons was again in turmoil. The feud between Diefenbaker and Pearson was in full flower — Diefenbaker believing that the upstart Pearson had usurped his power in 1963 — and the Speaker of the House, Alan Macnaughton, was no match for him. On 12 May Pearson called Knowles into his office. Like the conversation with Walter Harris back in 1956, this one too began casually and without warning turned personal. While discussing the general difficulties the House was experiencing in running its business smoothly, Pearson offhandedly suggested that Knowles might be put in the chair. Like the earlier remark of Harris, this one too he took in the same light manner in which it was made. But Pearson had obviously delved more deeply into the matter than his tone suggested. He added that there was a Senate vacancy in Quebec and he could easily appoint Macnaughton, the present Speaker and member for Montreal-Mount Royal to fill it. Pearson went even further. He had, he said, discussed the matter with some of his Quebec colleagues who all said that their high regard for Knowles outweighed the fact that he knew little French. Pearson was serious and Knowles had to be so in turn. This time, however, he did not say he would consider the matter. He had made his decision years ago and it remained the same. Moreover, as he pointed out to Pearson, imagine the howl in the House if he accepted from Pearson the nomination that he had refused from Diefenbaker in 1957. There would be no end to the wrangling and the House would be in even worse shambles.

Pearson's suggestion in 1964, like that of Harris in 1956, was unofficial and never became public. In fact, Knowles simply stored the two away in his memory, knowing full well that any public revelation on his part would simply bring the retort that the initiator had just been making conversation. But Pearson was obviously doing more than chatting. Since that time there have been other suggestions from other people that Knowles would make an ideal Speaker. But for him those three occasions are the only ones that count. And he has no regrets. Indeed, he thinks his days on Parliament Hill would have been numbered had he accepted any one of the offers. In 1956 he would have come to blows with the opposition, in 1957 probably with the government, and in 1964 he would have been caught in the cross-fire of hostility between Pearson and Diefenbaker. Each would have required his resignation. And to be separated from parliament would be like cutting out his heart. Little did he know that summer day in 1957, as he pondered and rejected Diefenbaker's offer of the Speakership, that the blow to the heart would come from his own constituents just seven months later.

12
DEFEAT

31 March 1958

The campaign had been long and wearing. February and March are not ideal months for anything, let alone an election campaign on the Canadian prairie. The storms, the snow, the wind, and the biting chill all limit extensive campaigning particuarly of the kind that Knowles likes best — shopgating. Still he had done what he could, including a number of cross-country trips as he had undertaken less than a year earlier in the campaign of 1957, on behalf of the CCF leader M. J. Coldwell. Now it was election day. He was making the usual rounds of the polling stations, attending to any problems, and generally "getting a feel of things." Everything was normal, except for the turnout which seemed unusually high. Even that caused no worry: perhaps his ten thousand vote majority over his nearest opponent in the last election would be increased.

Only late in the afternoon was he alerted. By then he was in a polling station in a home of the solidly CCF Weston area of his riding. A remark from the election official struck him: "Isn't it interesting, Stanley, there's exactly the same number of voters as we had by this time last year."[1] Knowles grasped the implication immediately. The vote was normal in the solidly CCF areas of the riding, but elsewhere it was higher. This will mean fewer CCF votes, he calculated as he called Alistair Stewart, the CCF candidate in Winnipeg North, to warn him about a probable reduction in their majorities. Stewart had the same feeling. Nonetheless, the reduction would have to be immense before it demolished his majority of the year before.

That, however, was precisely what happened. The votes started coming in shortly after the closing of the polls and Knowles prepared to keep close tally. As always, he could discern the trend from the very first polls. The first one came from the immediate neighbourhood of his campaign headquarters and had always been solidly in his favour; this time it defeated him badly. To a candidate seasoned to the temper of his riding, this meant trouble. But the extent of it had yet to be seen. Another two or three returns from polls, a scant half hour after the closing of the polls, and he knew the outcome. After five electoral wins in Winnipeg North Centre, preceded by six for J. S. Woodsworth, the voters were going to give him a taste of defeat.

It was both the biggest shock and the biggest surprise of his life. He had had no indication whatsoever of what the day held in store for him. Indeed for months before the election all the indications seemed to predict quite a different result. In the election of 1957, the CCF had increased its standing in the House of Commons; Knowles' own majority had climbed. Indeed all his opponents in the riding had lost their deposits by not winning at least half the number of votes of the winner. Even the parliamentary session, brief though it had been between the two elections of 1957 and 1958, had been a good one. The CCF had acted as the real opposition, given the total dispiritedness of the Liberals under St. Laurent, then in second place to the minority Conservative government of John Diefenbaker.

The Liberals had actually avoided any occasion to bring down the minority government. When the CCF, thanks to Knowles' skill in knowing just where to place discomfitting amendments, forced the MPs to take sides in a vote, the Liberals would either support the Conservative government or duck out of the chamber just before the vote so that there would be insufficient numbers to defeat it. This occurred both on issues of purely symbolic meaning such as the challenging of Speaker's rulings or on more substantive matters such as government taxation measures.

Knowles was sure that the performance of the CCF in that parliament would count with the electors in an eventual election. He even dreamed of the CCF surpassing the Liberals to become the official opposition. All the indications pointed to a perpetual decline for the Liberals. When Knowles chanced to be travelling with Walter Harris on one occasion, he had to disillusion the former Liberal finance minister who was convinced that the Liberals would return to power in the next election. "Walter," he remarked, "You'll be lucky if you retain seventy-five seats."[2] And he was right. The Liberals kept on plummeting from their one hundred and seventy-one seats after the election in 1953 to one hundred and five in 1957 and then forty-nine in 1958. Of course the CCF also declined from twenty-five to eight in the latter election but before that verdict Knowles' perception was limited to the Liberals.

He even thought the way Diefenbaker had treated parliament on the occasion of the dissolution could be turned to CCF favour with the electorate. He is still disdainful of the manner in which Diefenbaker brought on the election in 1958. It was all perfectly legal, he admits, but it was tricky and secretive. Late in January 1958, it was clear that an election was in the offing and the opposition kept pestering the government to know the date. Diefenbaker preferred to spring a surprise. The day that would turn out to be last day of the session, he and George Hees and a few other cabinet ministers were scheduled to fly to Winnipeg in a Department of Transport plane. There was no political significance in that so the opposition paid no attention. Later in the day, however, it became known that the plane, once aloft, had changed direction and headed for Quebec City. Now the trip acquired political significance: the governor general just happened to be in residence at the Citadel in Quebec and his permission was required for the dissolution of parliament. The opposition therefore surmised that parliament would be dissolved soon and the date set for an election. But still they did not know when or how the announcement was to be made.

Diefenaker, however, did know and he enjoyed playing the game down to the last minute. In the late afternoon of 1 February just as the house was to adjourn for the day, he rose to make an announcement and began commenting upon the nature of his minority government. An opposition member interrupted, wishing to know, as was normal at that time of the day, the order of business for the next sitting of the House. The Speaker allowed the prime minister to continue and he began listing the many virtues of his government and its need for a clear majority from the Canadian electorate. His remarks had turned into a political speech. As such they seemed to call for responses from the other parties in the House. Lester Pearson prepared to speak, and Knowles, then deputy leader of the CCF, also took his cue. But neither was given a chance to utter a word. Winding up the praise for his own government, Diefenbaker terminated by saying that "the present parliament of Canada has been dissolved by proclamation under the Great Seal of Canada bearing date the 1st day of February, and members and senators are discharged from attendance."[3] How Diefenbaker had pulled such a stunt was left to everyone's speculation. Either he had had the seal affixed to the proclamation of dissolution before he rose to speak, and if so, he was speaking illegally, or he had arranged with the officials in the governor general's office to have the seal affixed at a given moment, perhaps just as he was announcing the *fait accompli* to the House. In either case, he certainly succeeded in silencing the opposition. Knowles was immediately on his feet to protest but before he could say more than "Mr. Speaker," the Speaker himelf indicated "that this House of Commons has no further existence." He had only to leave the chair, for that parliament no longer existed. The commons stenographers stayed long enough to record a "Shame" and the combined comment of Knowles and Liberal James Sinclair: "What about the rights of parliament?"[4]

The dismayed Knowles was convinced that Diefenbaker's behaviour would dismay the voters too. The Conservatives had, after all, taken an active role in the pipeline debate of 1956 where so much had been said about defending the rights of parliament. Now Diefenbaker, like the Liberals before him, seemed to be quite content, indeed actually gleeful, about pulling the wool over parliament's eyes. What Knowles failed to recognize was that his passion for and devotion to parliament is not necessarily shared by voters across the country. Not that he expected Diefenbaker to lose in the election of 1958. Indeed Diefenbaker had done one very popular thing by raising the old age pension from the Liberals' niggardly forty-six dollars to a more respectable fifty-five a month. Knowles' own older constituents in Winnipeg North Centre would be grateful and he could hardly begrudge them the increase. Nonetheless he expected the CCF to do well in the election and he assumed that he would too.

For him, personally, there was also the matter of the Speakership. He believed he had made the right decision in turning it down the previous summer and he expected his electors to agree with him. He was supposed to be their champion and the Speakership would have effectively muzzled him. But his constituents may have been more desirous of voting for Diefenbaker as an expression of thanks for the increase in the old age pension; many of them were also caught by the Diefenbaker vision for Canada that was so much part of the election campaign in 1958; some, it seems, even thought that their MP had insulted the prime minister by rejecting his offer of high honour and recognition.

How the Canadian electorate and the Winnipeg voters would react was quite unknown as the House dissolved at the beginning of February in preparation for an election on 31 March. Knowles was as active as the weather permitted in his own riding and more so than he has since been campaigning across the country. In most elections before the 1960s, the most senior MPs in every party campaigned extensively right across Canada. The speaking, the engagements, the meetings, were all more of a shared experience rather than being centred on the leader. Knowles blames the media in part for this change in campaign practice. The concentration of press, radio, and, after the late 1950s, television, on the leader alone has led to that person having to undertake much more than he used to. For the other party members, the change has made campaigns considerably less hectic.

In 1958, however, Knowles was expected to be all over the country as well as in his own riding in Winnipeg. Given Coldwell's continuing frail health, he began to undertake some of the leader's national engagements as well. Before doing so, he checked with his perennial campaign manager in Winnipeg, Mrs. Eva Cove. Would it be all right if he were away from the constituency more often? Mrs. Cove thought all was well; indeed she was more worried about her candidate's health than about the constituency. Her worries too were misplaced as Knowles tripped off to Quebec where he actually made speeches in French, into the Maritimes to speak in Cape Breton, into Ontario, and on to national television. Everywhere the reception was good: the crowds were enthusiastic, the candidates optimistic, and the editorialists favourable. It was a good campaign and all the signs pointed to a substantial increase in both the popular vote for the CCF and its representation in the House of Commons. He could even name the seats across the country that the party would surely capture.

In fact the number of votes for the CCF dropped by fifteen thousand, the popular vote by more than a percentage point, and the party's representation in the Commons from twenty-five to eight. What had happened? For one thing, close to seven hundred thousand more voters cast ballots in 1958 than in 1957 and they probably all voted Conservative since that party in fact gained almost twice that number of extra votes since the election of 1957. In many ridings indeed, the Liberals simply disappeared: where three-way contests had often permitted CCF candidates to win, two-way contests guaranteed their defeat. That was the case in Winnipeg North Centre where the Conservative candidate, running third in the previous election, picked up a mere few hundreds votes from Knowles but scooped up nearly all the Liberal votes and the new ones as well. With that, John MacLean won the riding for the Conservatives. He was as surprised as everyone else by the outcome.

The search for an explanation continued for days. Knowles had perhaps been away from the riding too often. But even had he been there, his presence might not have made any difference, since everyone, including himself, assumed that the seat was safe. Perhaps if he had sensed trouble and stayed in the riding, he might have saved the seat. But then he did glean national publicity for his activities in other parts of the country, and every candidate needs as much of that as he can get. Nonetheless, he was not physically present in Winnipeg at all times. The weather also limited the shopgating: even when enveloped in his huge beaver coat, there were only so many mornings that he could tolerate an hour or so outside the factory or shop gates with Winnipeg winds defying all thermometers. Perhaps too the voters and campaign workers relaxed this time believing their man to be unbeatable. Complacency, however, rarely turns into electoral victory as one of Knowles' campaign workers tried to tell the others. They were not to take this election for granted, they must face the possibility of defeat through inertia, they had to get out and urge supporters to the polls. For his pains, he was shushed by his fellow campaign workers: how could he think such things?

Although Knowles jokingly dismisses jinxes, like other politicians he has a grain of superstition in him and the election of 1958 fostered it. That was the first campaign in which he had the same opponent twice in a row; others had given it one try and gracefully retired. In 1958 the second-time candidate won. When the situation recurred in 1974 and Knowles had to contend once again with a second-time candidate, he was very careful indeed. Since 1958 too, he has not left his riding during a campaign. He has even refused to have adding machines in his campaign headquarters on election night. They had been introduced in 1958 to spare the candidate all that arithmetic. But says he, "They let us down," and therefore there were to be "no more adding machines."[5] He may even have determined not to have a tearful daughter in his campaign headquarters again; in fact that year was the only occasion when tears were required.

Many years later Knowles conceded that it had been a tough night. Never one to display his emotions, he was able to conceal his own while soothing those of the people who had worked for him. He called upon all his ministerial talents for the task. His first remarks to the press thanked his constituents for the sixteen years he had had as an MP. But it all sounded so final that he picked up the defiance of one of his campaign workers: this night was not the end, but the beginning of the preparation for the comeback at the next election. Knowles reiterated the comment all evening as it became clear that the government was to have a huge majority. All the more reason, therefore, to begin building a stronger CCF since

"no more adding machines." The candidate does his own election tabulations. Winnipeg 1968.

the country would need it in preparation for the next round. The comment became a soothing ritual as radio and television all wanted statements and the press required photographs. He bore it all. He had been used to hiding hurts since 1919.

In fact he was shattered by the defeat. Politics and parliament were his life and now that life was removed. Parliament was also his job; he had no other. How would he finance his family in Winnipeg, his children's schooling? What would he do? The worries mounted as the calm exterior persisted. And so successful was he at the latter that a newspaper headline remarked "Stanley Knowles isn't sorry for Stanley Knowles."[6]

There were immediate things he had to do. He had to go the next morning as he always did after an election to the shopgates to thank those voters who had given him their votes. This time he would try to get to as many as possible, where necessary leaving a sign STANLEY KNOWLES THANKS YOU FOR *YOUR* SUPPORT. He had the sign with him as he stood outside the entrance to the CPR shops in Weston. It was a dreary, drizzly morning and normally the incoming workers were glad to reach the bit of shelter provided by the inhospitable entrance to the tunnel which led under the CPR yards and into the machine shops. That morning they saw their former MP standing there and many of them could not face him. Instead they hung back, looking for another entrance, clambering over the tunnel to cross the tracks in order to avoid greeting him. They were as shocked as he was by the outcome but they were not as skilled in hiding their emotions. The riding that had belonged to them for thirty-seven years, that had returned Woodsworth six times and Knowles five, was no longer theirs.

Knowles also had a meeting to attend that night at the Winnipeg and District Labour Council. One of the members spoke of the election and referred to all the things Knowles had done for workers in his years in parliament. He mentioned the offer of the Speakership, including the salary, that he had turned down in order to work for the people of Winnipeg North Centre. "And last night," thundered the man, "they said their thank you to him."[7] The meeting then called on Knowles to speak. He admits that his carefully controlled emotions were dangerously close to the surface that time and he spoke with difficulty.

There was, however, only so much winding up of an election to be done. He would have to start thinking about work. His annual salary as an MP (eight thousand dollars plus a two thousand dollar expense allowance) would come to an end and he was not even eligible to draw the three thousand dollar pension for former MPs since he had had to borrow from his payments into the fund. What should he do? There were some suggestions of trade union jobs, even murmurings of a church. But he was not prepared to return there. Perhaps the CCF would take him on as a paid organizer to assist the rebuilding of the shattered party. A whisper or two suggested he replace Coldwell, who was also defeated in the election, as the national leader of the CCF at the party's biennial convention due that summer. Knowles dismissed the latter possibility, unsure of his own qualifications for the job, unsure of his own health, and uneasy about the idea of "fixing" things in advance of the convention. He did like the idea of working for the party. Back in 1934 he had made the decision to combine his minister's duties with the growing personal duties he felt towards the fledgling socialist movement; shortly thereafter he had made a complete commitment to that movement and left the church behind him. He could do it again. In 1958 he was prepared to take on a party job at a paltry salary in order to be part of that movement's continuing struggle.

But there was another possibility for his immediate future, more acceptable to his close friends and, it turns out, more acceptable to his enemies, some of whom happened to be within CCF ranks. Shortly after the election, Knowles received a call from Claude Jodoin, the president of the Canadian Labour Congress. The CLC was holding its own biennial convention in Winnipeg later in April; Knowles knew that since he was in fact to be a delegate at the convention. What he did not know was that the present executive vice-president was not going to stand for re-election; indeed an amendment to the constitution of the CLC was to be proposed at that convention providing for two executive vice-presidents. Jodoin wanted Knowles to run for one of those positions. Curiously enough, when relating this incident, Knowles did not raise the question that came up in reference to the possibility of his becoming leader of the CCF: "fixing" things in advance of a convention. Perhaps that consideration was a later rationalization after his unhappy experiences within the party over the next few weeks.

For it became evident during that time that much as he was prepared to sacrifice himself for the party, the party executive and national council were not that interested in having him. As soon as word of the CLC proposal was known, they began backing away from the suggestion initially made by David Lewis that Knowles come on staff. First there were financial difficulties: shouldn't Knowles try to obtain his MP's pension, even if he was in arrears in his payments, so that the party could pay him that much less? That had been the arrangement in 1941 when he was a Winnipeg city councillor and provincial secretary of the party. Now, it was worse. Nasty telegrams threatened to take the matter before the national convention of the party if he did not clear out by taking the CLC position. It was decidedly messy and Knowles' recollections carefully glossed over the entire incident.[8] Instead he shouldered the decision himself: could he really stand the travel, the pace, the demands, the general "knocking about" that a party organizer has to do? Could he really handle the job? He had consulted his Montreal doctor who had pronounced him as fit for one job as the other; Knowles interpreted that as meaning he was not a particularly fine specimen of health at all. He insisted that the CCF both wanted and needed him but that there were people within the party who suggested that he could do just as much for the CCF by taking the CLC job. Moreover, the CLC would pay.

Only after lengthy discussions, telephone calls, meetings, arguments, persuasion, pleading, and talk, did he agree to the CLC proposal. The decision took two weeks and he was reluctant to the end: reluctant because his first attachment was to the CCF and yet the party, although he would not state it publicly, did not reciprocate the attachment; reluctant too because the CLC position would be something entirely new. Ever since working as a typesetter before he was twenty he had been a member of a trade union but he had never been active within a union and now he would be moving in right at the top of the labour movement in the country. Would he be accepted? His supporters insisted that he had done so much in parliament for trade unionists in Canada, that the position was a natural one for him and would be seen as such by union people all across the country. Besides, there was talk in the air of creating a new political party that would combine the union movement and the CCF. Someone would have to be working on that from the union side. What better person than Knowles?

The decision was made and announced to the press and on television from Knowles' home in Winnipeg. He was straightfoward: yes, he was available for the job; yes, he would like to have it; yes, there would be other candidates; and yes, there was the possibility that he might not win. His contesting the position was in fact facilitated by his being a delegate to the CLC convention; indeed had he not been a delegate, he could not have run at all.

It would not be the first union convention he had attended as an official delegate. The most recent had been the founding convention of the Canadian Labour Congress in 1956. That meeting, held in Toronto, had joined the two major Canadian union centrals — the Trades and Labour Congress and the Canadian Congress of Labour — into one single national body, the CLC. Knowles was a delegate from his own union, the International Typographical Union, local 191 Winnipeg. Partly the choice had stemmed from the respect which local union members had for him; partly it stemmed from their inability to pay the expenses of a delegate. As an MP Knowles would at least have free rail transportation to Toronto. In 1958, however, the situation was somewhat different. It was known months in advance, long before the federal election, that the CLC convention of 1958

"What better person than Knowles [to] combine the union movement and the CCF?" (Cartoon by Kuch, *Free Press*, Winnipeg, 1961)

would be held in Winnipeg. Knowles' union there could easily finance a delegate; he told the members so and they agreed. He did, however, let it be known that he would like to be a delegate to the convention; perhaps there was a poor typographical union local elsewhere in the country that was in the same situation as the Winnipeg one two years earlier and would like nothing better than to have an expense-free delegate. In fact there was, in the small Ontario town of Galt. Long before the federal election, then, Knowles knew he was to be the ITU delegate from Galt. He also expected to be an MP again by the time of the convention. The only difference that the election made to his appearance at the CLC convention was that instead of being merely the delegate

"added a new suit . . . and even put on a bit of weight . . ." Executive vice-president, Canadian Labour Congress. Ottawa c. 1960.

from the Galt local of the ITU, he was also a candidate for the
position of executive vice-president of the Congress.

The convention had first to pass an amendment to the
constitution, to enlarge the executive from one vice-president to
two. As expected, there was some opposition at the convention.
Delegates wondered why the position was necessary and how
much it was going to cost. Fearful lest the amendment fail, the
other candidates for the position all came to Knowles to tell him
that if there was to be only one executive vice-president, he
should be it. When he asked the other major contender, William
Dodge, why it should go automatically to him, Dodge replied
simply, "Because I've got a job and you don't."[9] Perhaps Knowles
registered the contrast between the warm reception at the CLC
and the cool one in his own party. In any case, the opposition to
the amendment disintegrated and it passed. The two positions
were then filled by Knowles and Dodge. Knowles held the job for
four years, standing successfully for re-election to the post in
1960, but not running again in 1962 because he was ready to
confront his Winnipeg electorate again in the federal election that
June.

By then he had added executive and administrative experience
to his parliamentary practice. He had travelled extensively and
spoken for the Canadian union movement throughout Canada
and abroad. And he had also played a major role in creating the
New Democratic Party in 1961. Moreover, he worked regular
office hours, had an evening meal with his Ottawa family, added a
new suit or two to the threadbare blue serge of his parliamentary
days, and even put on a bit of weight, none of which he had done
as an MP. Knowles will not go so far as to say that the defeat of 31
March 1958 was a Good Thing. But he does concede that it
speeded up the creation of the NDP. The CLC was already
interested in the idea of a new political party in the late 1950s, but
had the CCF not suffered such heavy losses in the election of
1958, it might not have been so willing to reconsider its position
and to look about for possible allies elsewhere. And had Knowles
not been defeated, the organizing of the NDP might well have
taken longer. He enjoyed his four years with the Canadian Labour
Congress but by the end of them he was anxious to wipe out the
shattering personal experience of 31 March 1958. "Remember
1958," he reminded his campaign workers at every subsequent
election: "Let's be sure it does not happen again."[10] It hasn't.

13

A NEW PARTY FOR CANADA

31 July 1961

The old Ottawa Coliseum had been rented for the occasion and Canada was about to witness its largest political convention. Delegates and groups from all over the country were gathering in the huge auditorium. People who had never been politically active before, people who had never had anything to do with the old CCF, they were all there. They had been discussing this new party idea for the last three years and they came prepared to discuss constitutions, programmes, names, and leaders. They brought with them the accumulated documentation of three years of study, some of it prepared by the national committee for the new party and some prepared by themselves. Their resolutions numbered almost seven hundred. For the next five days they would work hard at making history and at fashioning a new democratic socialist party for Canada. To open the convention was the one who had kept the whole idea alive and moving towards this culmination for the past three years, the chairman of the national committee for the new party, Stanley Knowles.

For him too that day was the tangible and exciting end of more than three year's work. One of the tasks he had been assigned when he took on the position of executive vice-president of the Canadian Labour Congress in April 1958 was precisely this. He was to work out the practical sequel to the CLC's resolution that there was a need in Canada "for a broadly based people's political movement, which embraces the CCF, the Labour movement, farm organizations, professional people and other liberally minded persons interested in basic social reform and reconstruction through our parliamentary system of government."[1]

That resolution in itself was the result of years of political evolution within the union movement in Canada. Back in the 1930s one of the fondest dreams of the CCF had been that the labour movement might ally itself officially with the socialist party. But the dream was never realized. The old Canadian Congress of Labour, the smaller of the two national union centrals in the period before 1956, did go as far as recognizing the CCF as its political arm in 1942 and encouraged its members to support the party. But the older, larger, and more traditional Trades and Labour Congress was bound by its similarities to the American Federation of Labor and to the heritage shared by both of them: that unions should have no direct ties with political parties but should instead try to get the best for their members out of whatever party happened to be in office. Individuals were of course free to act in any political way they wished and there were strong CCF members within the TLC but as a body it had shied away from endorsing the CCF much less affiliating with it.

However, when the union movement was considering a merger in the mid-1950s it had to face the issue. If the CCL and TLC joined forces what would their political position be? The CCL was not willing to give up its affinity to the CCF; the TLC was not willing to develop an affinity it had avoided all these years. The question was a major one in all the preliminary talks and planning that preceded the formation of the Canadian Labour Congress in 1956. Knowles had in fact taken part in many of those talks, informal chats that went back at least to 1954.

At the founding convention of the CLC the issue was debated and resolved with a compromise statement about political action. The new CLC did not name the CCF but it did encourage its members to continue their political practices. As for the Congress itself, it would study the whole question. Behind the scenes were discussions about the possibility of an entirely new structure for a political body that would, from the very beginning, combine the union movement and the CCF. The discussions were known but they were informal and they continued after 1956 in much the same fashion as they had before. Again, Knowles was part of them.

By 1958 the CLC was ready for much more direct action. At the convention in Winnipeg which elected Knowles to the vice-presidency, the Congress also debated the resolution about a "broadly based people's political movement." The debate was long and serious as some delegates, who happened to be CCF members already, worried about the watering down of their socialism, and others worried about a loss of union independence.

The resolution, however, carried with a substantial majority. The union movement thus took the lead in calling for a new political party in Canada, just three weeks after the major setback to the CCF in the federal election at the end of March.

Since many of the same people were involved in both the union movement and the CCF, it was not surprising that the CCF should follow the lead of the CLC. The CCF too had been evolving since its foundation in 1932. It did in effect water down its socialism as wartime and post-war prosperity seemed to eliminate the need for nationalization as a means of ensuring a more equitable distribution of wealth. And yet it also succeeded in promoting numerous social welfare benefits. It claimed to be closer to the people and its party organization was certainly more democratic than that of the Liberals or Conservatives. But despite its electoral success in Saskatchewan where it formed the provincial government from 1944 until 1964, it rarely attracted more than about ten percent of the vote in federal elections and had indeed registered a steady decline since a high of more than fifteen percent in 1945. With the loss of most of its MPs in the election of 1958, the party was ready to assess its future in a somewhat different light. The overture from the CLC seemed to

Knowles, Thérèse Casgrain, M. J. Coldwell with portrait of J. S. Woodsworth in the background. CCF convention, Montreal 1958. (Courtesy of Photo Illustrations of Canada, Montreal)

suggest there might yet be room on the Canadian political stage for a reform party of the left, one that — thanks to the labour movement — might be able to reach more people. In the summer of 1958, therefore, at the CCF convention held in Montreal, a parallel resolution to that of the CLC was passed. It even repeated the same words about the need for "a broadly based people's political movement" and stressed the "identity of the CCF program with the social objectives of labour."[2]

Since both the CLC and the CCF resolutions included instructions to the executive to get on with the job and report back by the next convention two years later, it remained only to find the link between the two. Knowles was to be it. As vice-president of both the CLC and the CCF he was the obvious choice to chair a national committee for the new party. For the next three years he co-ordinated the activities of that twenty-member committee consisting of ten people from the CLC and ten from the CCF. He chaired committee meetings and ensured that the ideas expressed there were realized. He badgered sub-committee chairmen to keep them at their task of drafting programmes and constitutions. He supervised the activities of an organizer whose job it was to arrange study groups all over the country. He presided over the details for the founding convention. He spoke all over the country, contributed pieces to the popular press, and even wrote a book. And when it was all over he tidied up.

Not that that was his only job during his four years with the Canadian Labour Congress. As one of two executive vice-presidents, he had departments to supervise that matched his interests, talents, and experience. Where the other vice-president, Bill Dodge, oversaw the largest department in the CLC, that concerning union organization, Knowles' more public and political background attached him to what might be termed the external affairs of the Congress. Individual directors headed the four branches for which he had responsibility — legislation and government employees, education, public relations, and international affairs — and like a cabinet minister, Knowles let them run their departments without interference. If there were problems the directors came to him; he then spoke for them at executive meetings of the Congress and took their concerns into the public arena. For example, he watched over the drafting of the CLC's annual brief to government with its proposals for legislative changes in such fields as minimum wages, hours of work, holidays with pay, housing, and the old age pension. Knowles had previously been urging such matters on the government from the opposition side of the House of Commons; now he was doing the same thing from down the road in Ottawa and with the backing of the union movement across the country. Often indeed he had to undertake the popularizing of the legislative proposals among union members themselves; that too was his former political work in a new guise.

Indeed, the educational functions of the CLC were extensive and were also part of Knowles' responsibility. Seminars and courses for union members were organized all across the country, with instruction in everything from trade union principles and collective bargaining to parliamentary procedure and public speaking. Plans were also under way for the formation of the Labour College of Canada officially inaugurated in 1962 to provide summer-long university-level courses for union members in labour history, political science, economics, sociology, and labour law.

As with any executive position, there were numerous meetings to attend. The CLC executive met; the executive council, a somewhat larger group, met. The nine provincial federations of labour of the time each had annual conventions and someone from the head office of the CLC was expected to be there. The various city labour councils had meetings and they too wanted someone from the CLC executive. When the press sought statements from the union movement, it too came to the executive. Then there were all manner of invitations that came pouring in to speak to this gathering or that luncheon. It was all part of the public relations task, much of which fell to Knowles. Although he dislikes both after-dinner speeches and the boards of trade to whom he had most often to give such speeches, he did consider it a challenge to speak to some of the most powerful members of a given community and to convince them that the union movement was not as bad as they thought.

In the realm of international affairs, Knowles was responsible for the policies of the CLC regarding similar union centrals in other countries. He also had to maintain some of the direct contacts with those bodies. He therefore travelled to Europe, to South America, to Scandinavia, and to England to attend union conventions in various countries. He was also, in the language of the International Labour Organization the "workers' delegate" from Canada to the annual meetings of the ILO in Geneva in June 1959, 1960, and 1961. Delegations to those meetings are made up of representatives from government, management, and labour, and their respective advisers; they are officially named and their expenses borne by the government. But the ILO stipulates that the management and labour delegates cannot be chosen by government but rather by their respective representative body. Thus when the CLC indicated its wish to have Knowles as the worker's delegate on the Canadian delegation, the government had to agree. Prime Minister Diefenbaker was obliged to swallow his annoyance with Knowles over the refusal of the Speakership and let him go. On other occasions, however, such as the meetings of UNESCO in Paris in 1958, Diefenbaker refused to name Knowles and reportedly snapped that he wouldn't nominate him for dog-catcher.[3]

The purpose of the ILO — one of the few enduring institutions of the peace arrangements in 1919 after the First World War — is to improve the standards and conditions under which people work. Such a purpose necessitates demands for improved safety, health and living conditions, wages and pensions. All of those had been Knowles' concerns as well since the early 1930s. As he admits, "Everything in the field of social progress moves too slowly"[4] but the ILO does at least provide an international forum to start things moving. And when ILO conventions are passed and ratified by member countries they tend to become world standards. Although the ILO attempts to avoid politics, it is never entirely successful and has become less so since the time when Knowles was there. Still, says Knowles, "politics isn't that bad a word."[5] Moreover, political affinities between delegates have the various workers' representatives from different countries displaying more in common with each other than with the representatives of management or government from their own country. That was certainly the case for the Canadian workers' delegate and his advisers in the early 1960s and Knowles took advantage of it in organizing the one or two social occasions that are required in any kind of international gathering. He had each member of his group invite a counterpart from a different country and they would have a small dinner party together.

In many ways the jaunts to the ILO were a holiday for Knowles. For besides his full-time job as executive vice-president of the Canadian Labour Congress, Knowles was also pursuing the new party. To do so was not a matter of incompatibility of aim but rather one of time. There were never enough hours in a day. But during his annual stay in Geneva, he could let the new party idea take its course. The respite was good for him and necessary for the new party.

There were, for example, still a number of sceptics within the union movement itself. All one million members of the CLC were not necessarily favourable to the CCF or to a new party. One of Knowles' many tasks, therefore, was to convince the unconvinced among the union membership. He had to make clear something which is still the case today: the CLC as an organization never intended to affiliate with the new party. It wanted to maintain its own independence and freedom to criticize or support, depending on policies or issues. But it did intend to give leadership and direction to its own members about what it considered to be a sensible course of political action. Members were always free to make their own political decisions and individual union locals could decide for themselves whether to affiliate to the new party or not. The executive of the CLC would be prohibited from holding concurrent executive positions in the new party. What was developed in the late 1950s is the pattern in the 1980s: the CLC is not affiliated to the NDP but it does say publicly — and often strongly — that the party is closer than the others to the interests of working people. Technically, therefore, as Knowles is careful to point out, the CLC is not the father of the NDP, but, as he hastens to add, it certainly facilitated the birth.

Many of the people involved were also old friends and colleagues. On the national committee for the new party were CCF members in the CLC group and union members in the CCF group. Many of them had been at both the CLC and the CCF conventions and had had a hand in the drafting and passing of the parallel resolutions. Only one of the CLC members, Frank Hall, was actually unsympathetic to the CCF to begin with but after working on the committee, he became very enthusiastic. Knowles recalls that at the CLC convention in Montreal in 1960 where the political question was hotly debated, he asked Hall to identify a particular speaker. "I don't know" was the reply, "but I think he's one of ours." Knowles turned to him in great delight and said, "Frank, this is a wonderful moment."[6]

Hall's eventual enthusiasm reflected that of the members of the national committee. Of that group Knowles remarked that it "did one of the nicest jobs of organization, education, propaganda if you want to call it that, and hard work that I've seen done."[7] He also acknowledged in the preface to his book *The New Party* that "During my years in Canadian politics I have experienced nothing more exciting than the development of the New Party." Those lines, written in 1960, are still true for him more than twenty years later. He also thinks that the experiment was successful: the building during those three years led to a number of NDP provincial governments and to a strong voice in the federal House.

Although the national committee knew the direction in which it was heading, it was also determined that the new political grouping be as much a "people's party" as possible. Discussion about the purpose and the means of the new party was to take place in small groups all across the country and the eventual party was to be an outgrowth of that process. The first of a series of brief publications sponsored by the national commitee was a pamphlet entitled *A New Party for Canada?* which raised a number of questions about the very need for such a venture and provided the basis for local study sessions. From those study sessions would then emerge the design for the next step. The format pleased Knowles; indeed he encouraged it. There need be no rush — in fact the initial tentative timetable of two years stretched to three — for there would not be another federal election for at least four years. Moreover, the pattern of small study sessions drew on a CCF tradition and Knowles knew of it from his own activities in Winnipeg in the early 1930s. He still believes such a format to be necessary: "When political parties and political party organizations can spend time studying issues of substance instead of just organizing for elections, canvassing for members and holding events to raise money . . . the situation is much healthier."[8]

Money was of course a major requirement in order to develop a new political party and canvassing for it was one of the tasks of the various members of the national committee. Gradually they were successful. Contributions came from unions and they were substantial. Knowles recalled seeing the first cheque for ten or fifteen thosand dollars; he had never seen a cheque for such an amount and he "nearly went through the floor."[9] The money permitted the hiring of organizers who then facilitated the establishing of small groups in cities, towns, and rural areas to ponder and propose programmes for the new party. As contributions grew, the national committee was able to do more printing, distributing and translating. Every document that emerged from the national committee was in both French and English, something that was quite rare in Canada at the time.

Once reactions from the various study groups were received, the national committee published more brochures. A study paper on the constitution of the party came next, followed by one on its programme. These documents also went the rounds of group discussion throughout Canada where they were altered, revised, thought over, developed, rejected, accepted. It took time but it was necessary. When the various reactions had been gathered by the national committee, an actual draft programme and draft constitution were printed and once again distributed across the land. Anyone connected in any way with the study sessions anywhere in Canada was encouraged to send resolutions for consideration at

the founding convention which would design the official programme. The resolutions could propose changes to the draft
programme and constitution or could be new resolutions dealing
with matters that had not been touched on at all in the preliminary
discussions. The resolutions rained in. Put together in a book of
one hundred pages for the convention, they were much more
voluminous than any of the publications of the national committee. The new party was intended to be and it actually was a
popular movement. Knowles will acknowledge that the national
committee gave direction, organization, and impetus, and he as an
individual did much of that too, but he insists that twenty people
could never have accomplished all that went into the making of
the New Democratic Party.

His favourite example of the changes the founding convention
made to initial proposals concerns the Senate. The national
committee had heatedly debated the position the new party
should take on the Senate. On one side were people like Knowles,
long time members of the CCF, who stuck to their original belief
that the Senate should be abolished. On the other were
newcomers, less convinced of the uselessness of the Senate and
who argued for reform. On a vote in committee the latter won. At
a subsequent meeting, however, it was decided to leave the
question of the Senate out of the draft programme entirely. There
was just too much division within the commitee itself. So the draft
programme went to the founding convention without any mention
of the Senate at all. The founding convention spotted the lapse
and immediately produced a resolution from the floor: something
had to be said about the Senate and that something should be total
abolition. Knowles was tickled, both because the resolution
matched his own sentiments, and because it indicated what could
come from the floor of the convention itself.

All the pre-convention activity attracted the attention of the
press, radio, television, and even publishing houses. That of
course was just what the national committee hoped for since such
publicity would be free. The now defunct *Star Weekly* asked
Knowles to take part in a printed debate about the new party.
Hugh Garner would respond in the negative to the query "Do we
need this new CCF party?" and Knowles would answer for the
affirmative. The two positions appeared in the issue of 6 August
1960. The *Globe and Mail* picked up the flurry of activity in July
1961 and ran a series on Canada's political parties; Knowles wrote
about the new democratic socialist party that was about to be
born. He also wrote for the *Canadian Commentator* and was even
asked to write a book about the new party for the Toronto

publisher McClelland and Stewart. His reaction was astonishment: in the midst of all his CLC and new party activities, how
could he possibly write a book? But the people with whom he
discussed it simply said he had to do it.

"How in the world does one write a book?" he asked himself
as he hid away one weekend in a CLC office without a phone. The
answer seemed simple enough "Guess the only way to write a
book is to start."[10] So he sat down and wrote the first sentence
"This is a book about an unfinished story in Canadian politics."
That sentence stayed as he went on to write, and subsequently to
alter, the others. He wrote at CLC headquarters; he wrote in
airplanes; he wrote in hotel rooms while attending meetings
across the country. And he finished in time to meet the
publisher's deadline, not knowing that publishers count on their
authors not meeting deadlines. The manuscript was ready by the
end of December 1960 and it went to McClelland and Stewart for
publishing and for negotiating with the recently formed Editions
du Jour in Montreal which wanted to inaugurate its new
publishing house with a French version of *The New Party*. At the
launching of *Le nouveau parti,* in the spring of 1961, Knowles
encountered Pierre Trudeau whom he had met in various CCF
gatherings before. To the Trudeau of 1961, Knowles' book was
not far enough to the left.[11] But the book, in French or in English,
was an indication of the interest and excitement that the new party
idea had aroused in Canada. Even Jack McClelland remarked to
Knowles after reading the first few chapters of the manuscript that
he was almost convinced.[12]

In the midst of all the activities — indeed part of them — were
the conventions to which the CLC and the CCF executive were to
report. The CLC met in Montreal in April 1960 and the CCF in
Regina in August; both wanted to know what progress had been
made towards the new party. Knowles was at both but more
comfortable with the first. There the political question was
debated heatedly but basically in a friendly fashion. The
delegates' enthusiasm was infectious; they were creating something new, and they instructed the executive "to assist by all
appropriate means in the preparations for and in the calling of a
Founding Convention."[13] The CCF convention a few months later
passed a similar resolution but a shadow hung over that body.
There had been simmering difficulties with the eight-member
parliamentary caucus, the handful of MPs who had survived the
Diefenbaker sweep in 1958, and the difficulties crystallized
around the question of the leadership at the convention. M. J.
Coldwell was still the leader although he no longer had a seat in

the House of Commons. There, Hazen Argue, as House leader, directed the tiny CCF group. It was time, the caucus contended, to have Argue become the party leader; indeed if he did not do so the caucus would not have him back as House leader.

Most of the members of the national committee for the new party, however, preferred to have Coldwell continue until the new party was formed and the CCF presumably coalesced with it. At that point a new leader for the new party could be chosen. They were prepared to offer Argue the somewhat more prestigious title of parliamentary leader. But Argue was not content. Nor was Coldwell willing to force a leadership election on the issue; he would consent to stay on as national leader until the founding of the new party only if the convention was unanimous. Since that unanimity was not forthcoming, he would not stand at all. Argue thus became national leader of the CCF. It was a bitter episode, one of the unhappier incidents that the CCF had experienced, and Knowles deliberately downplayed it in his taped recollections. Nor did the scar of that convention ever heal. It reopened only a short time after the founding convention of the new party when Argue, having been defeated by Tommy Douglas for the leadership, joined the Liberal party. Old CCF members have maintained their unhappiness by not having Argue's photograph among those of the other former leaders of the CCF.

Shadows and scars were, however, well concealed as the plans were made for the founding convention of the new party to be held in Ottawa in mid-summer 1961. Knowles once again supervised the activities and the CLC provided facilities and the expertise in organizing conventions. The motif of the new party appeared as a stylized parliament in green: the new party was going to instill life into the political process. And it was going to do it in both languages.

More than two thousand delegates joined Knowles in the Ottawa Coliseum on 31 July 1961. There he presided over the opening of the founding convention. He greeted the mayor, Charlotte Whitton, who arrived furious with the Chief of Police for being responsible for her delay in the city traffic. He arranged the seating on the platform: the members of the national committee were to be there and so too were the aspirants for the role of leader; he carefully sat Tommy Douglas and Hazen Argue equidistant from the podium. In the crowd he knew some faces but many more were new. They would be the people to take the old CCF one step further, to broaden its popular appeal, and to formulate its policies for the 1960s. For five days they would discuss everything from agriculture to the arts, from foreign

Accompanying the mayor of Ottawa, Charlotte Whitton, to the opening session of the founding convention of the New Democratic Party. Ottawa 1961. (Dominion-Wide photographs, Ottawa)

affairs to federalism, from full employment in a planned economy to the peaceful uses of nuclear energy, from consumer protection to progressive taxation. What they did not cover they left over to the new party's council and executive to cope with. As an officer of the CLC Knowles would not be on that executive but he had been around in the very early days of the CCF in the 1930s and now he was presiding over a new generation creating a similar but different party. He knew what the CCF had done for Canada in the preceding thirty years — indeed he had done much of it himself — and he hoped this new party, to be named during the convention the New Democratic Party, would be able to do as much in the next thirty years. No doubt he also hoped to be part of that activity. There would probably be an election in 1962.

For five days he was there, making sure that all went smoothly. And when it was all over, he was still there, compulsively clearing things away. The press caught him at it: "Last of all, when everyone else had gone, the slim, bent figure of Stanley Knowles prowled the deserted platform, tidying it all up. It was fitting that this man who perhaps had more to do with founding the new party than any other should linger a little while pondering it with his handiwork."[14]

14
ESCALATION

19 December 1969

Elected in all four of the federal elections in the 1960s, Knowles was in his usual place in the Commons late that December afternoon. He knew the government was about to interrupt the business of the day to make a special announcement and he knew that it would be of some interest to him. What he did not know was that the president of the Treasury Board was about to announce the winning of one of Knowles' twenty-five year battles. He had known it would be won some day and there had even been recent indications that victory was closer than ever. But still there had been nothing definite. Then came the announcement from Charles Drury. The government had decided to bring in legislation to provide for the escalation of pensions for retired federal public servants and other related groups. Knowles was close to tears.

Just that morning he had asked Drury what was probably his thousandth question on the matter:

In view of the action of the government of Ontario in granting substantial increases in the pensions of its retired civil servants, and in view of the concern for federal superannuates felt by members of all parties in this House, will the government now consider taking action to increase the pensions of federal superannuates?[1]

Drury could not miss the import of the question; some of his own Liberal colleagues were among those Knowles referred to as being concerned. He also knew what he intended to announce later in the day but he could not resist dangling his inquisitor along for a while yet. His reply did, however, contain more than the usual 'government-is-considering' generality: "As the honourable member is, I think, aware intensive discussions and consultations are now taking place on this very subject."² But he gave no indication that a major announcement on the subject was forthcoming. For once, Knowles did not trouble with a supplementary question. Drury's answer sounded positive. 'Intensive discussions' meant more than 'consideration' and had to result in something. He accepted the answer and no doubt began mentally formulating his thousand-and-first question.

On the other side of the Commons, Drury assumed that Knowles knew what was coming that afternoon. The parliamentary grapevine winds around all members and even if it had not reached Knowles, he had a direct contact in the Treasury board itself. His son David was an economist with the Board and was working on the very issue his father had been nagging the government about since David was a tot in Winnipeg. Surely Knowles must know. But he had not had the slightest hint. Certainly not from David: father and son had long since agreed that the MP might tell his civil servant son of his doings but the son would not reciprocate. Knowles had even driven to work with David that morning, the son knowing full well that his father was about to receive one of the great thrills of his parliamentary life later that afternoon. Not a word was breathed.

To his amazement and delight, therefore the announcement came in the afternoon: "Mr Speaker, I am pleased to be able to inform honourable members that the government will be introducing legislation, following the Christmas recess, to provide for increases in the pensions of retired public servants and their surviving dependants."³ And he went on to outline the escalation provisions.

Announcements like that do not come every day in parliament. But like any other, it did call for some acknowledgement by a spokesman for each of the other parties. Following the party standings, Robert Stanfield spoke for the Conservatives and then Knowles for the NDP. Stanfield's was a begrudging word of thanks; Knowles recorded his delight:

Mr Speaker, I have waited for about twenty-five years to be able to make the statement I am very happy to make. Like the Leader of the Official Opposition I could find areas for criticism, but the first word I want to say is that there are 35,000 retired civil servants and 17,000 widows of retired civil servants plus many thousands of pensioners from the RCMP and the Armed Forces who will say tonight. 'Well this is a Merry Christmas after all.'⁴

The speech continued and he could not refrain from mentioning that the pensioners of the CNR ought to be included and that the ceiling of two percent on the escalation ought to be lifted. But basically he was pleased. It had been a twenty-five year battle and he had won.

It all began in 1944. A small group of retired civil servants in Winnipeg had come to him to outline their case. Led by a Sam Carberry who lived long enough to benefit from the fight he was asking Knowles to undertake, the group pointed out the difficulties they had trying to make ends meet with their admittedly small but what was worse, fixed, government pensions. The amount of their pension was the same from the day of retirement to the day of death and already by the mid-war years they were starting to feel the pinch. Shouldn't the young member for Winnipeg North Centre take up their cause?

He thought so too. Not that there were that many retired civil servants in Winnipeg but there were thousands more across the country. Knowles knew that if one could just get the government to initiate such a step, private employers would be pressured into following suit. Moreover, there was the elemental justice of the argument behind the particular case: "Just as people in the working years of their lives have the chance to fight for and to get increases in their wages and salaries and with it some increase in their standard of living, so people who are retired should have that opportunity, should not be condemned to a fixed level of income for all their remaining years which, taken together with the rises in the cost of living, means a declining standard of living."[5] Knowles took up the cause, little realizing that he was engaging a good part of his energies for the next twenty-five years.

True, there were some small changes along the way. In 1959, for example, the Diefenbaker government passed a Public Service Pension Adjustment Act which increased the pension on a once-only basis and restricted even that fixed increase to certain long-time retirees. There was no mention of the principle of escalation for present or future retired public servants. A few private companies here and there introduced an escalating clause into their pension arrangements but even today barely five percent of the pension plans in the private sector have such benefits. There was also the Canada Pension Plan, passed in 1965, with escalation limited to two percent a year to begin taking effect in 1968. As of 1966 the same limited escalation was added to the Old Age Security. And even with Knowles' victory in 1969 which provided for the escalation of the pensions of retired civil servants and even with the removal of the two percent ceiling in 1972, still a decade later, only one-third of all pension plans in Canada provide any form of escalation. For most retired people, their standard of living declines as the cost of living soars. Knowles' principle is still far from being universally recognized.

In 1944 then he began what would turn into a twenty-five year public nag. He asked questions in the House of Commons and embarrassed ministers year after year by exposing their deliberately vague replies. He put written questions on the Order Paper and thereby forced officials in various government departments to dig up the statistical material he demanded. Indeed, his questions, coming as frequently and insistently as they did, became something of a standing joke within the departments in question. "There's the Knowles' question again — if he ever alters it, he'll throw the computers all out."[6] Always he wanted to know how many retired civil servants drew pensions of such and such an amount? How many retired RCMP? How many retired forces personnel? How many retired CNR workers? Nag, nag, nag.

The direct questions, verbal or written, and presented during question period were only part of the battle. Whenever he felt he had received an inadequate response and once the parliamentary day began allowing for it in 1964, he would bring the question up again during the half hour "late show" by which a certain number of questions with strict time limits on both query and response could be put to the government. Ten or twelve times during a session Knowles would be on the late show with yet another question for the Treasury Board president, the one responsible for civil service pensions. When Drury was in that position from 1968 he would always stay for the Knowles' question and answer it himself, unlike other ministers who frequently departed early and left their parliamentary secretaries to answer for them.

Then there were speeches on any and all occasions. During the debate following the Throne Speech Knowles was always ready with his argument for escalated pensions. During the budget debate too he trotted out the principle once more. Whenever any legislation came before parliament that touched pensions in general or those of the public service in particular, he would jump into the debate, arguing, insisting, demanding, cajoling, pleading. The government would have to learn, even if it took years, that the only way to shut him up was to do as he asked. As the years did begin to pile up, and Knowles' questions and speeches with them, people began to think this particular task was his sole reason for being. His single-mindedness sometimes disturbs even his supporters but they cannot deny that eventually it pays off and he wins.

Over the years too supporters on this issue began to pile up as well. Other MPs who had retired civil servants in their ridings were more than welcome on his one-man bandwagon. Gradually they climbed aboard: Conservative and Liberal MPs from Ottawa; Conservative, Liberal, and NDP MPs from British Columbia. Groups of retired civil servants across the country soon recognized that they had a champion in Knowles and when they formed a national association of federal superannuates, they followed his example by lobbying susceptible MPs and bombarding the government with briefs. When the Public Service Alliance of Canada was formed in 1967, it too took up the cause, urging in both general and special presentations to the government the necessity of adding an escalating clause to its pension plans. The Professional Institute of the Public Service did the same; indeed some of the more pathetic cases that came to Knowles' attention were from people who had been senior civil servants and who were now in desperate circumstances on their fixed pension. Added to the clamour were the voices of particular unions representing certain groups of public servants. The postal workers, for example, undertook extensive research into their international colleagues' pension plans. They stuffed their briefs with statistics to show that the government paid out less in pensions than the amount of interest that was credited to the public service superannuation account.

Confronted with such material the government fell back on actuarial excuses. As pension plan experts insist, there must be sufficient credit in any superannuation account to cover pensions for all present and former employees should the employer go out of business. Knowles' reply is that may be all very well for private companies (and this is another of his arguments in favour of state pensions) but it is absurd for governments. Governments do not go out of business; countries do not go out of business. Moreover, pensions are not, as too many people continue to think, paid out of a fixed pot of actual dollars set aside for that purpose. They are a pay-as-you-go proposition: working people now produce goods and services, part of the benefits of which go to presently retired people in return for the contribution they made to the economy when they were working.

The continuing campaign of questions, speeches, briefs, lobbying, and explanations had eventually to lead to some result. Whenever an occasion in the House permitted and anything to do with pensions was being sent off for committee study, Knowles would request that his demand for escalation be added to the committees's work. That approach was finally productive after the

Canada Pension Plan came into being in 1966. One of the questions raised by its introduction was the relationship between it and existing pension plans. The CPP was not intended to supersede other pensions; indeed it was instituted to ensure that those people (still today more than half of all the employed in Canada) whose employers offered no pension at all would have some retirement benefits when they ceased working. But what about those people who did have pension plans? How were they to be fitted in with the CPP? There were two possibilities: either keep the CPP and the other pension plan separate — "stacked" in pension jargon — or join the two together in an "integrated" plan.

The federal government decided on integration for its various public servants' pension plans and prepared the necessary legislation for the parliamentary session of 1966-67. At the same time, the issue of collective bargaining in the public service was before the House, along with other matters concerning the civil service. To deal with the various pieces of legislation the government established a special joint committee on the public service in May 1966. Knowles was among the MPs and senators named to it. In his own mind, the committee would be an ideal place for discussing the escalation or retired civil servants' pensions. But that was not among the many matters referred to it. Knowles raised the possibility in House in June and elicited from Edgar Benson, the national revenue minister, an agreement that if the joint committee completed its huge work load it might well look at the question of escalation. Knowles held Benson to what he considered a commitment and reiterated it througout the autumn of 1966 while the committee waded through the four complex bills it was considering. By January 1967 he was beginning to think the government was stalling: the parliamentary session had to come to an end soon and the committee would vanish. Even when he did succeed in having the question referred to the committee at the end of the month he had to wheedle the committee chairman into calling a meeting and then the government itself into ensuring the committee reported back to the House before the end of the session.

It was a close call. The committee, with the addition of some new members who were particularly interested in the question, worked steadily with Knowles goading it on. Not only did it have to convince some of its own members of the value and necessity of the measure — Conservative senators on the committee, protectors of the financial community, were as aware as Knowles of the long-term implications of such a move — but it also had to

cope with thorny practical problems. How far should escalation
go? Should it be applied equally to all pensions? Should it be
scaled, with longer retirees receiving higher escalation? How was
it to be paid for? And did the committee deliberately wish to
establish a principle for the future? The questions were vast and
complex. Could the committee ever agree among itself let alone
produce a report and urge the government to action?

Just as it began to agree on a position, the parliamentary clock
began to run down and with it the life of all unfinished business.
Knowles was anxious: this was the closest he had come and the
committee had almost arrived at an unanimous agreement. But
now the members were scattered for a brief Easter recess and they
would only return for a brief sitting on 8 May, just the time for the
government to bring the session to a close. Knowles pleaded with
cabinet ministers that it would be unfair to have all that work
wiped out and convinced the government House leader to have
one more meeting of the committee on the very morning of 8
May. There it completed its report and rushed it off to the Commons
for presentation. The report recommended unanimously that
escalation be added to the pensions of retired federal employees
by an amendment to the Public Service Pension Adjustment Act
of 1959. No sooner was the report tabled than Knowles wanted to
know when the government would take action on it. The
somewhat testy reply was that after all the report had only just
arrived but that the government would consider it. Knowles
thought he had won the battle. Some newspapers thought so too
and began printing stories about the twenty-three year battle of
the member for Winnipeg North Centre.

But nothing happened. Knowles therefore reached into his bag
of tricks and prepared to keep pestering the government for the
next twenty-three years. In the bag of tricks now he had the
committee report from the spring of 1967 and he could keep
referring to it. The government even gave him the chance to make
a lengthy speech when it introduced a series of highly technical
amendments to various pension acts covering different groups of
public servants in March 1969. When introducing the amendments Treasury Board President Drury actually apologized that
there would be no amendments to the Public Service Pension
Adjustment Act, as the committee report from 1967 had urged,
but he did assure the House that the government was continuing
to study the matter. At the time Knowles merely registered one
more rebuff but he realized later than things had in fact been
moving, albeit at the normal snail's pace of most social legislation.
But he did make his speech, most of it emphasizing what was not

in the legislation before the House. And he was gratified by the fact that almost all the speeches following his echoed the same sentiments, some even using his own words. The speakers came from all sides of the House, many of them indeed had been on the special committee with him to study the question of escalation in the early spring of 1967.

And then came the great surprise and gift for him when the announcement was made in December 1969. Legislation followed in March 1970 in the form of a Supplementary Retirement Benefits Act to provide for the escalation of the pensions of seventeen different groups of retired government employees, something Knowles had been pleading for since 1944. To his chagrin, however, one of the groups included were members of parliament. He had no objection to their pensions being escalated, but this bill did more than that. It actually introduced a new formula for the pensions of former MPs which would raise the amount from the former figure of three thousand dollars a year to nine thousand. He was disgusted and even ashamed. While escalation now seemed admissible for others, MPs were to have a better pension as well. Needless to say, he was caught; he could and did fight that aspect, but he could not oppose the entire bill. At least the principle of escalation had been established for a large group of people. And Knowles was sure that it would eventually be extended to other pension plans. The principle that he had recognized back in 1944 and had agreed to fight for was now law.

The shortcoming was that the escalation was limited to two percent, the same ceiling that had been affixed to the CPP and the Old Age Security. Knowles had not liked the limit at that time and he liked it even less now. Perhaps the government was merely tossing him another bone to worry for the next quarter century. Certainly he set to it immediately. It was all very well to make the two percent retroactive for retired civil servants although only in the sense that the first pension cheques to go out under the new law were adjusted to represent the amount the pension would have been had it been escalated since its inception at two percent per year. His old friend Sam Carberry in Winnipeg got a fat cheque. But still, if a fixed pension is wrong, so too is fixed escalation. Knowles argued that fixed escalation was a contradiction in terms, and given the inflation of the 1970s and the increased longevity of people, it was also an insult. By 1972 the Liberal government appeared to agree for it removed the ceiling from the Supplementary Retirement Benefits Act, the Old Age Security, the Guaranteed Income Supplement, and the Canada

Pension Plan. Since then escalation has matched the rise in the cost of living as measured by the Consumer Price Index.

Even then Knowles refused to let go. He argued that the pensions of employees in enterprises that come under federal government jurisdiction should also be escalated and without a ceiling. Bank employees, railway employees should all be covered by such a scheme. Where the CNR might choose, out of the generosity of its heart, to add an escalation provision once in a while, but for a limited period of time, Knowles insisted that it was not good enough. He would like to see the various Pension Benefits Standards Act — umbrella legislation at both the federal and some provincial levels that regulates private pension plans — amended to include the provision for escalation.

Even if all that were done he would still not be content. The formula used for the escalation of pensions leaves him unhappy. The calculation, although attached to changes in the cost of living, is always slightly out of date. The quarterly increases in the Old Age Security, for example, are based on a comparison of the Consumer Price Index for the previous three months with that of the three months prior to that. Surely, Knowles will contend, in an age of computers we ought to be able to match the pension sums to this month's rise in the cost of living, or even to next month's. And then he begins to speculate about whether the cost of living is an accurate index for the needs of retired persons. They have special needs; shouldn't a special index be devised for them?

Ultimately he contends that the cost of living should not be the index at all. Rather the standard of living should be the criterion for the escalation of pensions. When a cost of living formula is used, it simply means that retired people are enabled to maintain the standard of living that was theirs at the time of their retirement. The cost of living index, based as it is on the Consumer Price Index, is simply the percentage rise over a given period of time in the prices of a particular set of commodities. A person retired in 1949 is thus at least assured that he can still buy a pound of butter. But supposing he wishes to buy a coloured television? Such an item was unknown in 1949 and represents an increase in the standard of living. When other people's standard of living continued to rise in the early 1970s, why shouldn't that of retired persons?

The same question has been asked by two different groups of people and unwittingly confirmed by a third. After much consultation among veterans' associations and government officials in the early 1970s, it was proposed that the pensions for disabled veterans be equivalent to the average salary of people in

the five lowest categories of the civil service. In 1973 the
government did so but limited the comparison to one year after
which the pensions would, like other government pensions,
increase solely by means of escalation as attached to the cost of
living. The veterans claim this is not good enough. If their
pensions are to be similar to certain salaries in the civil service at a
given moment, they should go on being similar. As those salaries
are increased so too should the basic level of the disability
pension. Needless to say, Knowles has many friends and admirers
in the various veterans' organizations.

A second group that raised the same issue was the National
Council of Welfare. A government appointed and financed body,
the Council nonetheless has a certain autonomy in its work and its
reports. One of those reports, in the early 1970s, was on income

"if necessary, he's ready and armed for the fray." Ottawa 1982.
(Reprinted with permission, *The Toronto Star*)

security and part of it concerned senior citizens. The Council urged that for pensioners the cost of living index should at least be adjusted to reflect what they actually have to buy. But it would prefer to see pensions increased according to increases in the standard of living with the calculation done by using the wage index or the gross national product as guides.

In 1975 members of parliament showed that such calculations were quite possible, at least for themselves. By doing so they proved Knowles' point but they also infuriated him. That year he succeeded in blocking a proposed fifty percent increase in MPs' salaries. The government retaliated by suggesting a thirty-three percent increase in the salaries and a provision for their escalation according to the rise in the Industrial Composite Index. That index is based on wages and is a more accurate guage of the rising standard of living than is the Consumer Price Index. Under pressure, the government did limit the increases thus calculated to seven percent. But the entire proposal as implemented was an acknowledgement that the Consumer Price Index was inappropriate for members of parliament. For other Canadians, however, already favoured just by having escalating clauses in their public pension plans, it was quite good enough.

Although Knowles frequently looks as if he had no blood in him at all, let alone any heat to boil it with, this question makes his blood boil. He can even produce some strong, albeit quaint, language to express his anger: "By all the gods of war, I don't intend to sit quiet or rest when we can do that for ourselves and can't do it for pensioners generally."[7] He hopes it will not take another twenty-five year battle, but if necessary, he's ready and armed for the fray.

15
BEST SUPPORTING ACTOR

25 August 1974

He was in Brandon that day, attending to some of his functions as Chancellor of the University, a position he has held since 1970. By evening he was back in his hotel in time to catch the national news. The first item was the death of M. J. Coldwell, former leader of the CCF and a close colleague and friend. Although the news bulletin did not mention it, Coldwell took part of Knowles with him into death. It was more than having been mistaken for him and frequently greeted on the street as "Mr. Coldwell" — as indeed he has been taken for Mr. Woodsworth and even Mr. Douglas and sometims for the former Conservative leader Robert Stanfield ("We're both tall and thin and look a little lost," he mused.[1]) He had worked beside Coldwell in the House of Commons from 1943 until 1958 and the link between them was more than official: it had developed into a close personal friendship. Then too, there was Coldwell's influence upon him. Indeed he claims that all the leaders of the CCF and the subsequent NDP — to all of whom except the first he has played the supporting role — would be on any short list he made of people who have influenced his life and for whom he has great respect.

Woodsworth and Coldwell were both of Knowles' father's generation and he reserved for them the esteem in which he had held his own father. For Coldwell, with whom he worked much more closely, he added the affection he also had for his father. Woodsworth was more awe-inspiring: he was not a brilliant orator but commanded attention because of his presence and saintly ways. Knowles first met him 1929 at a conference of the

Student Christian Movement in Jasper, Alberta. That summer Knowles, aged twenty-one, had just completed his second year of studies at Brandon College and had charge of a summer mission field for the Baptist Church at Reston, Manitoba. He was to be the one Brandon student delegate to the SCM conference, where political, social, and religious topics were discussed. Indeed in the days before the establishment of political clubs on campuses, the SCM was a centre for budding social gospellers, young people anxious to attach their religion to contemporary social questions. SCM conferences always had major figures as invited speakers. In 1929 at Jasper, J. S. Woodsworth lectured on the economy and social conditions and he joined the students in their discussions. Everyone — young Knowles included — was impressed with the directness and honesty of the man.

So impressed was he indeed that he cast his first Canadian vote for Woodsworth. During the federal election of 1930 Knowles was living in Winnipeg North Centre and the enumerator assured him that he had the right to vote. After all, his parents had been born in Canada and he had come to the country before he was twenty-one: of course he could vote. Knowles was delighted although his father in Los Angeles was less enthusiastic. To vote in a foreign country, even if the elder Knowles would have approved his son's choice of candidate, meant pulling away from the United States. That, his father was convinced, was a mistake. The son voted anyway.

When the time came for Knowles himself to run in an election — in 1935 — the question of his national status arose again. Was he in fact eligible to run? He took the problem to his member of parliament, just as so many constituents have done then and since. Woodsworth recognized that the question of Knowles' citizenship was one for the secretary of state, Charles Cahan, but he did not think that he, as an MP, should approach the minister. To Woodsworth, the role of a member of parliament was to make policies and develop legislation; it was not to be a case worker, administrator, civil servant, or ombudsman. Perhaps it was right that Woodsworth should pass from the scene in the early 1940s; since then the MP's role has become very much what he shunned. Perhaps one-third of Knowles' time is spent on such non-legislative matters: a sample of his correspondence revealed eighty-six replies (all of which he wrote himself) from his office in a three-day period and of that number over a third entailed additional correspondence with officials of the government or civil service. In 1935, Woodsworth passed the query about Knowles' status on to his colleague A. A. Heaps who took the matter up with the secretary of state. Cahan wasn't sure: perhaps Knowles was a Canadian, perhaps he was not. Since he intended to run for parliament he had better straighten the matter out by being naturalized. So he did so and became an official Canadian in 1935.

He and Woodsworth then campaigned beside each other in the election, Woodsworth in Winnipeg North Centre and Knowles in Winnipeg South Centre. The ridings adjoined and the candidates undertook certain functions together, sharing radio broadcasts and shopgating. People were in fact used to seeing the two together. Knowles had frequently invited Woodsworth to speak at the forums he had held in Central United Church before the board announced it could not afford the heat for the auditorium. And Knowles had often been at the Woodsworth home, a virtual open house on Maryland Street. There Woodsworth gathered students and young people about him to discuss religion, politics, and social issues, or sometimes just to chat about a recent trip he had made. Among the young people he may well have spotted Knowles as a spiritual son. He was greatly disappointed when the young minister was defeated, but urged him to find something to keep him alive and active in the CCF until the next election. In the meantime he would put him on his list of recipients of Hansard and Knowles could acquaint himself with the ways and means of the debates of parliament.

Woodsworth's wish to have Knowles as a colleague in the House of Commons was not to be realized. He gave what assistance he could in the election of 1940 but once again the younger man was defeated. Shortly after, in May 1940, a stroke silenced Woodsworth's voice in the House of Commons. For someone who had used the public word all his life, first from the pulpit, then from the platform, and then in the Commons, he was devastated. He wanted to resign on the grounds that he was unable to perform what he believed to be an MP's function — speaking. But others in the party argued that Woodsworth after all had no other source of income and a by-election necessitated by his resignation might develop into an unseemly scramble while the old man was still alive. Woodsworth struggled with the handicap, overcame it in private, but never in public. When he was well enough to return to the Commons in November 1941, he was greeted by kind words from Mackenzie King but Hansard recorded no response. Shortly thereafter he had another stroke.

Knowles had two final encounters with Woodsworth. One was in the autumn of 1940 when the Woodsworths were in Winnipeg to distribute the contents of their family home in preparation for a move to Vancouver. Would Stanley take the old washing machine? And would he take J.S. out to the two-room school that was named for him in the Brooklands area of his riding so that he could donate his dictionary? Knowles did so, speaking for Woodsworth and explaining to the pupils who the frail gentleman standing by the wall was. And then he took him home unaware that the incident would be revived in a droll manner a few years later. The second encounter was just before Christmas in 1941 when Woodsworth was on his way from Ottawa to Vancouver and passing through Winnipeg by train. By then he had had a second stroke and could not leave the train but others could come to him. As they did, Woodsworth was more pleased by a grimy train worker climbing aboard to say hello as soon as he knew Woodsworth was there than he was to see Knowles and other political associates. To them he urged a continuation of the battle against war profiteering and for post-war planning. Both items appeared in Knowles' campaign literature in the subsequent by-election in Winnipeg North Centre to fill the seat vacated by the death of Woodsworth early in 1942.

After winning that by-election Knowles was introduced to the House of Commons in January 1943 by the next leader of the CCF, M. J. Coldwell. Coldwell had been acting leader during Woodsworth's illness and was made the official leader at the biennial convention of the CCF in the summer of 1942. Knowles had first met him during the election campaign of 1935 when Coldwell and Tommy Douglas, both defeated in bids to win seats in the Saskatchewan provincial legislature in 1934, were taking a fling at the federal house. Knowles was impressed by Coldwell's polished oratory, genuineness, and sincerity; he concurred in the view in party circles at the time that Coldwell was the natural successor to Woodsworth as party leader. In that election Coldwell won the Saskatchewan riding of Rosetown-Biggar which he represented for the next twenty-three years.

Just after the election of 1935 Knowles had his first close contact with Coldwell. The national council of the CCF met in Winnipeg to discuss the results. They were disappointing for the fledgling CCF; the campaign had gone so well that the party had dared to hope it might form the official opposition. It was the beginning of many such dreams and the seven seats won in 1935 were a long way from realizing the dream. The national council debated the party's future and there too Knowles was impressed with Coldwell's intellect and skill with a small group. Subsequently he met Coldwell at national conventions of the party and secured his help when he ran unsuccessfully in the election of 1940 and again in the successful by-election of 1942. Later, in the House of Commons, the two became fast friends — so much so that Knowles expected him to call whenever he was passing through Winnipeg.

A year or so after his election, he greeted Coldwell on one such occasion and drove him around the city. He went by the tiny Woodsworth school and told him in minute detail (the way Knowles tells all his stories) of the last occasion he had been there with J. S. Woodsworth for the presentation of the dictionary. Coldwell absorbed it all, more thoroughly than Knowles realized at the time. Two years later Coldwell was once again in Winnipeg and this time accompanied Knowles into the school, where the latter was to speak. Before doing so he introduced the leader of his party and asked him to say a few words. He could hardly contain his surprise as Coldwell launched into his remarks: "As I stand here today, I think of the last time I was here. I remember it very well. It was the last public appearance that Mr. Woodsworth made. I remember his coming into this room and standing back there while Mr. Knowles presented the dictionary on his behalf for he wasn't able to say a word."[2]

The younger MP was startled and embarrassed. Here was his leader, a man whom he admired and respected, making up this story! Is that what politicians did after they had been in the game a while? Would he start doing the same thing? Whatever would the audience think? Knowles assumed the pupils might not know the difference — it had been at least three or four years since he was there with Woodsworth — but the principal was the same. He would know that Coldwell was concocting a story. What would he say?

Fortunately Coldwell also began looking a bit puzzled. As they were leaving the school in the company of the principal, Coldwell admitted his perplexity. "Stanley, I'm a bit puzzled about that occasion when Mr. Woodsworth's dictionary was presented. I don't see how I could be there at that time because I was in Europe at the meetings of the Commonwealth Parliamentary Association."[3] Knowles, tremendously relieved that he did not have to make Coldwell into a liar, explained that in fact he had not been there. Either Knowles' graphic description or Coldwell's own photographic retention of detail had made him think he had been present. Coldwell roared with laughter and continued to do so whenever Knowles retold the tale.

Coldwell's ability to laugh at his own mistakes was one measure of the man. But there were other indications and

Knowles came to admire them all, working as he did so closely with Coldwell first as party whip from 1944 until 1957, then as deputy leader during 1957 and 1958 and throughout the period as a member of the party's national council. Coldwell had a sense of dedication to the CCF cause, an assuredness of the very rightness of it all, that affected everyone around him. He was convinced that one could in fact create a society which was both democratic and socialist, that such a society could indeed distribute the benefits of modern technology to everyone. And he was sure it would happen one day and that the parliamentary process would bring it about. He did not fuss as much with the rules as Knowles did — a small party only needs one such person — but his belief in parliament was unshakeable. So fierce was that belief and so appalled was Coldwell at the shambles parliament became during the pipeline debate in 1956 that he, the epitome of the well-behaved, respectable gentleman, could be seen on one occasion shaking his fist in rage at the Speaker. Coldwell was just as determined to put the social democratic cause in the best possible light. In a country where the press and even the government could interpret a peaceful work stoppage such as the Winnipeg General Strike in 1919 as a bolshevik revolution, socialists had to tread warily. Even Woodsworth had been considered a bit strange: the old-fashioned beard that he wore might well be hiding an anarchist. But no such thoughts could be harboured about M. J. Coldwell. He was urbane, gentlemanly, one of the best speakers in parliament, and received invitations to speak to service clubs and other organizations as far removed from socialism as they could be. No one could doubt the respectability of the CCF with someone like Coldwell at its head. He was a militant fighter but he fought with velvet gloves: one of his main battles was for health insurance as he watched his wife being slowly devoured by multiple sclerosis. Knowles, who knew something of the disease himself after 1946, was impressed by everything about Coldwell.

So too were many other people for after Coldwell was defeated in 1958 and left the leadership of the CCF in 1960, he was offered many functions. The Liberal government named him to a special committee on election expenses in 1964 and some of the results appeared in legislation a decade later. He was also named to a special committee on national defence whose work and results were largely secret. He received honorary degrees and even an honorary membership in the Privy Council, the Queen's advisory council in Canada which normally contains only present and former cabinet ministers. There were even suggestions that he be named to the Senate although most of them came from people who had no power to implement them. Knowles kept a close eye on Coldwell whenever such suggestions were made. Both the old CCF and the NDP were opposed to the Senate and advocated its abolition. How could Coldwell even consider the possibility of a Senate seat? Knowles carefully pointed out that the qualifications for a Senate seat probably precluded Coldwell: one had to own property in the province which one represented in the Senate and was the then solidly CCF Saskatchewan likely to allow Coldwell into his home province if he became a senator? Fotunately for Knowles, the offer never came and he was glad: neither the CCF nor the NDP could ever have justified Coldwell's acceptance of a Senate seat. Still, it might well have been the ultimate mark of respectability for a socialist leader.

As party leader, Coldwell was different from Woodsworth. Woodsworth had been an isolated figure, a leader blazing a trail and inspiring others to follow and to do the necessary building. Coldwell had been caught by that inspiration and although he had some of the same qualities he had much more of the concern for and attention to detail that are required for the building of a national party. Woodsworth himself, Knowles speculates, would probably say that Coldwell was a better leader in that respect. Once launched by Woodsworth, the party had to be solidified by someone like Coldwell.

Knowles' respect for Coldwell was reciprocated, and he confirmed it at the very end of his life. He requested that Knowles and Tommy Douglas, the two preachers of the party, conduct his funeral service. The service was in Ottawa to be followed by cremation and the burial of the ashes in a cemetery in Regina. Would Stanley see to the details? It was fortunate that he did so, for there was almost a hitch that upset the Coldwell family but which Knowles is sure Coldwell would have enjoyed. Sometime before his death Coldwell had complained to Knowles about the inordinate length of time mail took to get from the House of Commons to his apartment just a few blocks down Metcalfe Street in Ottawa. Couldn't Stanley say a word about it to the postmaster general? He did so, only to receive the normal post office reply: regrets and the hope that it would not happen again. Apparently it didn't while Coldwell was alive. But then came the time to send his ashes by mail to Regina for burial on 10 September 1974. Ever attentive to detail, Knowles checked with the undertaker in Regina a few days before the scheduled ceremony. Everything was in order except that there were no ashes. The post office admitted that the parcel had gone astray but assured Knowles that it would be found and delivered on time. It was. And the family, annoyed but amused, agreed that their father would have enjoyed the story too.

And why was Knowles not number three on the list of leaders of the CCF? In response to that unexpected question he hesitated just the fraction of a second and then, in a tone that suggested the questioner ought to be as aware of the political facts of life as he is, said "Well, because there are better people around to be the leader."[4] He sees his talents best used in the supporting role, the number two position as he terms it. He backs the leader, attends to detail, ensures that nothing is forgotten, keeps things running smoothly in the caucus and on the floor of the House. An effective leader has to be freed of much of that work and Knowles is more than pleased to be able to do it, indeed to be needed to do it. He also admits that for him political life on the hustings is not the most enjoyable task; a party leader, however, has to undertake it with enthusiasm. As for parliamentary life, he loves it. He is never willingly away from the House and he relishes all its complex workings. Party leadership would demand too much public bustle and take him away too often from parliament. Besides, ever since 1946 there has been the nagging question of his health. Leadership was not for him.

Leadership was, however, a natural for his old college chum, Tommy Douglas, premier of Saskatchewan from 1944 to 1961. Knowles can recall the very day they met, 27 September 1927, when he was entering Brandon College for the first time but coming into second year of the B.A. programme and Tommy, who had made up his high school programme at Brandon College and had just finished his own first year there, was also beginning second year. The two would joke about it later, Stanley saying he spent three years at Brandon and Tommy six and yet they both emerged with the same degree. They were friends from the beginning.

There were in fact many parallels in the lives of the two men. They had both been printers, both linotype operators, both members of the International Typographical Union. (Unlike Knowles, Douglas let his membership lapse. "Tommy's a Scot," quips Knowles with great amusement.[5]) They both became ministers and maintained their ministerial connections although they both soon abandoned religious for political preaching. They ran at the same time for the House of Commons in 1935 although the victorious Douglas got there first. It was a happy relationship, the two complementing each other to an extraordinary degree. Douglas was an orator, Knowles is not (he says he tries, but

Tommy did not even have to try); Douglas was an organizer, Knowles an attender to detail. Douglas engaged in flights of rhetoric and sometimes of fancy; Knowles, in his own words, is a plodder. The complementarity goes back to their Brandon days, when Knowles, even then playing the number two role, was Tommy's cheer-leader in student elections. Douglas took the honours in dramatics and debating; Knowles took them in academics. At graduation when Knowles took all the medals,

Once again championing Douglas, this time at the founding convention of the NDP. Ottawa 1961. (Cartoon by John Collins, *The Gazette*, Montreal)

Tommy complained that when he tried to take some too he was told to put them back.

The friendship continued while the two were ministers. Douglas was in Weyburn, Saskatchewan and Knowles in Winnipeg but they saw each other frequently. Knowles was best man at the Douglas wedding in 1930 and they exchanged their student ministries to permit the young couple a brief honeymoon in Winnipeg. He then encouraged Tommy to run in the Saskatchewan provincial election in 1934 and after defeat there, to try again in the federal election of 1935. Douglas had wanted to complete post-graduate work in the United States but Knowles did not want to go to Ottawa alone. He may also have wanted some company in resisting the admonitions of the church. When the few strong voices of criticism in Douglas' church indicated that a change of minister would be required if he ran for election he decided to do precisely that. He was elected and acted as party whip for the CCF group in parliament until 1944.

At that point Douglas returned to Saskatchewan to dumbfound the dubious churchmen of less than a decade before. For he came back to lead the CCF to provincial victory in the Saskatchewan election of 1944 and thus inaugurate the first democratic socialist government in North America. He was premier of the province until 1961 and the list of accomplishments is long. He pioneered hospitalization and medicare in North America in the face of a bitter doctors' strike and organized hostility across the country. He introduced labour legislation, farm legislation, encouraged industrial development, and extended gas and electricity lines into the rural areas. He was a strong voice in federal-provincial relations.

In 1961 he returned to the federal scene as the first leader of the New Democratic Party, Knowles again championing him, this time over Hazen Argue, the contender at the founding convention of the party. His departure from Saskatchewan may, however, have been too abrupt for he was defeated in the federal election of 1962, the one that returned Knowles after a four-year absence. Douglas then found a suburban Vancouver riding which he represented until 1968 and then a Vancouver Island riding until 1979. When he indicated he would not run in the election that year, Knowles was desolate. You can't leave me alone here, but Douglas, about to be seventy-five, did.

By then the NDP had had two others leaders: David Lewis, like Douglas a contemporary of Knowles, and Ed Broadbent of a younger generation. Knowles first heard of Lewis from a conversation with Woodsworth in the early 1930s: there was a brilliant young man from Montreal studying at Oxford on a Rhodes scholarship. While the temptations of Britain and an academic life might be great, Woodsworth expected Lewis to return and work for the new CCF since he knew him to be a committed socialist. By the late 1930s Knowles had met Lewis and Woodsworth's assessment held true. He was extraordinary, endowed with a sharp, brilliant mind, and tremendous ability. He could have gone anywhere in government, business, or the professional world but chose instead to devote his life to the minuscule socialist movement in Canada. For a pittance he worked as national secretary of the party from 1938 until 1950 when he went into private law practice in Toronto in order to pay off some of the accumulated debts and to educate his children. But he maintained an official position with the CCF and was national chairman of the party when the New Democratic Party was formed. Along with Knowles, he was one of the main instigators of the new party.

After several unsuccessful election attempts in the 1940s Lewis was elected to the House of Commons in 1962 from the Toronto riding of York South. During one of the earlier attempts, it appears that the electorate did not find him far enough to the left for in the Montreal Cartier by-election in 1943, he lost to the Communist Fred Rose. His victory in 1962, however, was shortlived since he was defeated in another federal election the following year. In 1965 he was back in the House and the caucus made him deputy leader. There, for perhaps the first time, he and Knowles worked together on a close daily basis. Their paths had run parallel within the CCF and the NDP for years, the more flamboyant Lewis concerned with party organization, Knowles more interested in parliamentary practice. Now they combined their talents in the House. As House leader, Knowles smoothed the parliamentary way for his more combative colleague. That combativeness, and Lewis' re-election in 1968, made him a serious contender for Douglas' job when, as was expected, he relinquished the leadership after ten years.

Lewis was not the only contender for that job in 1971. A great number of candidates appeared, all considerably younger than he and some professing to be more radical: Frank Howard, John Harney, Ed Broadbent, and Jim Laxer. The latter, representing a left-wing splinter group within the NDP known as the Waffle, surprised everyone by running second to Lewis. Perhaps Lewis knew then that his leadership would not be lengthy; it was time that the next generation of socialists in Canada began running the party.

In his three years as leader, possibly cut short by an awareness of the disease that would take his life in 1981, Lewis managed a breakthrough for the party. In the election of 1972 the NDP gained the largest number of seats that it or the former CCF had ever had. Its thirty-one seats placed it in the exciting and powerful, if awkward and eventually damaging, position of balance of power between the Liberals and the Conservatives. From that position the NDP was able to extract all manner of things from the Liberal minority government of Pierre Trudeau. The electorate, however, sensitive to the cry for majority government, turned away in 1974 and the party dropped to sixteen seats. Lewis himself lost his and with him, as Knowles said at the time, parliament lost the only MP who could make Trudeau squirm. On his defeat Lewis suggested the party seek a new leader and although he remained the nominal leader until the convention of 1975, there was an interim leader who would in fact step into his shoes that year.

Ed Broadbent is his junior but Knowles plays number two to him very happily too. Broadbent was not even born when Knowles first ran for parliament in 1935 and he was not a member until 1968. Before then he had been a professor of political science at York University. On one occasion he came to see Knowles to discuss political life with him. Was there a place for professors in politics? Could one do an MP's job and still have time to study and think and write? Knowles assured him that if one made the time it could be done. He was encouraged that such people were appearing on the scene.

Once in parliament, Broadbent was different. He sided with the back bench in a party which, like the others, has internal conflicts between its front and back bench, its old guard and young turks, its establishment and its radicals. Knowles recognizes that by age and experience he belongs with the old guard but in contrast with the others he considers himself the real radical: "I'm the guy who wants a new heaven and a new earth here."[6] In spite of that he and many of his generation were uneasy with the behaviour, tactics, and language of the left-wing nationalists around the Waffle, of whom Broadbent was one. Although he and Broadbent now joke about their different approaches at the time, what Broadbent saw as an open discussion of ideas, Knowles interpreted as disruption in caucus. Knowles appreciated Broadbent's forcefulness but he also noted the difficulties he could occasion within the parliamentary group. In 1971, Knowles was not at all sure that Broadbent should be seeking Douglas' position as leader. Knowles was at that point backing Lewis.

By 1975, however, things had changed considerably. On a gamble, Broadbent had been made chairman of the caucus during the minority parliament from 1972 to 1974. Says Knowles, who has seen many, he was the best chairman we've ever had. He held the caucus together, had ideas, but at no point assumed that he was the leader. It was natural then that he should be looked to when David Lewis decided to leave after the 1974 election. Since there was no party convention scheduled until 1975, Broadbent

"Broadbent . . . gives him a warm, happy, confident feeling." Ottawa 1979.

had the unenviable task of being a temporary, parliamentary leader. There was some talk of one of the "old boys" taking on the interim leadership so that Broadbent would not be burdened with a rather unrewarding task that could easily jeopardize his bid for the leadership in 1975. But old boys Knowles, Douglas, or Andrew Brewin were not interested. So Broadbent had to give leadership without assuming that he was the permanent leader. Again he did it well and his election as leader in 1975 was a natural consequence.

Knowles was pleased. Pleased that the party he knew back in the 1930s has been able to attract new young people like Broadbent. Pleased that people like Broadbent are there to ensure the continuation of the work begun fifty years ago. Pleased too at one of Broadbent's instant reactions to an issue shortly after he became parliamentary leader. The grapevine around Parliament Hill was predicting a huge pay increase for members of parliament, perhaps as much as fifty percent. Knowles passed the rumour on to Broadbent. His response was immediate and instinctive: "I didn't join the socialist party for this sort of thing. I didn't come to parliament for this. Stanley, we just can't stand for this. We're in this movement to try to lessen inequalities of income, not to increase them and especially not our own."[7] When the issue subsequently became public and Broadbent continued his stance, the press thought he was putting on a show. Knowles knew better. He was convinced that this man's socialism was there where it counted, at the very centre of things. In order to make socialism the centre of things, Knowles and his contemporaries had given much. Families, health, and the bank balance all would have been eased if they had made different choices. But they did not do it just to stage a one-act play and then draw the curtain. They had always known they were building for the future and they had always known that another generation would have to continue the task. On the day of Coldwell's death in August 1974, just a month after Lewis' defeat, Knowles did not know who in the next generation would take up the task. That someone of the ability, perception, and dedication of Ed Broadbent should emerge gives him a warm, happy, confident feeling. He is sure that Woodsworth and Coldwell would be as pleased as he is.

16

POLITICS AND THE FAMILY

2 October 1981

The battle is a personal one now, but to help him fight it Knowles has his personal, political, parliamentary, and public families on his side. He did not know they were there on the morning of 2 October when he suffered a cerebral hemorrhage at his Ottawa home but they were all with him. Usually he had managed to conceal his illnesses; only during the election campaign of 1963 had one of them become public knowledge. This one, however, belonged as much to the public as to him. Indeed, at the time, the public knew more about it than he did. Radio, television, and newspapers flashed the state of his health across the country; hourly bulletins from Ottawa's Civic Hospital chronicled his reaction to the stroke that had felled him. He recognized his son David and he recognized the couple in whose home he had lived in Ottawa since 1944, but the rest was confusion. An operation to relieve the pressure on the brain and remove the dead brain tissue in the vicinity of the rupture saved his life, but the long-term effects of the stroke were unknown. For days he did not know where he was, much less why, and only weeks later did he understand what had happened. One of the first things he knew within a week of the stroke was that his parliamentary family was reconvening "next Wednesday," 14 October.[1] But he was unable to read the huge Get Well card from that family in the form of a giant edition of that day's Hansard containing only Speaker Jeanne Sauvé's best wishes and the signatures of MPs. Nor could he cope with the letters of concern from his vast public family: he was used to their bringing problems to him to solve; now that their worries centred on him, he was confused. Things were not quite right.

Just the night before he had been coping with their problems, as he had been doing for more than fifty years, first as a minister and then as an MP. Gradually that public family grew from its Winnipeg base to spread out over the whole country and he had handwritten replies ready to be typed and sent the next day to people in Nova Scotia, Quebec, Manitoba, Alberta, and British Columbia. The letters were personal more than political as he sorted out a pension calculation for one, prodded the Pension Commission for another, explained the complexities of veterans' pensions to someone else, sympathized with a single sixty-four year old woman about the inequity of the spouse's allowance, and shared yet another's criticism of the Liberals for an increase in the postal rates ("Let us hope that their days are numbered," he wrote[2]). One of the last letters before he turned in for the night — it was near the top of the pile beside his bed — contained a rare personal reflection:

> There are so many things that give us cause for concern about our country and our world, but there are also many satisfactions, particularly those that come from trying to help others. . . . May good things come your way as well, but the best of all is the satisfaction of doing one's best.[3]

And then came the darkness out of which Knowles has been struggling ever since.

The struggle is not entirely unknown to him, although his manner of coping with it is different. As an infant, he was not supposed to live at all and languished until his parents experimented with goat's milk. And he was not yet forty when another death sentence was passed. Shortly after his return from Europe in the late winter of 1946, he collapsed at a luncheon in Ottawa's Chateau Laurier at which he was the guest speaker. His personal and political families assumed it was fatigue while he, having experienced numbness in his legs just a day or so before, thought that the end had come, particularly since the lights in the room coincidentally dimmed just as he did. The diagnosis was multiple sclerosis, a degenerative disease which attacks the central nervous system. There is no known cure and no specific treatment; most victims are eventually incapacitated and confined to wheel-chairs with their life-expectancy considerably shortened. Knowles fought it with sheer will power. He buried emotions, feelings, and sensations for fear that a stray tingling might announce a triumph for the disease. He wore heavy shoes, perhaps to ensure that his feet stayed where he placed them. Even his habit of lugging

excessively weighty baggage on any trip may have been an
assurance that he himself would stay put. Then he filled his days
with work, work for others, so that the disease had no time and
maybe even, with a nod to his religious background, no excuse for
claiming him. Few people knew of the struggle and fewer still of
the emotional cost. Along the way he acquired a few other
ailments — the Meckel's diverticulum, a malfunctioning gall
bladder, a temperamental spine — but he controlled them all with
living habits as austere as his public image sometimes portrays.

A stroke is not so easily subjugated, although Knowles
obviously intends to try. Indeed, watching him cope makes one
wonder at the very location of his will power; it must be other
than in the brain for that plays him some cruel tricks now. He is
dismayed by them, as he misses the import of a remark or cannot
follow a three-way conversation or struggles with television and
the morning paper, but he is also intrigued by the process. Just as
he once attempted to convince a sceptical child that the very
movement of a little finger was a marvel, now he puzzles over the
meanderings of his brain. Just how does it work? Will some other
circuit take up the message that has come to a dead end down the
damaged path of the stroke? Are there parts of the brain not used
before that can be willed into service? And can he exercise that
will? Maybe he can and maybe he can't. He's trying.

In that effort he counts on the support of the many families
that have intertwined with his political career. Like his Winnipeg
constituents, his family too has spread from a spot on the prairies
to take in politics, parliament, and perhaps even the country itself.
Such an extended family has frequently meant divided loyalties
and even emotional conflict for the immediate Knowles family of
whom there are now, after the death of Mrs. Knowles in 1978, a
daughter and family in Winnipeg and a son and family in Ottawa.
But they have always rallied to their father's assistance, he
knowing full well that he has made unusual demands upon them
and they ultimately proud of his unusual acquisition of other
families of different sorts and in different settings.

In order to bring his own family all together on a rare occasion
in 1974, he even had to conjure up a different setting for them.
And he also had to organize it long in advance. For three years he
planned a trip to Nova Scotia with his wife, children, and
grandchildren; they would visit his father's birthplace one
hundred years after the event and they would roam about the
southwestern tip of the province, digging up distant cousins and
peering at crumbling tombstones. It would be the first time in
many years that the entire family had been together. Indeed he

could hardly remember the last time, so interrupted had the family been by politics and politics by the family. This trip he would cherish and perhaps his family would see, despite the absences over the years, just how much the family tie meant to him.[4]

The plans were carefully designed and nothing, he insisted, was to interfere with them. He would fly from Ottawa; his wife Vida would fly from Winnipeg and join son David and his family in Ottawa for the drive to Nova Scotia; daughter Margaret and her family would fly from Winnipeg directly to Halifax. From there a rented car would be added to the cavalcade and the family would descend the south shore towards Shelburne, Barrington Passage, and Upper Woods Harbour. The entire trip was to be Knowles' treat. He had already given copies of a recent local history — Edwin Croll's *History of Barrington Township* — to his family before they went and he was going to take along a recent genealogical survey of the Knowles family produced by a descendant in the United States.[5] They would visit relatives who had connections with the Cape Sable Historical Society. For them all, he hoped, and certainly for him, it was to be a sentimental journey.

Family reunions, let alone sentimental journeys, are, however, as Knowles well knew, luxuries for a politician. And this one did not escape the demands of politics: in the late spring of 1974 Prime Minister Trudeau put an end to his minority government by calling an election for that summer. The family, resigned over the years to such things, looked at Knowles as if to say "Here we go again." But he assured them the trip was still on. The election was set for 8 July and the family would leave the following weekend, win or lose. When NDP leader David Lewis passed through Winnipeg during the campaign, Knowles pleaded with him not to have a meeting of the newly elected NDP group too soon after the election; his family engagement was pressing. Lewis assured him there would be no rush to call the MPs together but he did add jokingly that if the NDP formed the government everyone's plans, family or otherwise, would have to be scrapped to face the new situation. Knowles was realistic enough to know that he could proceed with the organization of his sentimental journey.

Then the election itself played a trick. The NDP dropped from thirty-one seats to sixteen and Lewis insisted on an immediate meeting of caucus. Set for 17 July, it was right in the middle of the week of the long-planned trip to Nova Scotia. Knowles apologized to Lewis: he simply could not be there. The leader was equally adamant: Stanley simply had to be there. It was a typical conflict, the kind of thing Knowles and his family had known and gradually come to accept ever since 1942. This time it was his turn to mutter "Here we go again."

As he had done on so many other occasions, Knowles would once again attempt to combine both. It had not been easy in the early days of long train rides across the country. Even the first airplanes had not speeded things up much. In 1956, for example, in the midst of the pipeline debate, in which he was such a key figure, he was determined to be in Winnipeg for his son's graduation from high school. To do so meant flying all one night, being in Winnipeg for the day, and flying all the next night back to Ottawa. Now at least the planes were faster: he could easily accompany his family as far as Barrington Passage, see them safely ensconced in a hotel there, entrust their day's entertainment to his young third cousin, Elizabeth Smith, get back to Ottawa in time for the caucus meeting, and be back again in Nova Scotia by the evening. It was exhausting but it was quite the normal pattern and he at least was used to such arrangements.

Politics and the family: the Knowles grandchildren in Grandpa's home. Ottawa 1979. (United Press Canada Limited, Toronto)

The day after his return back and forth from Ottawa he accompanied his family to Upper Woods Harbour just a few miles from Barrington Passage. As they approached the old family property he told them the tale once again, cramming in all the details he had carefully pieced together over the years: the great-great-grandfather who had come from Cape Cod to Liverpool, Nova Scotia, and thence to Barrington Passage; the great-grandfather who had purchased the property at Upper Woods Harbour; the grandfather who was born in that building just over there behind the house; the father born there too one hundred years ago that summer; and then the lot of them scattering to the four winds. Here was the big yellow house built in 1896 and known to so many young Knowleses as the ideal summer vacation spot. He told the story too of his first coming to this spot, at the age of eleven, just after the death of his mother. The first night he slept in Canada had been in this house.

He took them up to the Big Rock, beyond the house and the barn, up on the hillside. Familiar to generations of Knowleses, the huge stone knew all the family secrets. Now, on a glorious day that matched his mood, he had his entire family on that Big Rock. The family caught his mood and the occasion; his son David wondered how anyone could leave such a beautiful spot. So his father repeated his father's remark about having to move a stone every time one wanted to plant a potato. The notion was incomprehensible to Knowles' prairie born family and they were all for having their father buy back the family home from the "strangers" to whom it had been sold many years before.

The sentimental journey continued. They visited graveyards and established family connections with almost every one of the inhabitants. Knowles' son-in-law, Robert Plaxton, stayed up half the night devouring the book of genealogy and regaled the rest with his ability to rattle off generations. The grandchildren caught the spirit and urged their grandpa to go into every cemetery they passed. Grandson Peter was wearing a T-shirt with the number twelve on it the day the family figured out that he was in fact number twelve in the direct line of male descendants of Richard Knowles from Cape Cod back in the early seventeenth century. They went on to Yarmouth, the big city of the area, and chatted with the old lighthouse keeper who remembered the boats that had ferried young Stanley and Warren Knowles and their father in 1919; both had subsequently been lost in storms at sea. And they visited relatives far and near. The roots were there and the entire family felt the pull of them.

What a contrast with the visit to Los Angeles in 1955. On that occasion he had taken his family — wife and two teenagers — to his childhood home. The experience was not the same at all. Where Knowles as a child had lived on the outskirts of a medium-sized city, he now returned to visit the deteriorating core of a huge metropolis. It was neither attractive nor interesting. It had changed too much and, although the place held memories for him, there was no joy for him or his family. In fact, Los Angeles came to seem more and more a temporary aberration in his family life. His roots were in Canada and since Nova Scotia never changed those roots were still tangible and visible even in the summer of 1974.

Later that summer he went back to Nova Scotia to be there on the exact day of the hundredth anniversary of his father's birth. On 21 August he climbed back up to the Big Rock at Upper Woods Harbour and attempted to capture his dad by a recital of the details of the family past. This time he was alone, as in fact he has been so much of his life in spite of all the families, and the recital eased the ever-present ache.

And yet he had always known that this was the politician's lot. As early as the birth of his son David in 1939, his family and his politics had always been jumbled together. David arrived just as his father had to depart to resign his position as minister so he could run for election. His daughter Margaret arrived in the midst of the election campaign of 1942: the victory she brought meant separation from the family. David was married just before another election in 1962. His first grandchild Susan arrived in 1965 in the midst of an interminable debate in the House of Commons on the Canada Pension Plan. The next day Knowles spotted a friend in the gallery and sent a note up to announce that he now had a grandchild. Congratulations, came the reply, and I hope you finish the debate before there's another one.[6]

If the links to family and to the past were ever present, so too were the lengthy separations. When Knowles was first elected, the parliamentary sessions were only about six months long. A family could conceivably move back and forth from the riding to Ottawa. But that meant maintaining two homes, disrupting children's schooling, and breaking, if only temporarily, the tie with the constituency. The alternative was to have "daddy" away much of the time. The dilemma is one faced by all federal politicians except those living in the Ottawa area.

The Knowles family tried the two alternatives. In 1943 the entire family came to Ottawa in January for the opening of parliament and lived for a few months in a house on Crichton Street and then rented a cottage at Woodroffe for the summer. But by the fall, son David was ready for school; was it a good idea to shunt him back and forth from one school to another and from one town to another? The parents decided not. Knowles therefore came alone to Ottawa and found a place to board for the few months of the parliamentary session.

His search for a place to stay coincided with an unbalanced budget in the home of an Ottawa school teacher. Knowles had met Marjorie and Walter Mann when he first came to Ottawa in 1943 to take his seat in the Commons. The Ottawa CCF, of which Walter Mann was the first chairman, had used the occasion to have a gathering. At the dinner in the parliamentary dining room the Knowleses and the Manns sat beside each other. Through the ensuing year, the two women worked closely together on the production of a CCF cook book, *Canadian Favourites*, now a classic and a document of Canadian social history for the recipes are designed for people of slender financial means and scarce wartime products. Shortly before the opening of the parliamentary session in 1944, the Manns heard that Stanley would be coming alone. Would he like to stay for the session? Marjorie Mann had vetoed the idea of a permanent boarder to solve the family's financial difficulties — a funeral had necessitated an unexpected trip to Toronto and the budget was in the red to the amount of thirteen dollars. A permanent boarder might never leave but an MP would stay only a few months. So Knowles came to live with the Manns. No one knew then that the parliamentary sessions would expand to fill the year. Nor did the Manns know of Knowles' steadfastness; almost forty years later, he was still there. Unknown to anyone in 1944, Knowles had acquired another family.

He could not know it either in 1944 but that family was to ease for him some of the tensions created by the combination of politics and his own immediate family. Indeed he came to feel sorry for other MPs when he saw the haphazard and unstable arrangements they were having to make for the times they were in Ottawa. Some of them came to look on his arrangement with envy. He was in fact part of the furniture at the Mann household; family plans for travel, for construction, for grandmothers' visits, and for moving were all made with him in mind. The Mann children accepted as normal the disappearance of the dining room when Stanley was to come. The major worry of a year's absence from Canada was what to do about Stanley. When the Manns added to their home, one of the new rooms was for him. When the daughters married, he had to perform the ceremony. And when Marjorie persuaded the family to buy a new home further from the centre of town she knew she would have to convince

Stanley as much as her husband Walter. Knowles sometimes says that the Manns are away so much that the home is in fact his and that they stay with him. When they were all there, around the breakfast table, or more rarely, the dinner table, puns were part of the menu, the three adults exercising their wit and the two girls groaning. As youngsters, the girls wondered vaguely why Stanley called their father Senator until they were old enough to grasp the strategy: when the CCF formed the government, Walter Mann would go to the Senate where his first action would be a motion for abolition. They also knew all about old age pensions long before they were teenagers if only from their father's fun with Stanley's preoccupations:

> Father: What did the elephant say to the giraffe?
> Daughter: ???
> Father: Old age pension.
> Daughter: ???
> Father: Don't you get it?
> Daughter: No.
> Father: You won't until you're seventy.[7]

Before the daughters were even conscious of Knowles as a permanent fixture in their home, one of his CCF colleagues in the House of Commons recognized the happy arrangement and wondered whether he really did pay the Manns for boarding there or whether they paid him to stay.

Knowles in fact collects families, clings to them, and yet maintains his distance. His family in Winnipeg was always there. His family in Ottawa was always there. His family in Los Angeles, consisting of a stepmother, brother, and sister-in-law was always there. His first Canadian family, the Baileys at Carberry, was always there. He keeps as many ties with all of them and their various members and relatives as he possibly can. He was thrilled when the Bailey farm was chosen as the site for a twenty-four hour visit by the Royal Family during the Manitoba centennial celebrations in 1970. That farm he knew thoroughly and although his dear Aunt Ida was no longer there, his cousins still had the farm and would entertain the Queen. He mentioned it to Queen Elizabeth when he met her a few days before the scheduled visit during a ceremony at Brandon University. There, he was amused by Princess Anne behaving just like a typical teenager. When the Queen spilled a bit of mortar that she was lifting to place a cornerstone, Anne remarked aloud: "Oh Mother, what a mess!"[8] Shortly thereafter, when the Royal Family had spent their day at

With "Queen Elizabeth . . . during a ceremony at Brandon University."
Brandon 1970.

the farm he encountered the Queen again at another gathering. She took his hand, remarked that she had met him at Brandon, and passed on down the line of people she was meeting. But then she turned back and added that the family had had a wonderful time at 'his' farm. Even from a distance — perhaps especially from a distance — all Knowles' collected families provide enormous but unspoken emotional sustenance for one orphaned at eleven, cast adrift at sixteen, stricken at thirty-seven with a disease which undermines one's self-confidence before taking complete physical hold, and now battered by a stroke. He is, he admits, "well blessed" to have so many families.[9]

His political family has provided similar delights and despair, excitement and, on occasion, estrangement. Although he worked for the CCF as a paid staff member between 1939 and 1942 and although his work was crucial in the forming of the NDP in 1961, he has never been emotionally at home within party organization. He is most at ease in the House of Commons, perhaps because of the combination of dispassionate argument and logical, if highly complex, process that makes that House run smoothly. Knowles has a talent for both and although each has its place in a political party, neither is at the top of any party's list of essential qualities. He might even be difficult to work with in a party setting, for his insistence on exactitude could easily alienate the fervent. Nonetheless he was devastated when in 1963 he was told he would be nominated for an executive position on the NDP's federal council and then the nomination was not made. He wept at the rejection but only one person saw the tears. Since then he has distanced himself from the party's inner political workings.

He is, as Tommy Douglas says, a "House of Commons man."[10] From that haven he can work happily with and for his political, parliamentary, and public families. Within the NDP caucus he is known affectionately as the den mother and he plays the role to the extent of soothing difficulties, sometimes even before they arise. He knows which issues are going to cause problems for which members and how they are going to react to certain questions. He maintains the peace and looks after things. He has an ear of total discretion open to anyone's worries or confidences; until recently he and Broadbent had their offices across the hall from one another, each one wanting and enjoying the proximity, the sharing, and the loyalty.

Knowles gradually acquired much the same role within the Commons itself. As House leader for the NDP he participated in inter-party discussions with his counterparts from the Liberals and Conservatives about the order of business, parliamentary problems, and the smooth functioning of the household. On occasion he has been known to put the welfare of his parliamentary family above that of his political family as he became more concerned for relationships within the Commons than for the individual advantage of his own party. He has decided notions about proper parliamentary behaviour, for example. Knowles clucked over Pierre Trudeau's insensitivity when he took over as prime minister from Lester Pearson in 1968. Pearson was one day short of a five-year term as prime minister and Trudeau could easily have delayed his takeover by twenty-four hours. Worse still, Trudeau then merely met the House in order to announce the dissolution of parliament. He did not give Pearson a chance to say a word of farewell and nor therefore could the opposition echo the good-bye. The breach of parliamentary etiquette disturbed Knowles and he told Pearson so when he saw him later outside the House. Pearson admitted having notes in his pocket ready for the occasion.[11]

Knowles actually thinks his parliamentary family behaves best when there is a minority government. That situation occurred

"Knowles — in shirtsleeves — helped confirm the familial image of the prime minister." Louis St. Laurent, David Knowles, and friend, Gimli, Manitoba 1951.

in 1957-58, again with three consecutive governments between 1962 and 1968, and once more from 1972 to 1974. During those times, he claims, much more is accomplished than when there is a majority government. While Pearson headed minority governments in the mid-1960s, for example, many highly contentious and yet socially beneficial laws were passed: a comprehensive medical care insurance scheme; a revised Labour Code; the Canada Pension Plan; amendments to the Criminal Code; a gradual reduction in the eligible age for Old Age Security; a new transportation act; and a new flag. The same thing happened when Trudeau headed a minority government in the early 1970s. Where fractiousness, arrogance, and contention marked the majority governments before and after, the two-year minority managed to increase the Old Age Security and the veterans' allowances, to confront the problems of foreign investment and energy policy, to establish regulations for campaign contributions to political parties. According to Knowles, Trudeau himself seemed to prefer the minority situation.[12] Knowles may well have liked it because it allowed him to reconcile his political family's partisan advantage (the NDP held the balance of power between 1972 and 1974 and was able to extract legislation to its liking from the Liberals) with his parliamentary family's proper behaviour. But he may also have preferred minority governments because they diminished the element of power in the family relationship in the Commons.

Personal touches therefore characterized many of his own attachments to his parliamentary family. He understood the attraction of Louis St. Laurent as "Uncle Louis" not only to the Canadian public in the 1950s but also to his own family. On a chance occasion in 1951 when St. Laurent was attending Icelandic ceremonies at Gimli, on Lake Winnipeg, and the Knowles family was vacationing at nearby Sandy Hook, his twelve-year-old son urged Knowles to take him to meet the prime minister. They had neither invitation nor official access to the gathering. But St. Laurent spotted them, left the local dignitaries and came over, so pleased that Knowles had come. The press caught the scene and Knowles — in shirtsleeves! — helped confirm the familial image of the prime minister. In 1973 he was asked to be an honorary pall bearer at St. Laurent's funeral.[13] In the meantime he had scolded another prime minister for not keeping his wedding within the family. Why had Pierre Trudeau run off to British Columbia to be married in 1971 when there were at least three qualified ministers in the House — including Knowles — who could have performed the ceremony? Trudeau wondered how it could have been kept secret under such circumstances and Knowles retorted that Standing Order 43 would have sufficed, a rule by which members can initiate some matter in the House without giving prior notice.[14] Five years later Knowles offered Trudeau birthday wishes and wondered if now were not the time to lower the eligible pension age to sixty for those who are out of the labour force. After all, Trudeau would be sixty in three years and he might well be unemployed by then.[15]

The scolding and the teasing were the lighter side of Knowles' own parliamentary behaviour. But when his family stepped out of line, he could become very angry indeed, although the anger was always one of responsibility rather than revenge. The pipeline debate in 1956 appalled him but his response was not one of rage but of argument, persuasion, and erudition. An Ottawa paper singled out one of his speeches for its "knowledge, logical sequence, moral indignation, and at times a touch of beauty" and ranked it with the finest parliamentary pronouncements in many a year.[16] With the same indignation he chastised his colleagues for their eager dipping into the public treasury to increase their own salaries by an inordinate amount in 1975. Another newspaper pointed to him on that occasion as "one of the few standouts in a sea of moral mediocrity."[17] And had he been in the House in the late winter of 1982 he would have condemned both Conservatives and Liberals for their obstinacy in having division bells ringing for two weeks. He might not have found a solution since neither side seemed particularly interested in finding one but he would no doubt have given them what Trudeau called a "Sermon from the Hill"[18] on their obligations to avoid such squabbles in the family. If parliament could not govern itself, how could it govern the country?

"If parliament could not govern itself, how could it govern the country?" Ottawa 1970. (Cartoon by Rusins, *The Citizen*, Ottawa)

Indeed the purpose of preventing squabbles within the parliamentary family was to enable it to get on with the business of preventing disturbances within the Canadian family. In his later years in parliament, Knowles shared with his public family two issues that caused great disturbance: the constitution and the rights of women. Indeed, he attempted to make the peace within his own political and parliamentary families over the constitution as the NDP engaged in bitter internal arguments over the stand of most of its MPs, and those MPs in turn condemned both the Liberals' rigidity and the Conservatives' obstreperousness. All three aspects of the constitutional question that stirred up so much public controversy in the early 1980s — patriation, an amending formula, and a charter of rights — had in fact been on Knowles' mind long before some of his younger colleagues in parliament were even born. In 1949, for example, he had a hand in an amendment to the British North America Act. The purpose of the amendment then was to permit the federal government to amend those parts of the Act which concerned it specifically without having to go to London for permission. Since the federal and provincial governments had never been able to agree on an amending formula for the entire Act, this was as far as constitutional reform could go. But Knowles, encouraged by Frank Scott, the constitutional expert from McGill University, was fearful lest some future government attempt to overstep the bounds of propriety. He therefore suggested an addition to the limitations on the federal government's amending power: it was not to tamper with the constitutional provision that a parliament not last longer than five years and that there be a parliamentary session every year. The Liberal government countered with an exception to the first provision: in the case of war, invasion, or insurrection, the life of a parliament could be extended beyond five years but only with the consent of two-thirds of the MPs. Knowles agreed to the exception and his specification became part of the amendment, now Section 91, 1 of the British North America Act. For that, Knowles referred to himself on one occasion as a step-father of Confederation.[19]

In 1964 he was a bit more brutal. By private member's bill he proposed that the BNA Act also be known legally as the Constitution of Canada. The use of the title might even "hasten the day when we might have our own constitution . . . enacted in Canada and amendable in Canada . . . both in name and in fact."[20] The bill met the usual fate of private members' bills and was talked out. Later in the year, however, Knowles suggested that attempts at agreeing on an amending formula before patriation

'Let's Try This'

"In 1964 he was a bit more brutal." (Cartoon courtesy *The Globe and Mail*, Toronto)

were futile: the constitution should be brought home first and the means of changing it agreed upon later.[21] A cartoon portrayed a tiny Knowles wielding a huge sword to slash through a great bundle of knots (with Pearson and Diefenbaker entangled among them) representing constitutional ties to Britian.[22]

If he was a step-father in 1949 and an axe-wielder in 1964, Knowles was more of a go-between by 1981. Between parties in the House, behind the scenes in the federal council of the NDP, and in public at the party's federal convention that year, Knowles argued in favour of the constitutional resolution that had been worked out by an all-party committee of the Commons. He rejected the notion of some of his NDP colleagues that the provisions meant greater power to Ottawa, to the courts, or to the Senate, and pleaded with them not to stall the process of constitutional change, and particularly the enshrining of a charter of rights, as he had seen it stalled so often over the years.

Knowles could not follow the final stages of the constitutional process in the late autumn of 1981. But he was well enough to be among the parliamentary guests on 17 April 1982 when the Queen signed the Canada Act on Parliament Hill. Seeing things tidied up, if not doing it himself, had always pleased him and he was glad to be there.

There was still another area, however, in which his Canadian family required changes and tidying up, and for that Knowles may well have to stay around another parliamentary lifetime. It is unlike him to leave things undone but the issue of women's rights may well outlast him. He began on it early enough with specific references in the 1940s to widows of war veterans and civil servants. He raised the question of low pay for the Commons' cleaning staff, so many of whom are women. He badgered the government for five years before it consented to establish a women's bureau in the federal Department of Labour in 1954. And no sooner did the Royal Commission on the Status of Women make its report in 1970 than he began asking when its various recommendations would be implemented. Like others, his concerns developed from a notion of protecting women to an insistence on their equality. He never of course abandoned that first concern and one of his last acts in parliament before his stroke was an attempt to rouse the interest of the House in pensions for women over age fifty-five who are alone and not in the labour market.[23] But before then he was arguing more for their equality and against the various forms of discrimination that undermine that equality and do so frequently with the connivance of the federal government. And he was able to combine both his sense of protection and his sense of justice in his favourite topic of pensions by arguing for some change in the Canada Pension Plan to enable housewives to be covered, against the spouse's allowance because of its discrimination against single women, and for equality in the survivor's benefits of numerous pensions which remain at full value if the wife dies but are cut by as much as fifty percent if the woman is the survivor.[24] He won't let the government get away with the antique argument that widowers needed more money in order to acquire another wife whereas a widow could always attract another man to support her. And if MPs can improve the survivors' benefits of their own pensions, surely they can do so for others.[25]

". . . and tell him how much we love him." Speaker Jeanne Sauvé , 1981.

There is work yet to be done then before Knowles' public family is quite content. His personal family has long since been philosophical about the political demands on him. The frequently unbearable strains of the earlier years when lengthy absences occasioned grumbling about husband's or father's inattentions, when mother had full responsibility for raising the children, when the children were perplexed as youngsters and hostile as adolescents, when the parents themselves were increasingly distant and estranged, have all been absolved by time. The political family hovered over Knowles' illness: less than six months earlier, in May 1981, it had lost David Lewis; surely Knowles would not break so soon another of the links to the old CCFers of the 1930s. His parliamentary family sent its best wishes in early October and almost immediately started misbehaving and continued to do so after his return on 31 March 1982 for he was not quite himself. Still, all the members were on their feet as he stepped into the House that day and most of his public family caught the scene on television:

> MADAM SPEAKER: I believe the House has said it all. I do want to wish the honourable member for Winnipeg North Centre our warmest welcome and to tell him how much we love him.
> SOME HON. MEMBERS: Hear, hear![26]

He had come home.

NOTES

Chapter 1

1. Interview with Stanley Knowles (hereafter referred to as SHK), 19 August 1975.
2. SHK correspondence, Stanley Ernest Knowles (hereafter referred to as SEK) to SHK, 7 March 1933.
3. Interview with SHK, 19 August 1975.
4. Ibid.
5. SHK papers, card from [Li.K.?] to SEK, 28 October 1908.
6. SHK papers, card from SEK to Benjamin D. Knowles, 4 November 1908; "Maggie" [Margaret Blanche Knowles] to Benjamin D. Knowles, 26 December 1908.
7. SHK correspondence, SEK to SHK, 28 July 1929.
8. SHK papers, SEK to Benjamin Knowles, 24 July 1932.
9. SHK correspondence, SEK to SHK, 10 June 1928.
10. Interview with SHK, 19 August 1975.
11. Ibid.

Chapter 2

1. Interview with SHK, 19 August 1975.
2. Interview with SHK, 21 August 1975.
3. Ibid.
4. Ibid.
5. Ibid.
6. Comment to author, 29 April 1982. Knowles' brevity of emotional comment was as remarkable before as after his stroke on 2 October 1981.
7. Interview with SHK, 21 August 1975.
8. SHK correspondence, SEK to SHK, 27 September 1927.
9. SHK correspondence, SEK to SHK, 11 August 1929.
10. Interview with SHK, 21 August 1975.
11. Ibid.

12. SHK correspondence, SEK to SHK, 10 June 1928.
13. SHK correspondence, Ida Bailey to SHK, 29 July 1928.
14. Ibid.
15. SHK correspondence, SEK to SHK, 9 June 1929, enclosing a letter from Oliver J. Harvli, Pastor in North Hampton, Ohio, to SEK, 27 May 1929.
16. SHK correspondence, SEK to SHK, 9 November 1930.
17. SHK correspondence, SEK to SHK, 16 June 1929.
18. SHK correspondence, SEK to SHK, 28 July 1929.
19. SHK correspondence, SEK to SHK, 16 June 1929.
20. SHK correspondence, reference to two incidents in letters from SEK to SHK, 15 September 1929 and 28 July 1929.
21. SHK correspondence, SEK to SHK, 16 June 1929.
22. SHK correspondence, SEK to SHK, 28 July 1929.
23. SHK correspondence, SEK to SHK, 11 August 1929.
24. SHK correspondence, SEK to SHK, 18 May 1930.
25. Interview with SHK, 21 August 1975.
26. Ibid.

Chapter 3

1. SHK papers, SEK to Benjamin Knowles, 24 July 1932.
2. SHK correspondence, SEK to SHK, 15 January 1933.
3. Recalled by SHK in the interview of 20 August 1975.
4. SHK papers, SEK to Benjamin Knowles, 24 July 1932.
5. SHK papers, Benjamin Knowles to Ida Bailey, 7 April 1932.
6. SHK correspondence, SEK to SHK, 4 October 1932.
7. Ibid., SEK to SHK, 28 September 1930.
8. When his son accepted a poorer paying church for his student preaching in the autumn of 1930 Mr. Knowles reported to him what he had said to his wife and to people from his church: "you can say or think what you like about Stanley's modernism but you cannot complain but that his spirit is more to be desired and compares favourably with Jesus than any fundamentalist you can mention." Ibid.
9. Ibid., SEK to SHK, 26 August 1931.
10. Ibid., SEK to SHK, 11 August 1929; 15 March 1932; 16 January 1933; 5 December 1934.
11. Ibid., SEK to SHK, 10 August 1930.
12. Ibid., SEK to SHK, 26 August 1931.
13. Ibid., Anna Knowles to SHK, 28 March 1932.
14. Ibid., SHK to "Folks in the East", 13 October 1935.
15. Ibid.

Chapter 4

1. Recalled by SHK in the interview of 22 August 1975.
2. SHK correspondence, SEK to SHK, 29 January 1933; 2 February 1933; 28 February 1933.

3. SHK correspondence, SEK to SHK, 10 February 1935.
4. Recalled by SHK in the interview 22 August 1975.
5. SHK correspondence, SHK to the "Folks in the East", 18 October 1935.
6. Interview with SHK, 22 August 1975.

Chapter 5

1. Interview with SHK, 27 August 1975.
2. Ibid.
3. SHK papers, copy of a hand written, reproduced, "Personal Letter from Mrs. J. S. Woodsworth, To the Women Electors of North Centre," 14 November 1942.
4. Personal comment to author, 3 May 1982.
5. Interview with SHK, 27 August 1975.
6. Ibid.
7. Ibid.
8. Recalled by SHK, ibid.

Chapter 6

1. Recalled by SHK in the interview of 28 August 1975.
2. House of Commons *Debates*, 3 February 1943, p. 127.
3. Interview with SHK, 28 August 1975.
4. House of Commons *Debates*, 27 November 1944, p. 6594.
5. Recalled by SHK in the interview of 28 August 1975.
6. Coldwell read the petition when he presented it: House of Commons *Debates*, 16 May 1947, p. 3139. The Clerk's ruling came on 19 May 1947: *Journals* of the House of Commons #71. Knowles cited the ruling later in the debate: ibid., 26 June 1947, p. 4699.
7. Ibid., 18 June 1947, pp. 4282-90.
8. Ibid., 26 June 1947, pp. 4702-03.
9. Interview with SHK, 28 August 1975. As with the previous account, this one too has been clarified by reference to Hansard.
10. House of Commons *Debates*, 14 November 1949, pp. 1719-22.
11. Although I absorbed parliamentary procedure with my porridge as a child in the house where Knowles lived in Ottawa when parliament was in session, I have, for assurance and clarification, called upon the knowledge, precision, and great good-humoured assistance of Charles Robert of the Table Research Branch in the office of the Clerk of the House. He bears no responsibility for the result.

Chapter 7

1. Recalled by SHK in the interview of 2 September 1975.
2. Ibid.
3. Ibid.

4. Ibid.
5. SHK correspondence, copy of a letter from SHK to Lloyd Stinson, CCF member of the Manitoba legislature, 9 January 1946.
6. Recalled by SHK in the interview of 2 September 1975.
7. Ibid.
8. SHK correspondence, Vida Knowles to SHK, 16 February [1946].
9. SHK papers, copy of a cablegram from SHK to Co-operative Press Association, Ottawa [week of 18 February 1946].
10. Interview with SHK, 2 September 1975.

Chapter 8

1. Recalled by SHK in the interview of 3 September 1975.
2. House of Commons *Debates*, 12 April 1945, p. 817.
3. SHK papers, Report re pension rights of certain employees of the CPR and associated express and steamship companies (Johnstone Report) presented to Humphrey Mitchell, minister of labour, 7 December 1945, p. 17. Also in *Journals* of the House of Commons, #87 (1946): p. 747.
4. SHK papers, Bill 24: An Act to amend the Railway Act. The bill was given first and second reading in the House of Commons, 24 February 1947 and 20 May 1947.
5. Interview with SHK, 3 September 1975.
6. SHK correspondence, SHK to W. L. M. King, 19 May 1948.
7. House of Commons *Debates*, 17 June 1948, p. 5369.
8. Recalled by SHK in the interview of 3 September 1975.
9. House of Commons *Debates*, 17 June 1948, pp. 5389-90.
10. Interview with SHK, 3 September 1975.

Chapter 9

1. Interview with SHK, 22 September 1975.
2. House of Commons *Debates*, 14 August 1944, p. 6492.
3. Ibid., First Session, 13 April 1945, pp. 876-77.
4. This incident is referred to from a procedural point of view in Chapter 6.
5. House of Commons *Debates*, 20 February 1950, p. 62.
6. Interview with SHK, 22 September 1950. Knowles' "half mile" is equivalent to ten instructions given to the committee. House of Commons *Debates*, 10 March 1950, p. 665.
7. Recalled by SHK in the interview of 22 September 1975.
8. Ibid.
9. See Chapter 14.
10. Interview with SHK, 22 September 1975.

Chapter 10

1. House of Commons *Debates*, 25 February 1957, p. 1593.

2. Ibid., p. 1600.
3. Interview with SHK, 23 September 1975.
4. The most detailed account of the pipeline affair is William Kilbourn, *Pipeline: Trans Canada and the Great Debate, a History of Business and Politics.* Toronto: Clarke, Irwin, 1970.
5. Interview with SHK, 23 September 1975.
6. Ibid.

Chapter 11

1. Recalled by SHK in the interview of 7 October 1975. Knowles recounted the speakership story in a two-session interview about the many prime ministers he has known. I have chosen to emphasize the account.
2. Recalled by SHK, ibid.
3. Recalled by SHK, ibid.
4. Recalled by SHK, ibid.
5. SHK corrrespondence, SHK to J. G. Diefenbaker, 19 August 1957.
6. Sessional paper #178, 23rd Parliament, 1st Session, Vol. 782, 17 October 1957.
7. Recalled by SHK in the interview of 7 October 1975.
8. Recalled by SHK, ibid.

Chapter 12

1. Recalled by SHK in the interview of 1 October 1975.
2. Recalled by SHK, ibid.
3. House of Commons *Debates,* 1 February 1958, p. 4201.
4. Ibid.
5. Interview with SHK, 1 October 1975.
6. Winnipeg *Free Press,* 2 April 1958, p. 3.
7. Recalled by SHK in the interview of 1 October 1975.
8. The account and its implications come from private conversations with Knowles' landlady in Ottawa, who probably heard more than she ever wanted to know about the inner workings of the CCF.
9. Recalled by SHK in the interview of 1 October 1975.
10. Interview with SHK, 1 October 1975.

Chapter 13

1. Part of the resolution adopted at the Canadian Labour Congress Convention, Winnipeg, 21-25 April 1958. The resolution is reprinted in its entirety as Appendix A of S. H. Knowles, *The New Party* (Toronto: McClelland and Stewart, 1961), pp. 127-8.
2. Part of the resolution adopted at the CCF convention, Montreal, 23-25 July 1958. The resolution is reprinted in its entirety as Appendix B of Knowles, *The New Party,* pp. 129-30.

3. Kalmen Kaplansky, director of international affairs for the CLC from 1957, and then director of the Canadian office of the ILO from 1967, recalled this incident in a conversation, 1 June 1982. He was one of the labour advisers on the Canadian delegation to the ILO at the time Knowles was the delegate and he was able to clarify the structure of the organization for me. He also enjoyed travelling with Knowles for two reasons: in Europe Knowles name was pronounced Kanawvlays and that tickled Kaplansky's fancy; and to his continuing amazement Knowles could cut the top off a soft-boiled egg with one blow.
4. Interview with SHK, 2 October 1975.
5. Ibid. Part of the ILO account was also covered in the interview of 2 September 1975.
6. Recalled by SHK in the interview of 2 October 1975.
7. Ibid.
8. Ibid.
9. Ibid.
10. Ibid.
11. Recalled by SHK in the interview of 7 October 1975.
12. Recalled by SHK in the interview of 2 October 1975.
13. Part of the resolution adopted at the CLC Convention, Montreal, 25-29 April 1960. The resolution is reprinted in its entirety as Appendix C of Knowles, *The New Party*, p. 131.
14. Press clipping in Knowles' personal possession.

Chapter 14

1. House of Commons *Debates*, 19 December 1969, p. 2169.
2. Ibid.
3. Ibid., p. 2203.
4. Ibid., p. 2204.
5. Interview with SHK, 3 October 1975. The day was the fortieth anniversary of the death of his father; he had not forgotten.
6. Recalled by SHK, ibid. An example of one of his questions, which might well need a computer to furnish the response, is in the House of Commons *Debates*, 3 May 1965, pp. 829-30.
7. Interview with SHK, 3 October 1975.

Chapter 15

1. Interview with SHK, 8 October 1975. The interview about the leaders of the CCF-NDP was similar to most series of photographs of those leaders in that it gave no space to Hazen Argue, leader from 1960 to 1961.
2. Recalled by SHK, ibid.
3. Recalled by SHK, ibid.
4. Ibid.
5. Ibid.
6. Ibid.
7. Recalled by SHK in the interview of 10 October 1975.

Chapter 16

1. The author's observations from a hospital bedside, week of 5 October 1981.
2. SHK correspondence, SHK to Leonard R. Saunders, [1 October 1981].
3. Ibid., SHK to Joseph W. Johnson, [1 October 1981]. I am grateful to my mother, Marjorie M. Mann, the "landlady" referred to in the news bulletins about Knowles' stroke, for drawing my attention to these letters and to Doreen Salhany, Knowles' secretary, for providing me with copies of them. Ms. Salhany also facilitated access to Knowles' papers, for which I wish to thank her.
4. Knowles selected 18 July 1974, the day during the trip that he had all his family at his father's childhood home, as one of the important days in his life. The interview of 10 October 1975 is devoted to it; I have chosen to integrate it into an overview sketching Knowles' life to the present.
5. Virginia Knowles Hufbauer, *Descendants of Richard Knowles 1937-1973*. San Diego: Ventures International, 1974.
6. Recalled by SHK in the interview of 10 October 1975.
7. Recollection of the author.
8. Recalled by SHK in the interview of 10 October 1975.
9. Ibid.
10. Mentioned to the author in a conversation, 6 June 1982. Douglas added, "and the best there is."
11. Knowles recalled the incident in a two-part interview about the prime ministers he has known, the second of which dealt with Diefenbaker, Pearson, and Trudeau, 7 October 1975.
12. Ibid.
13. Knowles chose the date of the St. Laurent funeral — 28 July 1973 — as the starting point for his two-part account of the prime ministers he has known, the first of which dealt with Mackenzie King and St. Laurent, 6 October 1975.
14. Knowles recalled the incident, which occurred at a reception for the Trudeaus given by the Speaker, in the interview of 7 October 1975.
15. House of Commons *Debates*, 18 October 1976, p. 139.
16. The Ottawa *Journal*, 2 June 1956, p. 6. The speech referred to was on Thursday, 31 May. See House of Commons *Debates*, 31 May 1956, pp. 4507-11.
17. Editorial in *The St. Catharines Standard*, 25 April 1975.
18. House of Commons *Debates*, 31 March 1982, p. 15999.
19. Knowles recounted the episode in the interview dealing with St. Laurent, 6 October 1975. See House of Commons *Debates*, 2nd Session, 18 October 1949, pp. 892-3; 20 October 1949, pp. 959-60; 27 October 1949, pp. 1208-9.
20. SHK papers, copy of Bill C-97, an Act to provide for the British North America Act to be known also as the Constitution of Canada (First reading, 15 May 1964), Explanatory note.
21. Editorial in *The Toronto Daily Star*, 24 August 1964.
22. Cartoon in *The Globe and Mail*, 22 June 1964.
23. House of Commons *Debates*, 13 July 1981, p. 11450.
24. See, for example, House of Commons *Debates*, 5 May 1976, p.

13198; 6 May 1976, p. 13223; 6 March 1978, pp. 3495-98; 7 March 1978, p. 3513; 8 March 1978, p. 3561; 7 March 1979, pp. 3922-26; 20 June 1980, p. 2308; 17 July 1980, pp. 2987-88; 16 July 1981, p. 11586.
25.   Interview with SHK, 3 September 1975.
26.   House of Commons *Debates*, 31 March 1982, p. 15999.

INDEX

220   *Index*

Winnipeg, 14, 27, 32, 38, 39, 40, 41,
43, 47, 48, 49, 50, 56, 60, 63, 97,
136, 144, 147, 148, 150, 151, 152,
156, 162, 168, 169, 174, 180, 181,
182, 187, 193, 194, 195, 196,
200
Winnipeg Beach, 26
Winnipeg Free Press, 69
Winnipeg General Strike, 57, 96,
99, 103, 183
Winnipeg North Centre, 48, 54,
57-58, 60, 63, 64-65, 69, 70, 73,
76, 84, 97, 107, 113, 132, 136,
137, 138, 143, 145, 146, 169, 173,

179, 180, 181
Winnipeg South Centre, 45, 180
Women, rights of, 206, 208
Woodsworth, James Shaver (J. S.),
41, 44, 48, 50-51, 57, 58, 59, 60,
61, 62, 63, 64, 71, 72, 81, 97,
106-7, 108, 143, 149, 178-81,
182, 183, 184, 187, 188, 191
Woodsworth, Lucy, 58-59
Woodsworth School, Winnipeg,
181, 182

Yarmouth, N.S., 2, 12, 197